Also by Mathilde Apelt Schmidt

My Life on Two Continents

The Lake Dwellers

Happiness, a Matter of the Mind

The Old Castle in Austria

My Father, Hermann Apelt

The Legacy of a Great German Senator

Mathilde Apelt Schmidt

iUniverse, Inc.
Bloomington

My Father, Hermann Apelt
The Legacy of a Great German Senator

iUniverse books may be ordered through booksellers or by contacting:

iUniverse
1663 Liberty Drive
Bloomington, IN 47403
www.iuniverse.com
1-800-Authors (1-800-288-4677)

ISBN: 978-1-4502-9940-4 (pbk)
ISBN: 978-1-4502-9941-1 (ebk)

Printed in the United States of America

iUniverse rev. date: 3/9/11

Table of Contents

PART I – The Person

PART II – Excerpts

Introduction

Recently, while spring cleaning, I came across a very special book by the name of *Hermann Apelt, Reden und Schriften* (Hermann Apelt, his Writings and Speeches), compiled and edited by Dr. Theodor Spitta, my father's friend and co-worker in the Senate of my hometown, Bremen, Germany. It is, as to my knowledge, the only published book of his works that came to be published, thanks to Dr. Spitta, who was retired from his position as Second *Bürgermeister* (mayor) and created this labor of love after my father's death together with my mother, Julie Apelt, née Nielsen. The book was published in 1962 by the H.M. Hauschild publishing house in Bremen. It had been my Christmas present from my mother that year. I was very busy in the beginning '60s with raising my children and teaching German at the local high school and stored the book away without reading it then. Only after my children, evidently more interested in their heritage than I, made me aware of this book, I looked for it and found it. I was fascinated and could not put it down. I wanted to share this book with my family in Germany and abroad as well as make it easier to read for my American family. I immediately decided to translate passages from the book that I liked best and add material about my father that I had in my possession such as memories, personal letters, and handwritten notes my mother had sent me over the years. I also got in contact with state and university archives to search for more material. Altogether, I came up with the following book.[1]

Mathilde Apelt Schmidt
Castro Valley, August 2010

1 I chose the title *My Father, Hermann Apelt.* I selected Times New Roman font #12 for the writings by and about my father, and #14 for my personal remarks. Generally, I used regular fonts for the English text, italicized fonts for German and other non-English text, and for titles of works and sometimes for places, and italicized fonts in parentheses for my comments within the translated text.

My Father,
Hermann Apelt

PART I

Hermann Apelt, the Person

Course of Life[2]

Senator Dr. Hermann A p e l t

Born: July 10, 1876 in Weimar

Died: November 11, 1960 in Bremen

Married: August 23, 1909 with Julie Nielsen from Bremen

Education: Grand Ducal Wilhelm-Ernst-Gymnasium Weimar; *Abitur* (final exam before college entrance) 1895

Law studies: Universities Tübingen and Leibzig 1895-1899

First judicial state exam in Leibzig 1899

Doctor-promotion in Leibzig October 2, 1901

Military service in Erfurt from October 1, 1899 to September 1900

Junior barrister in Leibzig from March 13 to September 30, 1899; in Bremen from October 19, 1900 to July 15, 1903

Second judicial state exam at the Hanseatic Hall of Justice in Hamburg, early 1904

Attorney in Bremen from February 1904 to December 31, 1905

2 Taken from *Hermann Apelt, Reden und Schriften*, page 7

Syndikus (trustee) of the Chamber of Commerce in
Bremen from January 1, 1906 to December 8, 1917

Member of the Bremen Citizenship from 1909 to 1917
(Elected by the second class of citizens, the merchants)

As member of Bremen Citizenship he was placed in the office for
trade and navigation issues and deputation for ports and railroads

Served as soldier in World War I from August
20, 1914 to September 15, 1917

Was elected into the Bremen Senate on December 8, 1917
Was member of the Senate until the beginning
of the Nazi time, March 1933,
and after World War II from June 6, 1945 to the end of 1955;

Main areas of work: Ports, Navigation, and Traffic

During the Nazi era, since he no longer made an income working for the Senate, he worked as an attorney for family affairs.

Also

Member of the *Kunstverein* (Art Association) in Bremen since 1900;
Was elected executive on June 13 and first administrator
from June 7, 1922 to February 13, 1934.
During the Nazi era, he was dismissed from the first administrator
position and worked for the association as an accountant
until July 18, 1945. Then he was the first administrator
again and on November 11, 1957, he became an honorary
member together with Rudolf Alexander Schröder.

Member of the *Carl Schurz Gesellschaft* (Society) in Bremen.
Was president from its founding on March 2, 1949.

He was the founder of the Rotary Club Bremen in 1931 and became president in 1936. In 1937, the club had to disband because of the Gestapo. The members continued to meet on Wednesdays under the name *Bremer Tisch*. He was a member until his death.

He was active as president of the *Deutsche Gesellschaft zur Rettung Schiffsbrüchiger* (German Society to Rescue Shipwrecked People). This last organization has not been mentioned in the Course of Life but I feel that it was an important part of his life.

In addition, one of the rescue vessels was called *The Hermann Apelt* and a street by the harbor was named *Senator Hermann Apelt Straße.*

My Own Memories

I cannot deny that I was closer to my mother than my father. She was always there for me and I loved her with all my heart. My father had to work from 8:00 to 2:00, when *Mittagessen* (dinner at midday) was supposed to be ready. We ate (rather late for the main meal of the day) and after *Mittagessen,* he would lay down on our brown sofa in the sitting area. He started his nap, reading for a few minutes, then the open book fell onto his chest and he caught about half an hour of good, deep sleep. Naturally, we children had to be absolutely quiet during that time. No shouting on the veranda or in the garden, no running about. At 3:00, Father woke up, closed his book, removed his glasses, and was ready for his chauffeur to pick him up. He had never learned to drive, and Herr Ahrend and his black Rolls Royce visited us four times each workday. Father had his office in downtown Bremen, close to the Weser (the river that runs through Bremen). He worked a full afternoon into the evening, sometimes until 8:30. We had a light evening meal then and Father was usually rather tired. He only came to life when after the evening meal the family (my parents, my sisters, and I) sat in the living room and either read, embroidered, knitted, darned socks, or just enjoyed the last hours of the day together.

Most of the time he worked in his little cubicle by the cool light of a green lampshade surrounded by his beloved books and trinkets from traveling and hikes. There were some precious stones, bright yellow pieces of sulfur in a glass from Sicily, a little push/pull toy of two bears hitting a hammer on a block, and a flexible zebra that made strange movements when pushed by a button. The most meaningful trinket was a replica of the future Golden Gate Bridge, given to my father in 1928 by the building committee in California to raise money for that project. But sometimes he closed his books and joined us, conversing, or reading to us, or even playing a game with me. His cubicle was off limits for us children; he *had* to be left alone. Some evenings he worked there until after midnight, to the chagrin of my mother who had trouble falling asleep and depended on sleeping pills. She wanted Father to come to bed, "*Hermann, komm doch* endlich, *bitte!*" (Please, Hermann, why *don't* you come to bed!) I heard this quite often. Mother had a fragile constitution that was difficult for all of us. She also needed her nap in the afternoon, until 3:50 exactly, so between 2:30, when *Mittagessen* was over and 3:50 there was not a sound in the house, which was very hard for me who slept enough at night and had a hard time sitting still. Workdays included Saturday, but Sunday was precious. After Sunday *Mittagessen,* Father indulged in his once weekly cigar.

We hardly ever went to church, but both my parents were good Christians and loved to study the Bible. For Father it was part of his personality to be a good person—like Kant, he had the Ten Commandments anchored within. He would never do anything against these principles.

However, he had a few not so wonderful traits, too. Working hard and never letting a free moment pass without either reading or writing, except maybe when walking with my mother through our garden, produced a certain irritability in him, and probably was needed for balance. Whatever the reason, it was hard for the family to experience his sudden outburst of anger if something did not go according to plan. I certainly was often the cause of such temper tantrums. He could never let these feelings out at work or with colleagues; it had to happen at home. Maybe this was the reason I clung to my mother.

Still he must have loved me very much, as I was so much younger than my sisters were and spent more time with him than the others. I think that he admired my spunk and was proud of me for standing up to him. When I was older and my sisters had left home, he used to go on long walks with me. He told me stories from Greek mythology and gave me more literary knowledge than I could ever acquire in school. He made me an admirer of Goethe, Schiller, and other great German writers and poets. He even took me to the local theater. The first opera I saw with him, *Der Freischütz* (The Freeshooter) by Carl Maria von Weber, became my favorite one. When I was missing after the end of WWII, he was very concerned about finding me, and I was often included in events that had to do with his job. My parents took me with them on a trip to Italy, which I really did not quite appreciate because I was missing a coveted tennis match in Bremen. He had a special kind of humor and after a clever pun, he used to look at us with a veiled smile that broke into a laugh when we got it.

I wonder if I appreciated my father enough when I was young. I remember a conversation with my sister Dorothee, when I was twelve and she was twenty-one, studying medicine in Graz. We were on vacation together and she tried to enlighten me about the extraordinary achievements of my father and his outstanding character. She minimized his few flaws and for the first time I had an inkling of the greatness of this man, my father. That was in 1933, when he, together with the other members of the Senate, lost his job as a senator and had to rebuild his practice as an attorney. He certainly had enough reasons to be angry, but large, tragic events like the rule of the Nazis, did not faze him, just annoying little things, like the dropping of a fork.

All through the reign of Hitler and during the time of my studies in Hamburg, my parents sustained me with an allowance and fulfillment of all my little wishes, though, at least during the war, they did not have enough for themselves. Moreover, when I was finally done with my studies in Hamburg, I did not even stay home to help them cope—I took off to America! When I informed them of my marriage with Leo Schmidt, they had to realize that now three of their four daughters were living abroad, Cornelie (Nele for short) and I in the United States, and Dorothee in Argentina. Only Julie, who had married Christoph Kulenkampff, a regular *Bremer* (citizen of Bremen), had stayed in her hometown. My father had helped me to find passage on a freighter, which was free of cost. He even brought me personally to Brake to the pier where the *Magdalene Finnen* was waiting. It was strange to observe my father becoming increasingly smaller, until he disappeared completely after a curve of the river. I would never see him again because when we finally could afford my flight to Germany for Mother's eightieth birthday, he had been dead for four years. All during the busy years of child rearing, working as a teacher, and taking care of house and garden, I did not have much time to think of my father until now, when it is almost too late.

Was my father a happy man? I believe so. Though he never had his coveted son (my only brother died of an epidemic when he was only nine months old) and was always surrounded by women, he loved his family life.

About ten years ago, I adopted my maiden name "Apelt" as my middle name in order to keep my father's name alive, and now I am leaving this book for his descendants so they can remember his legacy to his beloved Bremen and Germany.

Letters from My Father and from My Father to Me

In: My Letters

My mother and I had always written letters to each other, and sometimes my father added on to those of my mother. Sometimes I got a postcard or letter from him. Likewise, I also wrote to him. Later, when I was in America, I had the chance to have the complete correspondence, or at least part of it since my mother had kept all my letters and my sisters sent them to me. I had kept most of my mother's and my father's letters. I had translated them into English and still have those translations on my computer. I named the document "My Letters." I chronologically divided them into thirteen books.

Book I
1921-1939

Father was vacationing in the Dolomites, in the Italian Alps, with our good friends and neighbors, the Ulrichs, who also liked the out-of-doors.

Postcard from Father, August 8, 1929 (I was eight then).
My dear sand-glacier companion,

Today I walked for six hours across real glaciers and ice. When you are grown up, we will do such a trip together if I am not too old then. However, you must shut your little mouth and watch carefully where you are going. Just think, on top of the mountain there was a little girl called Sophie, and she was only six years old.

Greetings! Your Father.

Letter from Father, Langenfeldt, August 20, 1929.
Dear Tita (my nickname as a child)!

Think of that, yesterday your father walked for three hours through this snowstorm. Hat and coat, everything was full of snow, just like Santa Claus, only that I didn't have a big beard—and besides, I had nothing to bring, except a knapsack on my back, but no presents in it.

And when I arrived down in the valley, the nice white snow had turned into an ugly mush and then into a regular rain, and all the Christmas wonderland melted down and what was left was a pack of wet clothes.

The weather had been too bad for Herrn Ulrich and Marie-Luise. They had stayed up in the hut that is standing between the glaciers—real glaciers made of ice, not only those made of sand like the ones on Sylt. *(That is one of the North Sea islands where our family spent many summer vacations.)* Since it had continued to snow all through the night, they were in danger of being snowed in and starving up there, because no provisions can be brought up and the food had been all eaten up. Therefore, they and all the other guests came down this morning, even though the snow kept falling and the path was completely under snow. Without a guide, they would not have made it.

Many greetings! Father.

In the summer of 1932, my father and I took a trip to the Harz Mountains, in northwestern Germany. Three postcards remain from that trip.

Poem from Father to Mother, Harz Mountains, July 21, 1932.

Der Vater und das Töchterlein.	Father and little daughter.
Eine Segelfahrt zum Wilhelmsstein.	A boat ride to the Wilhelm's Stein.
Bald Regen und bald Sonnenschein,	Some rain, some sunshine,
Steinhuder Leinen und Schok'lade.	Linen from Steinhude and chocolate.
Am Steinhuder Meeres Schilfgestade,	On the reedy bank of the lake,
Erquickung dann im flachen Bade,	Refreshing bath in shallow water,
Kaffee und Kuchen nach Begier	Coffee and cake according to demand
(Den Kuchen sie, den Kaffee er).	(Cake for her, coffee for him).
Sag, Liebchen, was willst du mehr?	Tell me, love, what more do you want?

Card from me to Mother, Harz Mountains, July 22, 1932.
Dear Mother!
Here at Steinhude is a beautiful mill. The lake is very shallow. The people in Wunsdorf are awfully nice. We took a trip on a boat to Wilhelmsstein, also visited the fortress on top of it. Tomorrow we shall go to the Harz.
Tita.

Card from Father and I, Harz Mountains, July 23, 1932 (written in the evening).
Dear Mother!
Now we are in the Harz. We already climbed 600 meters. It is wonderful here. Many blueberries grow here. Now we are in Romkerhalle, a restaurant, outside of course. Think of that, here is a waterfall! The Oker (river) flows by here.
Your Tita.
Father writes: Oh happiness, oh happiness!
Father.

There is only correspondence from me to my mother during the time from 1931-1939, since I had not kept any letters during that time.

However in an album, titled *Tochteralbum* (daughter's album), my mother sent me a few little poems in Father's handwriting. He used to make individual poems at Christmas and put them on the piano. All four sisters got those, but in the album, there are only two for me. Both refer to one of my vices, losing my wallet with money in it and bad table manners, but in a humorous, teasing way. I also must have twitched my eyes.

1931

Trotz der schwersten, ernstlichen Bedenken
Will der Weihnachtsmann auch dich beschenken.
Wirst du künftig—dieses hofft er sehnlich,
immer mehr der Susi Milarch ähnlich,
unterläßt Du künftig, mit den Wimpern
Höchst fatal zu zucken und zu klimpern,
Besserst künftig Du die Eßmanieren,
willst die Portemonais nicht mehr verlieren
—dann zum Lohne, mit dem lieben Vater
Darfst Du einen Abend ins Theater.

In spite of severe, serious considerations
Santa will now give you a present too.
If you'll in the future—he hopes so very much—
Try to become more like Susie Milarch[3],
If you in the future try not to bat your eyes
In a highly annoying way,
If you in the future improve your table manners
And will not lose your wallets,
Then, as reward you will be invited
To go some evening to the theater with your dear father.

---

3 Susie was the best student in my class.

I was ten years old then and I do remember going with my father to see the performance of *Der Freischütz*. This is still my favorite opera. My father had chosen well for my first performance at the *Bremer Stadttheater* (Bremen City Theater). Whether or not I had fulfilled all the requirements to earn this treat, I am not so sure. I must have been quite a brat.

The other poem is from 1935 and evidently, I was still losing my wallets.

Die Mutter spricht voll Gram und Weh:	Mother says very sadly
Bereits das zwölfte Portemonais!	Already the twelfth wallet!
Verlierst Du abermal die Säckl,	If you lose your purse again,
So gibt es welche mit dem Stöckl!	I might use the switch on you!
Ein Säckl aber gibts nicht neu,	But no new purse,
Und mit dem Geld it's auch vorbei.	And also no more money.
Denn wer das Portemonais nicht ehrt,	Because, who doesn't honor the wallet,
Der ist des Geldes auch nicht wert.	Isn't worth the money either.

I might mention that I still lose my wallet from time to time; my husband can attest to that. Only this time I am losing my own hard-earned money!

Book II
1940-1943

The Second World War started on September 1, 1939, and I had to absolve nine months in the *Arbeitsdienst für Mädchen* (work service for girls that was required under the Nazi regime). I was stationed several hours away from Bremen in a *Lager* (encampment) called Bühren, situated in the countryside and had letters from my mother telling me that everybody in Bremen was sick, including my father. I sent him a food package because in the country we had more access to food than in the city.

Letter from Father, Bremen, March 30, 1940.
Dear Mathilde!

Here you finally get a handwritten sign of life from me. It has gripped me quite badly. But thanks to Mother's wonderful care I lived through the bad fever and little by little I am gaining my strength back. The contents of your great package are also contributing to that. The chicken was delicious and we indulged in eggs. I have been quite spoiled by everyone. Today I was outside for the first time, in our garden, where I was surprised by the abundance of snowbells. I also found no less than four English fliers. *(Bremen had been attacked by the British.)* But unfortunately Mother has overdone her nursing of me; now she is in bed herself with a bad case of throat infection. However, after having slept well last night, she feels better already. We were very happy about your letters.

Father.

Letter from Father, Bremen, April 18, 1940 (for my 19th birthday).
Dear Mathilde!

So, on Sunday is the big day. I hope that Mother is in good enough shape to visit you. If not, you will have a nice time anyway since luck has it that your day falls on a Sunday. I wish you the best for your new life year; it is an important year that lies before you. The future of Germany and of all of us will be decided, and for you it will be decided what you will do with your life professionally. We hope that the *Arbeitsdienst* will agree with you as it has so far and you are happy in your group of comrades.

I am feeling much better. I am going to the office in the mornings, and otherwise get used to going back to my routines. Only in reference to food I am still pampered: additional meat ration, additional stamps for milk, a small glass of wine at noon, a small bottle of beer at night, and in between good tidbits from friends who stop by the house to visit.

Mother had her hands full with spring cleaning. I hope it is not too much for her. But now everything is done except the kitchen. Unfortunately, Mother's sleep is often interrupted at night.

Best wishes, your Father.

The Infamous Struggle for Eight Marks

The following series of letters shows the struggle the Germans had to bear with red tape, my own carelessness, and my father's persisting concern. Halfway through my time in Bühren, I was—together with a few other "maids"—transferred to a different camp, Ihausen, on the border of Holland. For some reason the administration in Bühren owed me some money. I wrote about this to my parents and my father took action:

Letter from Father to Führerin des Arbeitslagers Bühren bei Wildeshausen, RAD. (Reichs Arbeitsdienst) 11/171, June 19, 1940.

My daughter, Mathilde Apelt, was in your camp from January 5 to May 4 of 1940 as *Arbeitsmaid.* She still has a credit standing in the cashiers account there of 40,-- RM. (Reichsmark). My daughter asked to have this amount sent to me, either by transfer to my business account at the commerce bank AG in Bremen, # 1171, or by money order to my office: Attorney of Law, Dr. Hermann Apelt, Bremen, Schüsselkorb # 20/21.

Heil Hitler,
Signature H. Apelt,
Attorney at Law.

To Attorney H. Apelt, Bremen,
Bühren, June 26, 1940.

Concerns: Transfer. With same mail the amount of 32.--RM is being transferred to your account. You mentioned in your letter the amount of 40.--RM. However, by signing the statement here, *Arbeitsmaid* M. Apelt has confirmed the correctness of the amount of 32-- RM.

Heil Hitler,
Signature.

To the leader of the Arbeitsdienst Camp, Bühren bei Wildeshausen. RAD. 11/171
August 2, 1940, Apelt.
Concerning: *Arbeitsmaid* Mathilde Apelt.

After returning from a lengthy trip I found your obliging letter of June 26, 1940 concerning the credit that my daughter Mathilde Apelt has on your account. I herewith acknowledge the receipt of 32.--RM. About the amount of the money, there must be a mistake. I refer to the included written statement confirmed by my daughter. My daughter had given you a reminder about the 40.--RM, at which occasion she was informed about the 40.--RM.

I request transfer of the missing 8.--RM.

Heil Hitler,
Signature,
Attorney of Law

To Dr. Apelt, Attorney of Law, Bremen (hand-written),
Bühren, August 5, 1940.
Concerning: *Arbeitsmaid* Apelt.
Procedure: Your letter from August 1940.

On June 26, 1940, I sent to your account the amount of 32.--RM. The *Arbeitsmaid* Apelt has signed the amount of 32.--RM in person, so the mistake can only be that of *Arbeitsmaid* Apelt. If you would like a notarized letter about this, please let me know.

Heil Hitler
Signature.

After this, we gave up. Who kept the eight Mark???

Now a correspondence between my parents and Dr. Lembke in Malchow on Poel (an island in the Baltic Sea) in Meklenburg, the seed breeding farm that my parents wanted me to go to after the *Arbeitsdienst.*

From: Dr.phil.h.c.H.Lembke, Saatzuchtwirtschaft, Malchow auf Poel, Post: Kirchdorf in Meklenburg.
November 10, 1940.
Honored Madam,

Herewith I confirm the receipt of your obliging letter of November 8. Ever since I started my seed breeding business, I have employed only ladies in the area of this field and have found that they are especially well suited to do this kind of work. All ladies who have worked here have liked it very much. Many of them have continued this work in scientific institutes, for instance three of those ladies are now working at the Kaiser Wilhelm Institute in Müncheberg.

Fräulein Dettweiler has been working with me for a long time and is therefore well acquainted with all the problems and procedures. Besides her there are two young girls working as apprentices. One of these will have been here two years as of Easter and will likely go on to a scientific institute. Therefore, we would have a vacancy beginning at Easter 1941.

If your daughter should like to fill this vacancy, I would ask you for your decision as soon as possible so that I may hold the place open for her. I would offer her, in addition to free room and board, pocket money of 50 RM. Any other obligations such as taxes and insurance your daughter has to pay herself. We are always happy if our co-workers consider themselves as belonging to our family. Since there are also three ladies working in the office and two young girls are learning household as apprentices under my wife, we have ample youths on the premises.

Details about our business you might acknowledge from the attached brochure. I would be happy if your daughter decides to come and finds satisfaction in this career.

Heil Hitler,
Your devoted
H.Lembke, Signature.

After several letters written back and forth between my father and Dr. Lembke, also after my father had asked experts about seed breeding in Halle and in Gießen, and had informed himself about more scientifically inclined courses, he and my mother decided that this mostly agricultural approach connected with living in the country was the best thing for me. I did not have much to say about the matter and went along with it. So, in November of 1940 my father wrote:

Herrn Dr. h.c.H. Lembke
Saatzuchtwirtschaft, Malchow auf Poel, Post: Kirchdorf, i/Mecklenburg.
Very honored Herr Dr. Lembke!

Herewith I confirm the telegram I sent yesterday which said:

> I am enrolling my daughter Mathilde Apelt as apprentice to become a seed breeding assistant at your enterprise, starting Easter 1941. Letter follows, Apelt.

We had the opportunity to talk with the director of the Northwest German Feed Seed Breeding Company. He told us that the more theoretical course offered in Halle or Gießen is not quite what we had in mind for our daughter since she seems to enjoy the out-of doors and the practical aspect of this course. He advised us to do the practical part of the apprenticeship first, and then, if our daughter is inclined to do so, follow up with a course at an institute.

I now would be grateful if you could tell me when you want my daughter to start and what kind of clothing she should bring.

Heil Hitler,
Your devoted, H. Apelt.

Letter from Dr. Lembke to Father, November 26, 1940.
Honored Herr Attorney,

From your letter, I learn that you have decided to send your daughter to our place and we will be happy to enroll her in our seed breeding facility for Easter 1941. I hope she will be happy with her chosen profession and likes it here.

As I wrote you already, I shall give her 50 RM allowance every month and hope you agree with this. For clothing, I recommend sturdy shoes, solid dresses, and warm and waterproof outerwear. A pair of rubber boots would be recommended.

Easter falls on April 13 next year. It is up to you when to send your daughter. Should you decide to let her start on April 1 she would learn more about the important period of sewing and planting.

With best regards,
Your H. Lembke.

Father's reply to this letter, December 4, 1940.
Honored Herr Dr. Lembke!

Thanks for your friendly letter of Nov. 26 1940, in which you confirm the enrollment of my daughter in your training course. We would prefer if she would start on April 1. I shall let you know when exactly she will arrive.

We will follow your suggestions for her clothing. All the other instructions are agreeable with us.

With best regards, your devoted
H. Apelt, Dr. jur. Attorney of Law.

And one more letter from Dr. Lembke:

January 1, 1941.
Very honored Herr Dr. Apelt.

Because of vacationing of our office staff during Christmas holidays, I have only now the opportunity to confirm the receipt of your letter of Dec. 4. I therefore conclude that you agree with all our stipulations and consider your daughter enrolled as apprentice on my premises beginning April 1 of this year.

I hope she feels comfortable with her choice of profession and feels at home with our family.

Best greetings, your devoted
H. Lembke.

Then Dr. Lembke sent us a pamphlet showing all the types of plants that were bred in his business. They were mostly: *Raps* and *Rübsen* (for oil production), wheat, beets, oats, beans, barley, potatoes, rye, clover, and grass.

This concludes my correspondence in 1940.

In 1941, my father intended to visit a distant relative in Mecklenburg and announced his visit at my place of work on the Island of Poel. It did not happen often that he or my mother visited me; therefore, I was very excited about this. However, he did not make it to the Island, so I went to Wismar where he was visiting.

Letter from Father, Bremen, August 19, 1941.
Dear Tita!

Finally, my visiting you becomes reality. I intend to leave Bremen next Saturday, August 23 at 13:58 and to arrive in Wismar at 18:23. It would be nice if you could come over that evening and spend the night in Wismar. Please reserve a room for me at the Wedekin Hotel for two nights, Saturday to Sunday and Sunday to Monday and in case you are coming on Saturday, one room for you also. I will go on to Wendelstorf on Monday to Bertha Werner, if it fits with her plans.

Mother was happy about your letter that arrived here just before she left for Bunzlau for two weeks. *(My two sisters Dorothee and Julie were living in Bunzlau during the war; Cornelie had been living in the United States since 1933.)*

We have harvested cherries, currants, and beans. Apples, most of the potatoes, and quinces are still coming.

Goodbye and many greetings,
your father.

Father did not write any more during my time in Mecklenburg, Matlchow, and Pommern (Neu Buslar), where

Dr. Lembke's son-in-law, Dr. Rudolf Schick, also had a seed breeding farm. My mother visited me there once. I did not keep my mother's letters during that time either. After having finished two years as a seed breeding assistant, I had to decide where to work now. For a while it looked like I could work under Professor Sessous in Gießen, but this did not work out. Instead, I found a vacancy at the Genealogical Institute in Strassburg, in the Elsaß region, a German city at that time in 1943.

A letter from my boss in Poel in Mecklenburg shows that everyone was happy with my success in Kraftborn, Niederschlesien (now Lower Silesia, Poland), where I passed my exam with flying colors.

Letter from Dr. Lembke to Father, Malchow, April 25, 1943.
Honored Herr Dr. Apelt,

Just now, I received the news from my son-in-law that your daughter has passed the exam with "*sehr gut* (very good)."

I am, as you can imagine, extremely happy about this good result and I feel like expressing my best wishes to you. Though I was convinced that your daughter had the necessary knowledge that one can achieve in such an examination, it is also dependent on many circumstances and on whether or not the examinees have a talent for testing. When all these adversities have been circumvented, your daughter's diligence has now found its reward, and we all have a good reason to rejoice.

With great worry, we learned that the people in Bremen had another series of heavy air raids during the last weeks. We sincerely hope that you and your family have not been affected immediately. It is hard enough to endure these horrible events so close by, but when they lose everything and even dear members of their family then even the strongest persons will succumb.

Also, worries about your daughter overseas will depress you and your wife. Hopefully, you have received good news from her. We always have to consider our German people who are living as pioneers abroad and are subjected to the hatred and the pursuit of our numerous enemies. May a final peace soon end all worries and misery!

Wishing you and your family a quiet Easter time, I remain

Your devoted H. Lembke.

Meanwhile something was brewing about my future of what I was only faintly aware. That same Dr. Bürger who had steered my parents toward the seed breeding business in the first place and had notified my father about the available apprenticeship place in Malchow, and the same man who was with me at Kraftborn and had witnessed my (short-lived) glory there; he was now trying to procure a job for me where I could study in my field at the same time. He was the director of the *Nordwestdeutsche Futter-Saatbau-Gesellschaft m.b.H.* (Northwest German Feed and Seed Producing Company, Ltd.), whose main seat was in Hannover with a branch in Bremen. He had promised to help me find a job and he sure did. He wrote to Gießen where Dr. Sessous was the director of the *Institut für Pflanzenbau und Pflanzenzüchtung der Ludwigs-Universität Gießen* (Institute for Seed Production and Seed Breeding of the Ludwig University in Gießen*)*. The answer to his letter follows.

Letter from Dr. Sessous to Dr. Bürger, Gießen, May 20, 1943.
Honored Herr Doctor!

Unfortunately I cannot employ Frl. Apelt here since there will be no opening in our institute in the fall. *(Evidently, the job of the other girl had been rejected.)* Now I have here a request for a technical assistant in seed breeding from Strassburg. Herr Professor Dr. E. Knapp, director of the Institute for Genetic Studies at the University Strassburg, needs help with his genetic experiments and has asked me in this regard. I wrote today to Frl. Apelt and asked her to apply there. Maybe the job in Strassburg is even better for the lady; she could deepen her knowledge in genetics there. I am glad that I can counteract the disappointment of my denial of the job offer with this recommendation.

With friendly greetings,
Heil Hitler!
Your Sessous.

Book III
1944-1948

Meanwhile I had landed in Strassburg and had started working for Professor Knapp, a person with whom I never got along. After only a few months, I decided to work toward my *Abitur*[4], the last three years of High School that I had missed and that I needed to get into any college or university in Germany. I did want to go to a university and study. Just then, the German Educational Department in Strassburg started a course to prepare people like me, who wanted to go to the university, for the *Abitur*. I had already missed part of it, but they accepted me and offered to prepare me in half the usual time. In April of 1944, I passed the exam successfully. The program was closed after the exam because Germany was now at TOTAL WAR. The certificate of the *Abitur* became the most important paper of my life.

I have all the letters I had sent, thanks to my mother who kept them bundled according to years and I picked them up after her death. The family had gathered in Bunzlau, Schlesien, because they thought it was safer there. I only select one letter from me to my father shortly before the enemy took Strassburg. It expresses my utter dislike of my Nazi boss, Knapp.

Letter to Father, Strassburg, October 6, 1944.
Dear Father!

I received a letter from Mother from Bunzlau yesterday. How great that the journey went so smoothly, even the picking-up worked. It is nice for Mother to see all the grandchildren again, to enjoy both daughters and the peaceful life in Bunzlau. How do you cope as "grass widower?"

4 *Abitur* Maturity exam, necessary in Germany for acceptance at universities.

Mother wrote that Frau Schwarz is taking care of the household; does she take good care of you? I would love to come to Bremen now, but instead I am bound to stay here to do a very unsatisfactory job. Lately the boss has been so disgusting to me that I really almost feel like quitting and going into the armament factory; that is my only option. The boss thinks that I absolutely want to stay with him; that's why he is of the opinion he can treat me as he wants to. But I really have to weigh this; the work in the factory is probably the worst possible thing. Most people from the theater cannot handle it. They have to work for eleven hours per day on very heavy machines. I always think I might do it when he does <u>one more thing</u> to me. Right now, the political situation is so unsure. Because of the danger of bombings, we have packed much of the glassware in the institute and sent it to the Reich; but they say that the university stays here and that lectures will be held. In that case, the professor would stay here too. But we still don't know what will become of us. Most of the things we work with are gone. We just have to wait and see how it all develops. What turn will this disastrous war take?

Sabine *(my opera singer friend and roommate)* will soon leave Strassburg; the factory where she works is being transferred. That will be very sad for me. I had been so used to her and it was so wonderful to be together in the evening with a person whom I really liked, especially since I have to endure unpleasant things during the day. But there are also pleasant events connected with work at the institute: the activity outside, the nice colleagues, and all those healthy vegetables that we get out there. These are bad times. That's a fact with which we have to live. I am happy for Sabine that she is leaving; she has such a miserable life here and maybe she will find better circumstances somewhere else. In addition, here in the Elsaß (Alsace) the people do not like the newcomers from the Reich.

Do you have many attacks? We have alarms several times every day. On the 26th there was this terrible attack on Strassburg that destroyed so much, now the streetcars are not going anymore and there is no gas for cooking. Well, you know about all these things too. At least we have light and water; we are happy about that.

I hope you will have a healthy, strong grandchild. *(My sister Julie's second child.)*

Many greetings, your Tita

Postcard to Mother, Strassburg, November 1944 (last sign of life from Strassburg).

Dear Mother!

These are exciting days here in the Elsaß. All of us are packing suitcases. Tomorrow morning the three of us *(so Sabine and Schaußie—she also worked at the institute, as a gardener—must have come back)* will bring a large part of our belongings to Kehl with a handcart to send it to Germany. I'll send everything to Bunzlau. In case the situation changes, this work was for nothing, but if not, at least we have part of our stuff saved. We're staying here so far. Who knows what's to come. Just now it's alarm time; so much for writing! Tonight we will hear a great concert by the Berlin Philharmonic, the last opportunity to listen to something beautiful. How are you? I will put this card into an envelope; one has to be so careful now in the Elsaß.

Many greetings, Tita.

This is the last mail I have from Strassburg. I am not sure of the date; I only know it must have been sent in November. On November 23—the day of the siege of Strassburg—all the remaining Germans were captured and declared prisoners of war of the French. We were held in a French prison for 24 hours and then sent by American troops into France. There is only <u>one</u> letter from my mother in 1944 left in my possession that I have translated in its entirety. All the others are lost. And after that there was only one letter from me to my parents. In March of 1945, I appeared at the doorsteps of my parents in Bremen.

From Mother, Bremen, November 23, 1944.
Dear Mathilde.

For a change we had the alarm already early in the morning at 6:30, but so far they only came to the mouth of the Weser. So, I am sitting now after having had an early breakfast and have time for writing. I had written to you on Sunday and on Monday your dear letter from November 8 came, and on Tuesday the one from November 13 (both lost). So the mail seems to go a little faster. Today is Hedwig's birthday; that will be a celebration day for the Bunzlauers. And her beloved *Vati* (father) is there.

Yesterday the first letter from Wulf came. He is stationed near Leyden in Holland. After a journey of two days, they *(Mother, Julie, and her children)* came into an empty house that they now have to make comfortable little by little.

That the job agency is on your side is half the battle won. Just be patient, it will all straighten out. Think about how much worse off so many others are. Don't let it depress you, for these times will pass. It is too sad that you are so alone; everything is hard to bear nowadays. And how much we would love to have you here. It will all turn out better. Hopefully, the fact that you quit your job will remain. In case Strassburg is evacuated, will you go first to Tübingen? In Bunzlau you will live in the *Herrenzimmer* (gentlemen's room), that should be big enough for you. For Dorothee this is an advantage; she will not get other people to live into her house. It would be very desirable for her if you could come soon. She does not have it easy. The happiness of the first time after the birth is fading off and she feels very lonely. She would love to have you with her.

Now Sabine left and I can imagine that both of you were very sad about that. If only Frl. Schauß would come back soon. We do not like the feeling of knowing that you are all by yourself. Yesterday I met Laura Nielsen and we talked about you. She cannot believe that you are still in Strassburg; her brother has been transferred long ago to Leer. His wife is there, too. Their house had also been damaged.

What have you decided about your bank accounts in Strassburg? Will they transfer those? There won't be any in Bunzlau.

I could send you margarine, but that will be highly insecure. We had shortages too here, especially after severe attacks, now it is better again.

The Bölkens are always very busy. They had bad luck with their manager and their milkers, and those people were prosecuted and sit now in jail. Now the Bölkens have no manager and no milkers and have to do it all themselves. They don't write much anyway and not at all now. They are always asking how you are. *(I had worked for them to fulfill my* Pflichtjahr *(year of duty).)* When you come home, you must go out there and visit them. If you can come! Until then enjoy your Shakespeare. Whoever has time now to immerse into Shakespeare! Wonderful that you could get it.

You really stimulate us two; both of us want to read Shakespeare again. Did you ever read *The Merchant of Venice*? Isn't that brilliant!

We are indulging in apples. I am canning my last quinces now. But with the work on the *Parzelle* (plot of land near our home) and in the garden, I can't keep up since we had constant rain lately. Yesterday I had a nice time with Tante (Aunt) Lotte in Rönnebeck. I cleaned my room in Farge thoroughly for this winter. *(My parents had rented this room in case our house in Bremen would get bombed.)* Your room is our apple storage room. When you come, the apples go into Julie's room. Meta *(a boarder)* left, and we are glad to have the house for ourselves again.

Goodbye now and please, don't get so depressed. If you have a Bible, use it. It is always the most consoling book.

Mother

Now a letter from Chartre in France where I was held prisoner.

PRISONER OF WAR. Sender: Mathilde Apelt, German,
81g/527,968-H

P.W.J.B. France, U.S. Army

Letter to my parents, Chartre, France, December 22, 1944.
Dear Parents!

I am so happy that I can write you and tell you about my experiences. You can feel quite easy about me, as I am well and healthy. We, that means the members of the Red Cross, are American prisoners. My only sorrow is not to be together with you. I am longing for mail from you. Knapp was able to get across in time, also all the other assistants. Also Sabine got away in time. I had to leave most of my baggage in XXXXXXXX *(blacked out, probably Strassburg)*, but I have everything necessary with me. Please write to the sisters and give them my greetings. I recently met a wonderful person. Please don't worry about me, even if we don't see each other for a while.

Thousand greetings from your Tita.

I wrote down my memories of these three months in prison when I came back to Bremen after my ordeal and put this report verbatim into *My Life on Two Continents,* my memoirs that I put together in 1994 and published in 2006. (By the way, the "wonderful person" referred to in the previous letter was an American who was very kind to me. I lost track of him later.)

Now here is a report from an eyewitness, evidently a student of the Kohlrausch Institute for Physical Therapy. Since it was sent to my parents and is very interesting, I presented it in its entirety.

STRASSBURG, NOVEMBER 23, 1944

Letter from Ursula Strohm to my parents, Treptow, February 23, 1945.
Honored Frau Apelt, honored Herr Dr. Apelt!

In Bremen, you asked me for a report about my flight from Strassburg. I beg you to excuse me for waiting so long to do this, but I had to leave Bremen so abruptly that there was no opportunity to write before.

On December 16, I received the order from Hamburg to report to Königsberg on December 18. Since I didn't have a chance to take the state exam, I couldn't report there yet, and since I did not get an answer from Professor Kohlrausch, my father and I went two days later to Pommern to my mother and my sister to spend the holidays there.

By the end of January, I got another order to go to Königsberg, but since the letter came two weeks too late, I couldn't get into East Prussia anymore.

Two weeks ago, I finally received my approbation, but now I can't get away from here! The masses of refugees are constipating all trains and roads; day by day the vehicles are rolling, one behind the other—through Treptow! So close together, it is impossible to cross the street! And the horrible suffering! Four and five weeks the poor people and horses are on the way already; first through ice and snowstorms and now through bottomless mire. Where all of them are going, they don't know themselves! If they could only get across the Oder (river)! One can only hope that the Russians are forced to stand. What shall all these people eat when we lose all our agricultural areas? The Russians are trying to overrun Pommern too. Our big worry is that we will be cut off, that we will not able to get out anymore and fall into the hands of the Russians. Like at the siege of Strassburg, we have packed our necessary things. Who knows what is coming?

I am enclosing the report about Strassburg and also a map. Did you get news about your daughter in the meantime? I believe that now after the fighting in the Elsaß is over, a connection through the Red Cross is possible.

How different the situation is compared to the time of Christmas! Like a Christmas present, the offensive started in the west (Battle of the Bulge), and we counted on the liberation of Strassburg daily. They mentioned Gambsheim in the Army reports, that is situated about 18 km north of Strassburg. I know Gambsheim quite well; we visited it often by bike. But further than that our troops did not get.

I myself have not heard any news since then. If you would like to ask Professor Kohlrausch for advice, here is his address: Würzburg, Luitpold Hospital.

Wishing you may soon hear good news about your daughter,

Your Ursula Strohm

Here is her report to the public:

Since the invasion in France, Strassburg has visibly changed. The people in the Elsaß are becoming uneasy. Many Germans from the Reich leave the Elsaß since they count on a breaking through by American troops to the Elsaß. Strassburg and the rest of the Elsaß are only connected to the German Reich by the Rhine Bridges[5], across which day and night suitcases and packages are rolling into the Reich, and in the other direction goes reinforcement for our soldiers on the West front. This mood reached a zenith after the last days in September and the heavy attack on September 25!

Also for us, the students of Professor Kohlrausch, the ground under our feet became too hot. We begged Professor Kohlrausch to transfer the school to the Reich. So far, he had refused to do so since it would be desertion, but then he gave in and went to the Reich himself. The reasons

5 Throughout the book I use both spellings for the river: Rhine (English) and *Rhein* (German)

he gave for this were: 1. the closeness of the front, 2. the only escape route being the Rhine Bridge which could be detonated at any time, 3. the air-raids, 4. the low-flying enemy planes, and 5. the terrorists that made living in the Elsaß unsure. And a few days later all of us went home too. Only a few students stayed in Strassburg to treat patients.

On October 1, I left Strassburg with a friend and arrived after a 40-hour long journey in Bremen. On October 19, we were called back to Strassburg. The situation there had been stabilized, they told us; there would be nothing to fear. We were expected to have our state exam on December 15, 1944.

The weeks went by quietly, without severe attacks. But the fear and unrest within the population remained. One often heard mentioning of the valley at Zabern and most of us knew or felt that with its fall the Elsaß would be lost!

On Monday, November 20, news was spreading that the Zabern Valley had been broken through by American tanks! But nothing officially by the Army came over the radio. One hospital truck after another drove in front of the Bürger Hospital and transferred the wounded to Baden-Baden and further on to the Black Forest. Everyone knew some news; there was great agitation but everyone hoped that the troops could be halted.

On Tuesday, the November 21, we heard that the city of Zabern had fallen to the enemy. In the Army report, they mentioned that the Zabern Valley had been broken through. Professor Kohlrausch called us together and told us what the Army report had proclaimed. He himself drove that day to Baden-Baden to lecture there at a branch institute. He took his wife along and did not return by Wednesday. Before he left he told us that there was no reason to flee or even to be concerned, the troops would be halted! In the evening, a patient of mine came to us and begged us to pack our things for the worst case and to be ready. But even he did not believe in fleeing! He was a lieutenant and company chief and had the order to pack and be ready for the case they had to march out.

On Wednesday, November 22, it was rumored that the enemy was standing before Melsheim, which is 22 km from Strassburg. The lieutenant did not come for treatment on this day, so he did have an order to march. We quieted down because this meant that all reserves were thrown against the enemy.

On Thursday, November 23, we went to the hospital at 7:45 in the morning as usual to attend our lessons. There we learned that the enemy troops had overrun Melsheim and were standing closely before Strassburg!

During the night, several areas had gotten orders to evacuate, and we had not heard anything! We stood around, not knowing what to do and treated our patients. Only a few had come. About 9:00, we learned that we would have to undergo our emergency exam at 11:00! At 9:30, we were sent home to pack our flight baggage and bring it to the hospital. We were told that after the exam, we should leave together from there. My friend went right after that to her home to get her luggage from the bomb shelter. I went to a butcher on the *Rabenplatz*. During this time, the first shot fell in the suburb of Strassburg. This was around 10 o'clock. Nobody knew what this meant. But everyone felt that now the situation had become serious. I ran at once across the city to my home. Everyone either ran home or toward the Rhine Bridge. On my way, I asked a policeman where the enemy tanks were standing. He told me they were only two km from the center of town, at Krenzburg and Königshofen.

At home, my friend and I carried our luggage from the cellar and during this time our landlady came home too; she had been working at the Red Cross. Downstairs a military vehicle was waiting to bring us across the Rhine. In the truck we had to sit one upon the other, it was so crowded, and the baggage sat on the cooler! We started at 10:30. From the *Brantplatz* on, the stream of people became denser and denser. We could pass the first bridge across the harbor quite well, but the second bridge across the Little Rhine was constipated by a herd of sheep that was being herded across! At 10:45, we started to pass the large Rhine Bridge at Kehl. It was gridlock, bumper-to-bumper traffic, intermingled with bicycles, handcarts full of luggage, and people walking. An officer with a badge was regulating the traffic with a steady hand. In between German soldiers were running back and forth and installed cords for detonation; cases with dynamite and mines were standing ready for detonation.

In Kehl, the masses began to diverge and after driving one hour, we landed in Karlsruhe. In the evening, we went by cattle truck from Karlsruhe to Heidelberg and from there by express train to Bremen. On the train, we met a man who also had made it out of Strassburg. He had come with a special train across the Rhine Bridge a little before 11:00 and right after that he saw the three Rhine Bridges fly into the air. At 11:15, the first American tanks rolled up to the Rhine. At 11:15, the German artillery shot on Strassburg from Offenbach.

He also told us that the people in the Elsaß knew long before about the push on Strassburg and had horded foodstuffs days before. Indeed, three days before the fall of Strassburg there had not been any bread available anymore. It was also rumored that they had stocked up on wine in their cellars for the victory celebration!

Professor Kohlrausch wrote me these facts about the students remaining in Strassburg:

"As I am told by the *Gauleiter* (Nazi leader) that the Americans have taken over the protection of the Civic Hospital. There was unrest in the city for one day, but this subsided. The German women were interned for one day (in prison!), and then set free. They were able to move around in Strassburg until 5:00 p.m. I imagine that now it is possible to get information through the International Red Cross."

Ursula Strohm.

Now two letters my father wrote in an effort to find me. (They must have come back to him since my mother had these letters.)

Letter from Father, Bremen, December 4, 1944.
To the Center Information Office for Evacuated Persons.
re: Mathilde Apelt, born April 21st, 1921 in Bremen, profession: Seed breeding assistant at the Institute for Genealogy in Strassburg.

The Institute for Genealogy of the University Strassburg, where my daughter is employed, was in the process of transferring to Tübingen. My daughter had been left in Strassburg, together with a few other persons from the institute, to work at the experimental fields there. The director of the institute, Herr Professor Dr. Knapp, is now in Tübingen. My daughter was living in Strassburg, on Kirsteinstr. 1/4. Her last letter had the stamp of November 22, 1944; it had been written on November 21 and without apparent knowledge of the dangerous situation. *(This letter seems to be lost also.)* The only news about the fate of our daughter is the following telegram that we received after inquiry at Tübingen:

052 Telegram
3453 Tübingen 31 27 1550 November 28 14:30.
Zug 28.XI.44. 13:52

Senator Apelt, Strassplatz 15, Bremen

Fräulein Apelt was sent on Thursday, November 23, 1944, at 9:00 with packages to Kehl, afterwards not heard from.

> I left Strassburg at 11:00. I expect her to report to the University in Tübingen.
>
> Knapp.

Whether our daughter had left Strassburg with these packages, or if she only wanted to mail them, or whether she left Strassburg in time, we don't know.

You will understand our great worry. I am asking to search for the whereabouts of our daughter and to inform us as soon as possible by telegram. Reimbursement for the telegram for RM 2— is included in stamps.

Heil Hitler, Dr. Apelt.

Letter from Father to Dr. Knapp, Bremen, January 19, 1945.
To Herrn Professor Dr. Knapp, Tübingen, University.

Honored Herr Professor!

For your letter of January 6 that reached me yesterday, I thank you. I take it for granted that you received, in the meantime, the confirmation by wireless of the two letters you had sent me. I hope you have not undergone the trouble to write a third letter.

You will also have received my last letter in which I mentioned, among other things, the various places we had contacted to not miss any possibility. I learned through your letter that my written report to the government office was sent to your university. I did not receive an answer from the rector of the university.

The letters that my wife wrote to Frl. Hofstätter, Herrn Hangstein, and to my daughter have been returned to us. News about the treatment of Germans left in Strassburg is contradictory. I heard from various sources that they are treated quite decently. On the other hand, I found today the enclosed notice in our paper that gave us reason to be worried. Though I do not put much weight on just one newspaper report, you will understand that this kind of news is augmenting our fear. If you should by any chance hear about treatment of Germans from the Reich in Strassburg, please inform us.

Heil Hitler!
Dr. Apelt.

There are no letters from Professor Knapp. But my parents had received my letter of December 22, 1944 from Strassburg and knew I was alive and well. On January 29, 1945, we were released from France and brought back to Germany in exchange for American nurses captured by the Germans during the Battle of the Bulge in the middle of December 1944. I spent a few weeks in Bremen where I found our house overcrowded with two sisters, their husbands, and six children. They had to flee from Bunzlau because the Russians had invaded Silesia. Though my parents were overjoyed to see me again, there just was not enough room for one more person.

Therefore, I went back to Traunstein—my father brought me to the train station—and started working in a war hospital there.

Postcard to my parents, Traunstein, March 15, 1945.
Dear Parents!

The first sign of life from Traunstein! Did you get my telegram? It is wonderful in Traunstein. Helga *(a friend I made while in France)* was very happy; I might work in the same war hospital as she. I visited Herrn von Kummer and he is not very well. The journey was quite adventurous; we had to march through three burning cities: Marburg, Friedberg, and Hanau. One sees much misery on such a journey. From Hanau to Eberbach, I traveled through the Odenwald, a beautiful area. I met with nice soldiers who helped me carrying my luggage. How are you? How was Father's trip back on Sunday?

Thousand greetings, your Tita.

Letter from my parents, Bremen, March 28, 1945.
Dear Mathilde!

Today we received your first letter from Traunstein written on March 18 *(I do not have that letter).* It did not take very long. We are so happy that you had a chance to see the Gysaes *(friends from Bremen).* We have been there several times. At one time we stayed in the hotel, but the last time I lived with Tante Magdalene. Yes, the Gysaes know how to make life comfortable. They are already living together like an old married couple *(they were brother and sister)*, and so they became old rather early. You write that Herr von Kummer is very sick. Dorothee had heard in Bunzlau that he had died. That must have been on March 18, since she went to live in Farge on the 19th, and your letter is from the 18th. We lost all connections with the brother since Dorothee is in Farge and I don't see the Von Kummers anymore. Did he really die?

How great that we can write to you by military mail. You will be able to do the work in the hospital. Though one sees gruesome things when taking care of sick people (especially in a war hospital), it is a very fulfilling job. The human relationships that one develops doing this work will be enriching for you.

You had started to write about your experiences of the end of the war in Strassburg and your time a prisoner of war. Couldn't you continue this report? Or don't you have time for this? I find this very interesting, and I could send you the beginning.

Yesterday there was a very severe air raid in Farge upon the military buildings. We heard about it through Ursula Sander. Dorothee had just been to the restaurant in Farge with her children to eat. They have not been hit, nothing happened to them, but it must have been a horrible noise. The children must have been very frightened. And the attacks will surely be repeated. I would not be surprised if the Rohlands would come back to us some day. The happenings at the Rhein are also very depressing.

Now the food distribution is getting even sparser; we can expect bad times in the near future. We are working on the *Parzelle (a plot of land near our home)*; the Ulrichs could get hold of some Russian prisoners, so the digging will be done in a few days. It is fun. The garden will be ready soon too. We will stay here over Easter and together with the Ulrichs will dedicate ourselves diligently to the *Parzelle.* In the evenings, we will sit together and have a nice time. Maybe I will go to Farge to visit Dörte on Saturday.

Dr. Feinman's son Hans has fallen. Wulf is on this side of the Rhein.

Greetings, Mother.
Many greetings, Father.

I soon broke down because I had contracted scarlet fever and stayed as a patient in a Catholic hospital to recuperate. On the day of siege of the area of Oberbayern (Upper Bavaria), I had been at the hospital for six weeks and was free to go. I chose to go to a good friend of my parents, Rudolph Alexander Schröder, who was living with his sister Dora in Bergen, about 15 km from Traunstein. They took me in and gave me shelter until the war was over and everything was relatively safe again.

Letter to my parents, Bergen, June 7, 1945.
Dear Parents!

Tomorrow morning someone from here is going to Hoja; then many here want to try to send mail to Bremen. I shall be brief since there is not much time. I am not in Traunstein anymore; there I got sick with scarlet fever. Now I am completely cured and am living with the Schröders in Bergen where I am doing very well. Now I am waiting for a sign of life from you, and when I am sure that you have room for me, I shall go home at the next opportunity. How have you been, and what might have happened to you? The siege of Bremen must have been horrible (around May 7th). We heard that Bremen is now under American rule. We find that rather positive. Here the end of the war has been rather gentle, though just before the end we had some terrible air attacks, but only for a short time. In Upper Bavaria, no town had to be besieged; every city surrendered. The American troops are very popular with the people; they are polite and generous. If my American friend should come to Bremen and ask for me, (though this is highly improbable) please tell him that I am here in Bergen. How have the English troops been treat you? Regarding food, it is not very good here in Upper Bavaria, though in the country it is better, of course. Life with the Schröders is very nice; they are such pleasant people and treat me wonderful. We all hope that mail service with northern Germany is working again soon. There are many people from Bremen here in Bergen, family Bohner, Frau Hasenkamp with three children, Frau Kiepenhäuser, then a niece of the Schröders with two children. If only this letter would reach you!

Perhaps you could send us mail by ways similar to this; if one only had a sign of life! Was Dörte in Farge with all her children during the garrison? My plans are to go home in August and hopefully I get mail from you by then. Please send my greetings to all our relatives and friends from me and heartfelt greetings to you two.

Your Tita.

My Address: At Schröders, Bergen (Obb) Sonnleiten.

At this point, I traveled home to Bremen, this time to stay. This trip was an adventure in itself. I returned to Bremen in August of 1945 after trip partly on top of trains, on trucks, walking etc. It took about five days to get from Bergen to Bremen. I found my old home on Richard-Strauß-Platz in shambles; it had been destroyed on the last day of the war, on May 7, 1945. I found my parents living with Dr. Degner-Grischow, my father's lawyer colleague, at Parkstraße 74 in an attic apartment. I stayed with them all through the winter and into spring of 1946 when I had secured a place at the university in Hamburg to fulfill my dream of studying. It would become a six-year ordeal. But eventually it led to my marrying Leo Schmidt. Life works in mysterious ways! All of this is described in my memoirs, *My Life on Two Continents*, pp. 67-85.

Bombs had destroyed great parts of Hamburg including the university buildings. The buildings we had lectures in were in ruins. The hardest thing was getting shelter.

First letter to my parents from Hamburg, May 7, 1946.

I don't have many pleasant things to tell you about. I haven't found a room yet. Last night I spent very nicely at Hasso's uncle's place, Herrn von Reichenbach and they are very friendly people. Unfortunately, I could only stay for one night since they are getting a student to move in with them.

Einquartierung (billeting) is ordered by the *Wohnungsamt* (agency for providing lodging). Tonight I will sleep at Frau Dr. Vidal's home, friend of Frau Dr. Fischer, but also only for one night. What will happen tomorrow, I don't know yet. There is no way that I will get a regular room, only a very small room and those are very hard to get. Tomorrow the first lecture starts, which is botany. Dr. Mevius was very friendly, but cannot help me either. The Ackermanns are also unsure if they can keep their apartment. Well, time will tell. *(It looks like I had several acquaintances in Hamburg.)*

How are you? Has anything developed about the new help? How was the theater? Is Frau Bölken coming this week? If you write me, please use this address: Studentenwerk, Tesdorpstr. 20. There I am asking every day for mail. Polli wanted to stay until the end of this week. Please tell Frau Löning that he did not get admitted. So that's it for the first report, hopefully the next one is more pleasant. The only good thing is the weather.

Thousand greetings to everyone, your Tita.

All about a Stove Pipe
(It was freezing cold in winter 1946-47)

Postcard to Mother in Lesum, Heidberg-Adelenstift, Hamburg/Bahrenfeld, January 8, 1947 *(mother was sick and there to recuperate).*

Dear Mother!

For today just a short note, since I have very little time. The trip here was ghastly, four hours delay. Classes at the university start on January 13. My stove pipe doesn't arrive in Hamburg until the end of this week because the delivery van has broken down. But, in order to not sit in the cold constantly, I am doing the following now: there is an oven in our kitchen, but since the kitchen is occupied all day long until 10:00 in the evening and the oven is not lighted because none of the ladies have anything to heat with, I move into the kitchen at 22:00, heat the oven and work there until I get tired. During this week, I can sleep in every morning. With the electricity, it is like this here: twice a week, on Monday and Thursday, there is no power from 7:00 to 22:00. On the other days, power is on all day. Our water pipes have frozen since yesterday. Hopefully it will get warmer soon.

Tita

Postcard from Father, Bremen, January 12, 1947.
Dear Tita!

Thanks for your card. Hopefully the stove pipes arrived meanwhile. Luckily, it is thawing now. Here at home the water pipes are frozen and there is no electric light. The day before yesterday I was in Heidelberg and found Mother astonishingly lively. Unfortunately, there was a setback on the same day. It seems that my visits are bad for her.

Many greetings, your father.

Postcard to Father, Hamburg, February 3, 1947.
Dear Father!

How are you doing in this barbaric cold? Hopefully you have it cozy and warm in your office and not as icy as we have it in our lecture halls. But, since the lecture rooms are far apart, we have to walk quite a bit between lectures, which keeps us warm. Actually this is a nice, dry winter. In my room stands the little oven and burns industriously. Unfortunately there is not much fuel. That's why I am only home on Sundays and study with other students in their rooms. We are studying now analytic geometry in the n-dimensional space; "n" stands for all numbers in sequence 1,2,3,4,........n. That is very interesting. I will tell you more about it during vacation.

Greetings, Tita.

On the other side of a letter from my mother which ends:

… I am taking a coat of Father's apart so you can get a jacket out of it. It is very good cloth and should make a beautiful jacket.

Best greetings, Mother.

Included in this letter (Mother must have just used it for writing paper):

To: Herrn Senator Dr. Hermann Apelt, Bremen, Parkstr. 74.
Honored Herr Senator Apelt!

We learned with great joy that you have been elected again as the senator of our *Hansestadt* (city-state) Bremen as representative of the *BDV*

(Bremen Democratic Party, his party). We congratulate you for this and send our best greetings from the south.

With friendly greetings,
Democratic Party of the People
Landesverband Württemberg-Baden.

Now that was really good news!

Postcard from Mother, Bremen, Feb. 28, 1948 (just before the Reichsmark was changed to Deutsche Mark).

Dear Mathilde,

Thanks for your cards. I heard from Julie that you decided to go on the trip. I am sending 300 RM for travel money. I would like to know what part of the money you are using for the trip and what for your studies, because I record these amounts in different places.

Father earns 740 RM per month net, meaning without income tax. It seems to us you will not be eligible for help. If I weren't sick, it would be no problem. There are a few more things for you to take, says Julie: sausage, syrup and other things, she will tell me. On Monday, you would have to send the package off. It is really unpleasant that your little party is on the day before your trip. Please save the butter for the trip. Father and I plan to go on a trip this summer, maybe to Bodenwerder on the Weser.

Many greetings, Mother.

Postcard from Father, Bodenwerder, May 1, 1948.

Dear Mathilde!

Greetings from the room in which I became your successor. *(I must have visited Mother in Bodenwerder.)* I found Mother in very good health. She had consulted a neurologist who was recommended to her by Frl. Schütte, who had suffered a similar condition. She already went three times and had each time a shot to help her circulatory system. That had a very good effect and the pains almost disappeared. Unfortunately, this doctor is leaving for vacation, and the miracle drug is not to be had anywhere else. Weather-wise it is so-so, alternating rain and sun. Today it's quite cold. We enjoy the eggs you sent. Mother thanks you for that.

As always, your Father.

I was toying with the idea of writing my thesis (necessary to pass the teacher's exam) about my grandfather. For that, I needed to ask my father some questions about research materials.

Now from Father, dictated to Mother:

In the year 1847 Apelt, Schleiden, Schlömilch and Schmid founded the *Fries'sche Schule*. In the same yearbook #1 (Leipzig, edition Wilhelm Engelmann) was published and in 1849 book #2. I own both of these. If there are more, I don't know. After 1904, the following appeared: *Abhandlungen der Fries'schen Schule, Neue Folge* (edition Vandenhock and Ruprecht, Göttingen) by Hessenberg, Kaiser and Nelson. Of these, I own the four books of the 1st volume (1904-1906), the three first books of the 2nd volume (1907-1908) and also a special edition from the first book of the 4th volume (treatment of the history of philosophy of Fries and Hegel by Otto Apelt, 1912). The 4th book of the 2nd volume, as well as book 3 (1909-1912) and the following I don't own regrettably.

I didn't know about these later publications. I assume one could get them from the publisher Vandenholtz and Ruprecht still, and most likely, the library in Göttingen will have them.

Included are the leaflets Fries etc. Please keep safe.

Love, Father.

Now, if that isn't a thorough bibliography! Later I changed my mind and wrote my thesis on the importance of cotton to Bremen.

Book IV
1949-1951

I spent six long years in Hamburg before I graduated. Midway through I switched my studies from math and physics to geography and biology (I just could not make it in the exact sciences). The excursions offered in the new fields were wonderful, but also hard on my budget. My mother was frequently sick and could never visit me. My father did, but seldom and only when he had to be in Hamburg anyway. It was a busy time in his life and he had many official obligations.

Letter from Mother, Bremen, May 12, 1949 (while in the hospital).
Dear Tita.

Father will be in Hamburg on May 17. He has a speaking engagement in the morning, and has been invited out in the evening. He has to change for the dinner and would like to do that at your place, sometime between noon and evening. In case you are not there, please arrange that he can get into your room. It would be so nice if Father could see you. Do you remember that the 20 RM bills are soon devaluated?

Greetings, Mother.

Postcard to Father, Hamburg, May 14, 1949.
Dear Father!

I think that is so nice that you will come here on Thursday. I don't have anything then and can dedicate my time to you from 10:00 to the evening. I am expecting you then any time at my home. Do you know how to get to Vogelbeerenweg? Near Lattenkamp U-Bahn station, branches from Efeuweg. Could you ask Frau von Hundt to give you a little real coffee in a paperbag? I can make us a good coffee then. You might need that on a strenuous day like you will be having.

So, until Tuesday.
Best greetings, Tita.

Letter from Mother, Bremen, January 22, 1950.

Father didn't tell me too much about the party yet (for the Carl Schurz Festival). He came home at 2:30 in the morning, and, of course, I was asleep. At 7:30, he had to leave again for Hamburg where he will lay the cornerstone of a new building in the harbor. He is the senior of this department. This is pretty strenuous after a party night. I know this much: Father sat with the Jeffs and the French consul with his wife, also the Riddles (founder of the Lykes-lines). Julie also joined them and Father introduced her to Clem *(who became a dear friend of my father).* The Tiemanns and the Bölkens were there too. Father saw them briefly. It was very crowded, about 400 people.

Father came back from Hamburg completely frozen; he had forgotten to take his blanket. Now he is in bed to get warm, got tea with rum from Else and is quite happy.

Many greetings, Mother.

Letter from Mother, May 3, 1950 (bottom of the letter only).

... Father went to Hamburg on Saturday and had to speak at the Oversea Club. He is staying there overnight. He went by train this time since he has to hurry back on Sunday.

Greetings, Mother

Just to show how busy Father was in the summer of 1950, I have included excerpts from a few letters.

Letters from Mother, July 6, 7, and 19, and August 10, 1950.

... Father's birthday *(July 10)* will not be celebrated by us. He is too busy with his work.

... Father has weathered the strenuous July 10 very well. On top of all the work, there were so many phone calls and letters.

... Father goes to Rotterdam tomorrow, a nice change for him.

... Father is in Bonn now; I expect him back today.

Letter from Mother, Bremen, October 10, 1950.
Dear Mathilde.

Thank you so much for your card and that interesting letter. I didn't know that the Harz is geologically so interesting. Enclosed you find the last chapters of *Christiane Dee.*

Father goes to Hamburg on the 11th, has some meeting there, and on the 12th to Lübeck to another meeting, and then on the same day goes back to Hamburg. He now thinks it is impossible to visit with you. You will be too busy anyway to have company. But maybe it is possible that he sees you briefly.

Here we had a state visit from Francois Ponçet, from Saturday to Sunday. Father was still away. Therefore, Meinke showed him the ports. Saturday afternoon Prancois P. opened the German/French cultural center here in the first story of the *Amerikahaus.* It looks extremely inviting with many books. Rudolf Alexander Schröder came also for the initiation. Also some of the American consuls appeared. Mr. Toetdman was very nice and brought me home in his car after the event. *(John Toedtman, his wife Margaret, and son John, became good friends of ours. They treated me wonderfully when I was with my sister in Dayton, Ohio. Toedtman was in charge of the Culture during the American occupation of Bremen.)* In the evening, there was a small, nicely arranged ladies' party in the Gästehaus. Frau Kaisen was the hostess and did this task with grace, even gave a speech. I sat besides Madame Francois-Ponçet and actually had the best place. Madame P. is a lady of about 50 years, very blond and has bright-red fingernails. She wore a dress with deep décolleté and three strands of pearls. Nevertheless, she is a lady, and is very interested in our stories; and we told her several Bremen stories. I told her several facts about the *Kunsthalle* that she then visited the next day with her husband. I seldom had been to such a nice gathering of women. Frau Dr. Ley, Frau Mevissen, Frau Stiegler, all of the parties; Frau Consul Schoter and others. Later came Kaisen and Ponçet from the *Rathaus* (city hall) and then we ended the affair.

Sunday morning big speeches by Kaisen and Ponçet in the old *Rathaushalle* (hall in the *Rathaus*). Ponçet's goals are mostly the German/French understanding and a United Europe. *(Already thoughts of a United Europe in the 1950s!)* In the afternoon, the French visitors toured Worpswede.

Father came home exhausted after a lengthy night festival. He had been in Bayernzell for three days with beautiful weather. It must have been wonderful, but the sad thing is that he is not able to climb mountains anymore. He visited Emma's home and her grave. In Munich, he saw Willibalt Apelt (a cousin) and also Hasso Herlin briefly. And he saw many pictures in Munich at an exhibition of medieval paintings.

Frau Schön *(our housekeeper who was not above stealing)* is back again, but still looks rundown. I am finally getting ahead with the packing. Whether we are really moving on October 24 is doubtful *(my parents had decided to build up a house again on the same lot where my birth house had been destroyed on the last day of the war)* since the workers are stalling. The linoleum man tells us that the subfloors are still too fresh and have to dry out more before laying the linoleum *(not enough money for wood floors).*

So, on the 19th is your big day *(my zoology exam).* We don't have any illusions. Whatever happens, let us know. How are you with money? Please eat enough and don't push yourself so hard. Don't drink so much coffee; that is not good for you. What are you wearing? I am all for good appearance.

Loving greetings, Mother.

Letter from Father, Hamburg, October 11, 1950.
Dear Tita!

I am in Hamburg this morning because of business and social meetings. I don't think I have time to see you. But, to save time, I would like to change at your place tomorrow, Thursday, between 5:00 and 6:00 in the afternoon.

In case you should not be home during that time, please let your landlady know.

I just learned that I am free this afternoon. Please let Herrn Rusch, who brings you this note, know when and where I can meet you, at your place or otherwise?

Father.

Postcard to Mother, Hamburg, no date, but it must be after October 12, 1950.
Dear Mother!

Just now Father has changed in my room for the dinner. At first, we had a little uncomfortable collar incident, but now all is right. Thanks for your dear letter with the newspaper clippings. I didn't have time to read them yet. Father has given me plenty of money; I am touched.

So, the moving seems to stall. If it could only take place before November 1. Afterwards my lectures are starting. How nice that you could participate in a party, though it was only a ladies party. Could you ignore the red fingernails of your neighbor?

Many, many greetings, Tita.

Letter from Mother, Bremen, October 14, 1950.
Dear Mathilde,

Enclosed you will find your institute card. Father is not sure how it got into his briefcase. Hopefully you didn't miss it.

It was so nice that Father could tell me about you. Oh yes, I had packed the wrong collar for him and without your help he would have been lost! In the house I have to push a lot; the plumber has let us wait for the last two weeks and now everything is lagging behind. I have to sit on all the workmen. I don't think we will be ready for October 24, but maybe for the 29th. The furniture is all here as Niestädt tells me; the wardrobe for Frl. Partikel is finished *(that must have been our future renter/help for Mother).* Those things that were still here in the Parkstraße and needed painting have been sent by express to our cellar in the Richard-Strauß-Platz. There they get painted by our painter. That way it gets emptier here. We are working frantically, but can see light at the end of the tunnel. Then soon the big cleanup in the new house will come. And on Monday is a big washday.

Thousand greetings, good wishes,
Mother

In the summer of 1951, I had the opportunity to travel to Italy for four weeks with the Geographic Institute in Hamburg under the guidance of Professor Brünger. That was quite expensive for my parents, but my brother-in-law, Christoph Kulenkampff, was willing to lend us 300 RM. This did not sit well with my parents who were facing possible financial problems. My father was up for re-election in November and younger candidates were vying for his position. However, Christoph insisted and, after all, my father was re-elected on November 30, 1951. My father also traveled. He visited my sister Cornelie Ernst and her family in Dayton, Ohio. I started on my thesis for the state exam titled *The Importance of Cotton for Bremen.*

Postcard to Mother, Hamburg, June 8, 1951.
Dear Mother!

Thanks for your card. So, now Julie is with Nele! All the things they will have to talk about! I must share something with you that you will find unpleasant: I am listed among the ones who are selected to go on the Italy excursion. This trip to Italy will take four weeks and will cost about 200 DM. I did not commit myself for sure, since I have to ask you first. Before that, we are going on a biological excursion to the Rhein, that will last 10 days and will cost 50 DM. Together this is a lot of money and I don't know how this is possible in lieu of the soon to be expected retirement of Father.

I'd like to go to the Rhine in any event. Italy would be wonderful, and, considering the long time, it is relatively inexpensive, but the money has to be there. I myself don't have a *pfennig*, unfortunately. So, please write what you think.

Many, many greetings, Tita.

Postcard from Mother, Bremen, June 10, 1951.
Dear Mathilde.

The bill for your tuition came today, 162.50 DM; I will send the money tomorrow. Thanks for your card of June 8. The Italy excursion sounds very tempting. I have to know when you need the money; I don't have that much in the house. And doesn't this Italy trip interfere with the preparations for your exam? And when do you need the money for the Rhine trip? If you go to Italy, you won't have living expenses except the rent in Hamburg, so you could use some of your monthly 120 DM. Or not?

The election takes place in October. Julie arrived in Hamburg yesterday at noon and was met by all the Kulos. I couldn't let you know—heard of it too late. Christoph arrived on Thursday from Rio. Julie told us interesting things already last night.

Please let me know soon,
Mother.

Postcard to Mother, Hamburg, June 13, 1951.
Dear Mother!

Yes, all that money is horrible; I cannot tell you yet when we have to pay. Only last week it was decided who will be allowed to come along; of 60 applicants only 25 have been selected (it was chosen according to semesters absolved). It is not colliding with the exams. I am only applying this fall for that and only then get my thesis. This trip would be the best preparation. This last semester is so far my favorite one; that might have to do with the fact that I have learned so much and have a better overview. If I were filthy rich, I would go on studying like this all my life!

Tita

Postcard to Mother, Hamburg, June 26, 1951 (excerpt).

... I have to apply for a passport in the next days; I might need a few more papers from Bremen for that. I'll write you about this. First I have to be informed about what I need. The money has to be paid already at the beginning after all, isn't that gruesome! When I get to think about how much money this is, I get sick to my stomach. And all of it is supposed to be done as cheaply as possible; we will sleep in tents, cook ourselves, etc. It will be a real expedition. Meanwhile I almost told them I would cancel out because the whole thing might well be over 300 DM. The 200 DM doesn't include food. But I didn't want to write you that, but talked to Christoph about it yesterday. Now Christoph will give me the extra 100 DM. What do you say to that? Please, write to me soon as to what you think, if you think I shouldn't go so we could save all that money. Christoph thought that 300 DM is not very much for four weeks in Italy. But what will Julie say if Christoph gives me the money? I am not really sure yet what I should do and ask for your advice. Please don't mention this about the money to Kulos, I would not like that...

Letter from Mother, June 28, 1951 (excerpt).

This morning your two cards came. Christoph called me at once and told me that he would gladly would pay anything over the 200 DM for the Italy trip. It is a very generous thought, but I have to talk about it first with Father. So, beginning July, I shall send besides the monthly 120 DM also 200 DM for Italy.

Evidently, Father agreed to take the money from Christoph, but grudgingly. The trip was wonderful and Father was re-elected. He served until the end of 1955, when he retired.

Letter from Mother, Bremen, November 30, 1951 (beginning of the letter only).
Dear Mathilde.

Father has been elected into the new Senate…

Book V
1952-1953

Finally, in June of 1952 I passed my state exam at the University of Hamburg. I was not at all pleased with the outcome of this so very important exam. We were not examined by our professors, but by people from the school board who would be our employers. They asked us questions that were unrelated to our studies. One of those questions was: What does the word *Heimat* (home) mean to you? Is it the same as *Lebensraum*? Now that was a dumb question. I had not studied for that! I stumbled and failed that question. Still, my loving parents tried to soothe my ruffled feelings.

Letter from Mother, Neuhaus, June 18, 1952 (she was sick again).
Dear Tita.

We got your dear long letter with today's afternoon mail, and I started to read it from the end to get the result right away. I just sent a lettergram. The "satisfactory" was really taking a load off our shoulders. You definitely had bad luck. That you had to have the first days of your period during the oral as well as the written exam is too unfortunate. (Only men can be so stupid and set the dates of exams exactly four weeks apart!) …

Now from Father:

Dear Tita! We have thought much about you these days. How wonderful that the distressing examination is behind you.

Selig der Liebende,	Blessed be the loving one
der die betrübende	who has passed
heilsam und übende	the depressing but healing
Prüfung bestanden.	and teaching exam.

Mother has said all there was to say. I agree with every one of her words. Now two things:

1. Regarding "*Lebensraum*" and "*Heimat*" I tend to think as you do that there is a difference. So both of these concepts are not exactly the same. "*Lebensraum*" is objective; everybody has it at any time. But "*Heimat*" includes something subjective that is individual. Only for the child the two concepts are identical. But when the person changes his "*Lebensraum*" he might and he might not find a new "*Heimat*". If the two were identical, the word "*Heimweh*" would be meaningless.

2. Would you be able to come here for a few days to enjoy the wonderful mountain air? We will still be here for a good week since we leave on Friday, June 27. Why don't you get on the train tomorrow? Go to Göttingen and from there you take the bus to Neuhaus. Money is no object. So, might we see you?

Father.

P.S. by Mother: Please send a lettergram in case you are out of money, and we will send you some. Or even better, I will enclose 20 DM.

It had not been easy for my parents. They had supported me financially and otherwise during the six long study years after the war—my mother mostly sick, my father overworked. Still, they understood that I had tried my best and agreed to their further helping me to get a passage to America to stay with my sister in Ohio. I needed a change of venue and embarked at the end of July 1952 on the freighter *Magdalene Vinnen* at the port of Brake on the Weser downstream from Bremen. My father brought me to the ship and I will never forget watching him waving on the pier, getting smaller, smaller…

THE TRIP TO AMERICA

First postcard to Mother, from the *Magdalene Vinnen*, July 28, 1952.

Dear Mother! We are almost in Bremerhaven. Unfortunately, it is bad weather; it is raining. The departure was good; Father will have told you all about it. I like being on the ship. Our cabin is next to the eating room. We are sleeping together. Fräulein Lüpke (the only other passenger besides me on our little 6000-ton freighter) is very nice. She wants to go to California (I have her address already). The Captain's wife is going with us to Antwerp. This way she has the chance to see her husband a little longer.

Think of that, we might go via Lisbon! The last decision about that will be made in Antwerp.

The ship rides beautifully. There are also deck chairs. Thousand greetings, Tita

Because of the recommendations from my father, I was treated royally in Antwerp. The same happened in New York and practically all other cities where I went before landing in Dayton, Ohio, at my sister Cornelie (Nele) Ernst's house. Even my return home was taken care of (though I never had a chance to use this opportunity).

Telegram to my parents, from the *Magdalene Vinnen*, August 12, 1952.

Presumed arrival NewYork on Monday. Now Newfoundland. I am fine, hope you are too.

Thousand greetings, your Tita.

Letter from Mother, Bremen, August 14, 1952.
Dear Mathilde.

Just a few hours ago, we received your telegram from the ship, from the area of Newfoundland. That was wonderful, Father doesn't know yet. He is out until very late tonight, first to the foundation of the continuation of the *Mittelland Kanal* (Midland Canal) in Hannover, and then in Minden. How great that you might make it to New York by Monday. The main thing is that you are healthy. How was the voyage? And the last day with Mr. Grisar *(in Antwerp)*?

The enclosed letter is an invitation to a voyage back from New Orleans directly to Bremen, absolutely free, with the Lykes Line. Doesn't that sound fantastic! I have no idea how the climate is in New Orleans in winter, and how you would get there in February. Please, go to the agency of the

Lykes-Lines in New York and thank them. To do the trip twice would be too expensive. I would talk all of this over with the Ernsts. In New York, we will think of you under the care of Mr. Ewig; at least he can give you advice. The *Carl Schurz Gesellschaft* (Society) in Philadelphia also sent you a friendly invitation; maybe you could go there, too. *(Carl Schurz was a German American who became a senator in Washington after an adventurous life. My father was the president of this society in Bremen.)*

The Ernsts are really looking forward to your visit. Nele thinks it might be better to take the bus to Dayton; you would see much more that way. Father has so much to do since most of his colleagues are on vacation now with their families and he has difficulties with the *Mittelland Kanal.* I hope that next week things will get better. He was so happy about your long letter from Antwerp. He said, "That gives me great joy that she has such wonderful days." Otherwise, there is nothing new around here.

Best greetings, Mother

The two letters my mother mentions in her letter are as follows:

Letter #1:

Lykes Lines Agency, Inc. August 11, 1952.
Senator Dr. Hermann Apelt
B r e m e n, Kirchenstraße 4

My dear Senator Apelt!

When your daughter, Mathilde, went to the United States recently, we furnished her with a letter of introduction to our New Orleans office and we informed New Orleans that she might require passage from the Gulf on a Lykes vessel.

We are now pleased to inform you that our Principals in New Orleans advise us that they will do everything possible to arrange transportation for her on a vessel in the approximate position to meet her requirement. They further advise that they will be pleased to grant her a free passage to Bremen with the compliments of Lykes Bros. Steamship Company.

No doubt you will wish to advise your daughter of this situation.

With kindest personal regards, I am

Yours very truly,
Fred W. Riddle.

Letter #2:

Carl Schurz Gesellschaft, Inc. Herrn Hanstein.
420 Chestnut Street
Philadelphia, 6, PA

Honored Herr Hanstein,

On Saturday July 26, Fräulein Mathilde Apelt will leave for the United States on a freighter and will arrive in NewYork in approximately four weeks.

Frl. Apelt is the daughter of our president, Herrn Senator H. Apelt, whom you regrettably had missed during your last visit to Bremen. Frl. Apelt intends to stay for some time in the United States in order to prepare herself for her doctor's thesis about Bremen's cotton trade.

We would be very grateful if you could help Frl. Apelt while she is in the States and introduce her to all the places that might be helpful for her endeavor. Even if Frl. Apelt cannot come herself to Philadelphia, we would ask you very cordially to give her the addresses of your offices in NewYork and other cities. In this case, Frl. Apelt will correspond with you by writing soon after her arrival in NewYork.

You will understand that we find it very important that you take care of Frl. Apelt, since it would be very comforting for her parents. Our president and the other members of the board of *director*s are thanking you beforehand for all your efforts in this regard.

The Board of Directors
Parrau, Head Clerk.

Also:

Letter to Father from Mr. Nohmke, firm of Molson & Co in Bremen, Bremen, December 2, 1952. *Baumwoll Börse* (Cotton Exchange).
Honored Senator!

From our friends in Halletsville, Otto Goedicke and Co., we received the accompanying letter from which you will learn that your daughter had stayed for one night in Halletsville, on Monday, November 24. As you will see from the letter, she had a very good time there and she regretted that she could not stay longer.

We would like to have the attached letter back eventually.

Respectfully, Nohmke.

I could not find the attached letter. Father must have sent it back.

Letters such as these really helped to ease my ways in the various cities I was going to visit. In most cases, I received a royal treatment. It seemed important to the American business people to make a good impression on the Senator of Ports in Bremen. On September 1, I arrived in Dayton, at my sister's where I was warmly received. I enjoyed family life with her, but got a little bored by October. I had earned some money by babysitting and planned a trip of the United States that led me to most of the important cotton cities. In December, I reached California and met my future husband, Leo Waldemar Schmidt.

Letter to Mother, Lodi, December 19, 1952.
Dear Mother!

Now it's time for the Christmas letter. You might think that I am back with Nele by now, but I am still in California. I am now at the family of my student friend from Hamburg (Edith Schmidt) and will leave here tomorrow for Dayton. This family has emigrated from Germany this year and is living in Lodi, south of Sacramento. The father and the two brothers are working in a foundry here. The weather is not very good; today it is raining in droves.

I have seen the Yosemite Park from here and also was in San Francisco for a few days. That is such a pretty city! I was in Chinatown for quite a while; there you feel as though you are in the Far East. Unfortunately, I didn't have any money to buy some of the beautiful ivory things; they are very expensive. Actually, San Francisco is even prettier than New Orleans. The entire city is built on hills; a great problem for transportation within the city. For the steepest streets they have special "cable cars" with awfully loud and squeaky brakes. I also visited the town of Fresno.

The entire Californian valley is like a giant orchard. Around Lodi there are many vineyards and around Fresno many cotton fields. One day I was invited to see a cotton farm near Fresno and they picked me up with a small airplane to see everything. They wanted to be real nice to me and circled rather a long time above Fresno. But those sharp curves were too much for my stomach and I arrived airsick on the farm and had to lie down for two hours before they could show me the farm. So tomorrow morning, you can visualize me on the Greyhound bus to Dayton. For four days, I shall not leave the bus. On Christmas Eve, I will be in Dayton with Nele's family.

The oldest son in the family where I am now has asked me to marry him. He is very nice and very industrious. But I cannot decide; he is four years younger than I. In any event, first I am going back to Dayton. Someday I have to decide to marry someone since I definitely want to have children, but it is a hard decision. California is a beautiful country to live, but so very far away from all other places I know.

Now I wish you a happy Christmas,
your Mathilde.

Long letter to Mother, Dayton, December 26, 1952 (typewritten).
Dear Mother and Father!

You have not heard from me in a while. I stayed in Lodi, as I wrote already, until December 19 and left on Saturday morning. After about 85 hours on the bus, I finally landed in Dayton where Nelchen was waiting for me at the Greyhound station. The celebration on Christmas Eve was great; though not quite as sedate as you might imagine. There was no concentration to make music. The children themselves had decorated the Christmas room and arranged the presents. At 6:00 was dinner; then Daddy Ernst had to go to a meeting and then, after Daddy Ernst came back the patience of the children couldn't be bridled anymore. After a fruitless effort on Nele's part to recite the Christmas story (that all of them had learned this year) or at least sing a carol together, the children threw themselves onto the presents and in a few minutes, the whole room was a chaos of paper, ribbons, pralines, and presents. Among all of this, Sammy (the cat) sat happily in the lap of the family.

Meanwhile I have decided to marry. It is awfully far away from you all, I know that, but I am determined about this. It is better to do so and not to wait many more years. I shall marry into a very healthy family that comes from the east of Germany, has owned a foundry there, and had to flee already twice from the Russians. I already wrote you that I had studied together with his sister in Hamburg. Her brother is 27 years old, his name is Leo Schmidt, and he is a mechanic. Walter tells me that this trade has very good possibilities in this country. In any event, it has better prospects for the future than school teaching. Overall, the future looks better here than in Germany or elsewhere in Europe. My future husband has the wish to have children, just like I do. I would not have found a husband like him in Europe.

We might do it this way: I am going back to California next week, then we shall marry sometimes in January, and in February I am going back to Europe to get my immigration visa. It would be good to get on the list of emigrants as soon as possible. I would be very grateful if you could ask one of the consuls, Dur or McLaughlin, for advice. I could write to the consulate in Bremen myself, but I think it is just as good if you talk to one of the consuls. I talked to a lady here in Dayton who knows quite a bit about immigration. She tells me I need an "application blank for registration for permanent residence." When you talk to a consul, he will know what to do. In any event, I don't want to lose much time and wait unnecessarily long in Germany for a visa. So please send your next letter to California. My address there is:

c/o Waldemar Schmidt (the father)
208 Eden Street
Lodi, California, U.S.A.

Now you would like to know more about the family. The members of the family are: the father, 48 years old; the mother, 56 years old; Edith, my friend, 28 (still in Germany); Leo, 27; and Dagobert, 21 years old. Dagobert is engaged and his bride is also German and will come next year. So, we are a real big family. Leo is the same size as I, is very strong and very nice. He came here two years ago by himself. This was possible because his uncle, who is a pastor, is living in Lodi. So he got his affidavit from this uncle. After two years he was able to send the affidavit for his family. *(This is not correct. Someone else, a Mr. Kaiser, the person who Leo worked for at that time, signed the affidavit for the family. Leo could not do it because he was not a citizen yet).*

When the family arrived, they found a completely furnished house. The family has now been here for half a year. They also have a car, no, two cars. Leo has a nice Plymouth that he bought for $1800.--, and little Dago has just bought one for $800.--. Leo and the father are presently working at a foundry and are earning about $300.-- per month. The younger brother works at a metal factory in Stockton, about ten miles from Lodi. But they don't want to do this kind of work forever; it is too hard. Somehow, they would like to start something on their own again. But for this they have to learn to speak English better. That will come in time, and I could help with this since I have learned English quite well in the meantime.

Now you see the purpose for my studying; without it I never would have met Edith and therefore would have never come to Lodi. Even if the studies themselves should not be used by me, they have helped me indirectly with my life. Besides, I did not really study to become a teacher, but just to have been doing university work. I am so happy now with my life; it couldn't have developed better.

Walter is urgently advising me to get the doctors' degree. Then I could teach at a university later on in case my husband should be drafted or something else should happen. Of course, right now I am not in the right mood to concentrate on studying. I would rather take some practical courses like cooking or sewing. Well, we shall see. I could send all the material that I have collected on this trip to Bremen and assemble it there while waiting for my visa.

Now I am waiting for a letter from you to find out what you think about all of this. Maybe you are not too shocked. You might even have suspected something like this. But maybe not that I would be staying in California.

I wonder if Julie will let me keep her colorful dress; it fits so well with the California style and I love it so much. I would be happy if she gives it to me for the wedding.

Nele wants me to write the last hilarious thing the twins did. We were playing *quartet* (authors) with your economy port and shipping quartet (in German) and they asked for *Kanäle* (canals). There Madeline all of a sudden saw the light and piped up, "Daddy, isn't that where mother's name comes from?" Walter almost died laughing *(Nele's name sounds like* Kanäle.)

Meanwhile I received three long letters from Dr.Wagner (the director of the Bremen Natural History Museum who had lent me a camera to take pictures for a cotton exhibition at his museum). I believe he likes me. I have to write him today. I am so relieved that he got all those pictures and cotton leaves. And how are the *Schnuckies? (My salamanders from Hamburg. My mother had taken good care of them all this time, a piece of her daughter!)* They will finally have to go to the city aquarium for they will hardly get an imigration visa.

Now thousand greetings for the New Year, and for your birthday.

Your Tita.

And my parent's response to this news…

Letter from Mother, Bremen, December 27, 1952 (excerpt).

… And how about the proposal for marriage? Do you love him? That he is four years younger should not be a reason not to marry him. How good that you are talking the whole thing over with Nele. Please write more about this…

Letter from Father, Bremen, January 4, 1953.

Dear Tita!

Those were exciting letters indeed that you wrote us: the first one with part of the news, then the second one with all the news, and finally the letter from Nele that again told us about the not quite decided news. I do not have to tell you that our very best wishes accompany you. And you will understand that our feelings are mingled with happiness and sadness. For it is not quite easy for parents if the third daughter is leaving Europe behind and intends to settle several thousand kilometers further west. *(My sister Dorothee had immigrated to Argentina in 1948.)* It has cost your mother a sleepless night. In addition, we don't have any idea how "he" looks, how he speaks and writes, thinks and feels. Nevertheless, I am trusting that your healthy feeling will lead you to do the right thing and that your final decision will arrive at the solution that is best for you. And so it shall also be the best thing for us.

If everything is working out according to your last letter, then tell him, whom you will give your love to, that I shall welcome him as son-in-law. Even though we are not acquainted, my daughter's decision shall be enough guarantee. As the Bible tells us, "He went to find his father's she-ass, and he found a kingdom." So she could say, "She went to do her doctor's thesis and found a husband," or the doctor's hat became the bonnet. I have learned from the encyclopedia that California is derived from the Spanish "*caliente fornicalla*," meaning "hot oven." So my child will have it warm and at least she won't freeze.

You know already from Mother's letter that my empire of Amazons has been extended by one more little granddaughter. I have just seen the little person; she is such a complete and lively little human being.

And again our best wishes,
Your father.

Letter from Leo to my parents, no date, but before January 30, 1953 (maybe January 17).

My dear parents-in-law!

Fate has it that I cannot ask you for the hand of your daughter in person. So I shall do so this way. I thank you so much for the trust you have in me and ask you to bless our union and our future life. How much would I have liked to meet you, my dear parents, as you would have liked to meet me. However, it is not possible for me to cross the ocean again after such a short since it has only been two and one half years that I came to this country and started to build my future here. Abroad in Germany, all of us from West Prussia lost our possessions and had to flee to the area of Hanover. Because of the difficult and limited situation there, we could not see our future securely and therefore decided to emigrate. I was lucky enough to come here first and was able to receive my parents and my brother who came half a year ago, prepared and ready to facilitate getting familiar with the new country for them.

I myself have a job at a foundry and am earning my living with the work of my hands. I didn't have enough time yet to accumulate a large bank account since I helped my parents financially while they were still in Müden and sent money to my sister in Hamburg, and also had to acquire things for myself. But I have already learned to adjust to the customs of this new country and I have earned trust and respect. This means so much in this country.

In spite of this, I would not have married so soon if your daughter had not come into my life by chance or fate. Sometimes life is very hard that even as a young person one has made up his mind about one's future. Then, in Kurland, when I had to fight at the front against the Russians; I thought that I never would get out of this situation. My parents had given up on me as well, and when I, several months after the end of the war, found them near Hanover and surprised them, and was again back with my family; then I was so happy that I felt like I was on top of the world. But I will never forget to stand with both of my feet on this earth.

So now, I have met this lovable person and I want us to build our future together. I am well aware of the fact that she is several years older that I, but how fast does time travel. I will try very hard not to let her feel the age difference. My dear parents-in-law, how happy am I to have met Mathilde. And she is also happy; her radiant eyes tell me this. She tells me she has become a different person. She is happy about every little thing I give her and she makes me happy too.

Immediately after our engagement, we rented a nice room from the same landladies I lived with before, a couple of very nice older sisters. Here she will stay until we get married. During the day, when I am at work she thinks the time feels long, but when I come home, already at 4:00, we spend wonderful hours together that just fly by. In the evenings, after I bring her home, she reads all her mail to me. So today we read your dear letter of January 14 together in which you think so lovingly about us. Also your letter, dear Father, that you wrote a few days ago. I only wish I have the opportunity to see you at least once during your lifetime. Through your letters that Mathilde shares with me, I know you already and love you just as my own parents. I am only sorry that nobody from Mathilde's side will be at the wedding, but that is my fault. Why did I have to immigrate to California! During our honeymoon, we plan to go to Southern California.

Most heartfelt greetings, your Leo.

So we got married on January 30, 1953, in the small church in Lodi, California. None of my own family came—my mother too sick, my father too busy, and my sisters all raising their small children. I now had a new family: the Schmidts. However, we stayed connected through letters. Near the end of 1953 our first child was born, Leo Hermann Schmidt.

Now two official letters from the German and the American consulates.

Letter from Consul Dur; February 2, 1953.
Americal Consulate General, Bremen, Haus des Reiches.
Dear Senator Apelt:

In order to remove what appears to be some misunderstanding concerning the information I gave you a few days ago outlining the steps to be taken by your daughter in securing a visa if she marries during her present sojourn in the United States, I am outlining below the procedure to be followed:

If Miss Apelt marries her fiancé, who it is understood has been admitted into the United States for permanent legal residence, she is entitled to apply for third preference classification as a quota immigrant. Persons in this classification are entitled to preferential consideration under 20% of the quota to which they are chargeable and to third preference within any other portion of such quota not required for the issuance of visas to persons in the first and second preference class. The annual German quota is approximately 25,000.

In order for your daughter to secure preference status as the wife of a non-American who has been lawfully admitted into the United States for legal permanent residence, your daughter's prospective husband must submit a petition to the Attorney General after they are married. The required forms and information may be secured at any Immigration and Naturalization Service in America. These offices are located in every large town throughout the United States.

It may be possible for your daughter to secure an immigration visa after her marriage without departing from the United States, because section 245 of the Immigration and Nationality Act provides that the status of a non-American lawfully admitted to the United States as a bona-fide non-immigrant may be adjusted by the Attorney General in his discretion and that immigration visas may be issued to such people, provided the quota to which they are chargeable is undersubscribed. This office was informed today that the German quota is now current, which means that if it is not actually undersubscribed at the present time, it doubtless will be before long.

I wish to impress upon you that this office is not in a position to guarantee that your daughter will be able to secure a visa without leaving the United States in the manner outlined in the preceding paragraph because this decision rests solely with the Attorney General.

Sincerely yours,
Signature, Philip F.Dur, American Consul in Bremen.

Letter from the Immigration and Naturalization Service,
630 Sansome Street, San Francisco, California.
February 4, 1953.
Mrs. Mathilde Schmidt, 208 Eden Street, Lodi, CA.
Dear Madam,

You have been granted an extension of your temporary admission to the United States until August 16, 1953, as a visitor for pleasure.

Your passport, valid until February 1, 1958, is returned herewith by registered mail. Visitor's permit # V-1350711 endorsed to show action taken is stapled thereto.

Receipt is acknowledged of United States Postal Money Order in the amount of $10.--.

Upon your departure from the United States, please surrender Form 257A or Form I-94, or this letter if you do not possess either of the forms mentioned, to:

1. Canadian Immigration Officer if departing to Canada, or,
2. United States Immigration Officer if departing to Mexico, or,
3. Transportation company if departing elsewhere.

Your compliance with these instructions will greatly aid this Service in clearing your record.

Very truly yours, A.Kucklin,
District Director.

Letter from Father to Leo, Bremen, February 8, 1953.
Dear Leo!

Your dear letter of January 17 brought great joy to Mother Julie and me. I hoped to write in time so you would find this answer when you returned from your honeymoon, but this did not happen. I am rather occupied for my old age. Only Sundays are free for writing letters to family and friends, and sometimes even these are taken by official affairs. For instance, this morning I had to participate in opening an exhibition of French art in our art museum.

Your decision to get married was of course quite a surprise for us and you will understand that the joyful feelings were mixed with those of sorrow. But I am sure that Mathilde has chosen well and I trust in her healthy judgment. However, it is hard for parents, and especially for the mother, when three of our four daughters are married overseas. Mathilde now is in the beautiful, but far away California. I myself had been looking forward to having her tell us about her travels, and that I have to miss now. If we see each other again, all these experiences will be long behind her. **Because of our mutual interests, I had more in common with Mathilde than with my other children. I will miss this very much**. But it is part of being a father to bear such disappointments.

We thought very much about you on your wedding day. I hope that our telegram arrived in time. It is not so easy to pick the correct time, considering the difference in hours. You yourself will not have much time or inclination to write. But if Mathilde continues to describe to us how you are building your life and existence, we will be happy enough. Our thoughts are with you.

So we are sending you our heartfelt greetings. Also give our regards to your parents and brother.

Your Father Hermann.

P.S. We were very happy to have met your sister and now have a lively connection with a member of the so far unknown family of our son-in-law.

Letter to Mother, Lodi, February 8, 1953 (excerpt).

Dear Mother!

Enclosed are the notarized copies of our marriage certificate. My affairs here are as follows: I have been granted an extension of my visitor's visa for half a year, so that I may now stay in the United States until August 16, 1953. If I do not get another extension then I must leave. There is a new law initiated by Truman that he had issued just before he left office in order to save the nation from communist infiltration. There is a possibility that I might not get this extension. But in this case you can help me in Bremen to get my emigration papers as fast as possible. These papers could already be processed now and sent to California in case my signature is necessary. Leo would do everything possible on this side, like the affidavit of support and other papers. Please let me know what the consul thinks and how much time all this might take and how long it might be in the worst case. Hopefully there won't be another war. Right now, Leo and I don't even want to think of getting separated. And what if I should be pregnant in August? Do I have to go on this long voyage? All this seems so unnecessary, seen from here, especially since Leo will be a citizen automatically in two years and I can then stay as his wife. Maybe there will be a new law before August; one hopes so much from Eisenhower.

Tita

I became pregnant and the authorities managed to find a spot for me on the quota. I now became the proud owner of a "Green Card," allowing me to work.

Note from Father, Bremen, Kirchenstr. 4, April 21, 1953.
Dear Tita!

Today is the birthday of Frau Schmidt and the thoughts of the parents are all abroad in Lodi. Mother has celebrated the day by buying an exotic potted violet for herself. I myself have thought about my children while singing the enclosed happiness-promising, Californian-Sacramentalic refrain to the enclosed song.

Mother has been feeling rather low for several weeks. However, for the last a few days she has been feeling better and can get up for several hours regularly every day. Maybe it is this nice spring weather that is helping her.

With many greetings to both of
you, your Father.

Refrain to the Sacramento song:

Blow, ye winds, hioh, for Californio!
There's plenty of gold, so I am told,
At the banks of Sacramento.

Letter from Vice Consul Holm to Father, no date (must have been in May of 1953).
Senator Dr. Hermann Apelt, Rathaus, Bremen.
Sir:

Prior to his departure on a vacation to Rome, Mr. Dur referred your query concerning the issuance of an immigration visa to your daughter to me for reply.

There seems to be no particular problem to judge from the information furnished me by Mr. Dur, which he indicated had been received from you. The German quota is still under-subscribed according to information on file at this office, a fact that the Immigration and Naturalization Service office in Stockton can easily confirm by communication with the Department of State in Washington. With respect to a police certificate, I suggest that you submit either a *Strafregister* (criminal record) or *Füehrungszeugnis* (certificate of behavior) in the original with a translation thereof. These should contain a statement that it covers the preceding two years.

It is hoped that the information given above will be of assistance to you, and if there are any other questions that may arise, please do not hesitate to request any aid that you feel we will be able to render you.

Very truly yours,
Arvid G.Holm,
America Vice-Consul.

Letter to my parents, Lodi, June 5, 1953.

... Last Monday Leo and I went to San Francisco for an appointment at the consulate. They asked us several questions and I was sent to a doctor for an examination, blood test and X-rays. Now we have to wait for the final decision. The letter by the American vice-consul that you sent me sounds very positive. Doesn't it say that the German quota is not full at this moment? ...

Letter to Father, Lodi, July 8, 1953.

Dear Father!

In two days is your birthday and both of us hope you will spend it in best health. Are you having as much heat as we are? I can hardly wish that for you. It is up to 110 degrees Fahrenheit in the shade during the day; that is about 42 degree Celsius. Only the northern rooms in the house are livable. In the evenings, it cools down a bit, enough to let us sleep. I only wear a light summer suit; a dress is much too hot. Poor Leo works in a building with a roof of corrugated metal, and on top of that they pour iron in that building so that it is always a few degrees hotter than outside. He always comes home completely drenched. It's only really cool inside the stores (air-conditioned), in the water and in the movies. I am so happy that my baby comes in October and not earlier. Then the great heat is hopefully over.

Over the 4th of July holiday we made a nice tour to Lake Tahoe. We started very early at 4:00 in the morning and arrived around 9:00 at the lake. There it was nice and cool since the lake, originally a volcanic crater, is fed by the waters of surrounding snow-capped mountains. We spent most of the day in a rented boat on the water. In the evening, we danced at the village "El Tahoe." We stayed overnight in a cabin near the lake that we could rent for a few dollars. That was very comfortable. We had a bedroom, bathroom, and kitchen with gas stove, even an icebox. We bought groceries at the nearby grocery store close to the camp. The next morning we went back home over curvy roads, which was not good for me. It took us all day since Dago and Leo, our men, had to try out their fishing skills on the way.

We haven't heard from you in a while; hopefully a good sign. Edith wrote us that Mother had sent her a letter with enclosed answering card, the same method her mother uses in the worst case; we all laughed heartily. Tante Luise sent a charming letter and five beautiful edgings of Old Bremen. I shall write her, but maybe Mother tells her I have received it, and it made us very happy.

We sent a small package to you, containing coffee, chocolate and a shirt. Hope it arrives. This time we sent the coffee already ground, maybe then you don't have to pay duty. Please let us know if you do have to pay again.

We are swimming in fruit. Right now it's apricots and the peaches are starting. I have now 13 glasses *(canning jars)* with cherries and 24 glasses with apricots. We need lots of stewed fruit because Leo takes some in his lunchbox daily.

We hope you are having a great birthday with much cake and coffee.

Many, many greetings from your
Leo and Mathilde.

Letter from Mother, Bremen, July 16, 1953.
Dear Mathilde.

(This is a long letter from Mother and a short one from Father. I only translated the short one.)

Dear Mathilde!

Thank you so much for your letter, pictures, shirt and stockings. This is very elegant clothing! I shall wear it proudly as a present from my daughter with her self-earned money. My birthday was regrettably spent mostly on the train since I didn't come home until 10:30 in the evening. Mother was not feeling well. Meanwhile this has improved. Again, it had to do with our terrible weather here. We would have loved to share some of our rain with you. According to your description, California honors its name. This summer heat is your payment for the beauty of the landscape. We hope you are not suffering too much. I forgot to mention the coffee, thank you so much for that!

Many dear greetings, your father.

Telegram to my parents, Lodi, October 24, 1953.

Leo Hermann arrived everything is all right – Leo Schmidt

Letter from Mother and Father, Bremen, October 25, 1953.

Dear Mathilde, dear Leo.

Last night at 8:30 your wonderful telegram came telling us about the birth of your Leo Hermann. You can imagine how happy we are and how grateful we are that Mathilde has everything behind her. So it went well and the boy is healthy! The parents in Lodi will be just as happy. Please give them our best wishes. Tita had the right feeling that it would be a boy. And the doctor was not right with his heartbeat theory. The Kulos, who celebrated their engagement anniversary yesterday, were told last night by telephone. And at the same time Tante Lotte had a telegram from Montevideo that Dirk and Ruthilde have a little daughter.

Wulf stayed with us for three days and we enjoyed this very much. He left early on the 23rd for Düsseldorf, from there to Finland, and then to Switzerland. Beginning November, he goes back to South America. He looks heavier and also his hair turned gray. He was very balanced and in a splendid mood so that it was enjoyable with him. On the last evening the Darjes, Tante Lotte, and we sat together at the Kulenkampffs. Today is Julie Rohland's confirmation, regrettably without the father. Confirmations, according to Wulf, are celebrated in Argentinia almost like weddings, with long white dresses and masses of presents.

On November 5, Christoph is flying to Buenos Aires and stays for four weeks in Argentina. It will be a lonely winter for Julie.

We now wait for your next letter with excitement.

All good wishes, Mother.

And from Father from the *Braut von Messina (Schiller)*

Selber die Kirche, die göttliche, stellt nicht
Schöneres dar auf dem himmlischen Thron,
Höheres bildet selber die Kunst nicht, die göttlich geborne,
Als die Mutter mit ihrem Sohn.

Even the Holy Church; even the heavenly art can't depict anything
More beautiful than the mother and her son.

I dedicate this quote from Schiller to my daughter, Mathilde.
The Happy Grandfather

Letter from Leo to my parents, Lodi, October 25, 1953.
My dear parents!

We are having Sunday and I shall write a few lines to you, dear parents. It has been quite a while since I wrote you the last time. Since Mathilde became my wife, she takes over all our correspondence and does it for me. She knows that I am a reluctant letter writer; therefore, she doesn't mind doing it. We read the incoming letters together and we enjoy them and talk about their contents.

Since our wedding, we have become better acquainted and know each other better. Everyone agrees that our wedding happened a little too fast, but it seemed to be the right thing to do. The main thing now is that Mathilde does not have to go abroad anymore. It must be hard for you, dear parents, to know that she is not coming back to Bremen. Fate has decided that she is staying here. The final goodbye from home would have to come for her anyway and might even have been harder for you. God's ways are mysterious, and who knows when we will see each other in the future. How much would I love that and talk to you in person. Not long ago it would almost have been possible to meet you, dear Father, but it couldn't be, so we wait for the next opportunity.

Dear parents, I am trusting fully in you and hope you will trust me too. I shall always, come what will, stand at the side of Mathilde, especially now that she has given me a son. We are very different personalities. We come from different backgrounds. Mathilde comes from a merchant's and I from a farmer's family. *(He meant my mother's side. My father came from a teacher and writer's family.)* When I was 17 years old I wanted to become a farmer though my father owned a factory and wanted me to take it over. But the school of life has turned my life in a different way. Now I am here in America, and with my wife and son beside me I shall build up my future. Maybe soon we are able to have our own home where we will be happy and satisfied.

About everything that happened during the last days and in the hospital, Mathilde and also my mother will write you. We have received your dear telegram and thank you.

Many heartfelt greetings,
your son Leo.

Book VI
1954-1955

Letter From Father, Bremen, no date, (must have been in April 1954).
Dear Mathilde!

For the first birthday that you are celebrating together with two Leos, the big and the little lion, I send you the best wishes and greetings. We shall think of you with all our hearts. Recently I spoke with a man from Los Angeles, California, who also knows Lodi and Stockton. Mother has improved much after a time of rather poor health with help of good advice from three doctors. She is marvelously fresh and active.

We are looking forward to Dörte's visit.

With everlasting affection, your
always ageing Father.

Letter from Father (and Mother), Bremen, July 11, 1954.
Dear Tita!

Yesterday morning when I was still in bed, friendly violin music sounded in our bedroom into the ear of the 78-year-old one. It was our granddaughter, Hedwig, who had thought of this wonderful surprise. After dressing quickly and following the sweet sounds, I found myself in front of an overloaded gift-table, radiating candle brightness. It took me a while to get used to this entire splendor. Among the wonderful things, I detected a night garment that is so brilliantly colorful that I regret to wear it during the dark night, and cannot show myself in its lively colors at daylight. Something for the palate as well as the spirit. Thousand thanks for all your love and all the goodness for this old gentleman. Special thanks for the letter and the two photos. We especially love the picture of Leo Hermann in the bathtub, where his little head appears so radiant above the rim. We are only sad that he is not feeling well right now. We would appreciate if you could write us more about that. During the morning several visitors came, among others also friend Spitta. In the afternoon the three younger Kulos appeared (Hedwig had meanwhile left for Sottrum). So we had a good time together and played in the garden in the nicest weather: *Dreh Dich nicht um, der Plumpsack geht um* (Don't turn around, the "*Plumpsack*" (knotted handkerchief) goes around) and similar games, grandchildren and grandparents all together.

Our vacation in the *Knüll* was extremely successful, only it was regrettable that Mother had a little downfall again during the second half, and had to restrain herself with hikes. I am glad to report that she is feeling better now. With this, I shall close to let her write a few words.

So, once again heartfelt thanks and many dear greetings to Father, Mother and Son.

Your Father.

Letter from Father, Bremen, after Christmas (after Mother's letter of December 18, 1954).

Dear Tita!

Thanks and greetings! Thanks for clothes and food (coffee)! The stockings are so nice that I am debating to switch in my 79th year from boots to low shoes so the beautiful colors can be seen. I hope you had a wonderful Christmas!—as we had too. Only, one should not think about politics.

All the best to you, your Father.

Note from Father, Kassel, May 6, 1955.

We are saying: What Tita wants to do, she does it. First it's supposed to be a boy, and Leo Hermann appears. Then, it should be a girl now, and Doris appears! You don't believe how relieved Mother was when the news about the arrival of the little lady came here to us in Kassel. All the best!

The Grandfather

Letter from my parents, Bremen, November 7, 1955 (to Leo for his birthday).

My dear Leo.

Your birthday is near and we think of you often with many good wishes. In this new year of your life, there will be the realization of your wish, the purchase of a house. That makes us very happy. You will have so much more room. That it is so close to the lake seems very advantageous. Hopefully the book I sent you will come in time. We love this book very much. Just now it strikes me that you will be 30 years old this year; that is a very special part of your life. How will you celebrate this day? How nice that it falls on a Sunday. I already wrote Mathilde that the election turned out very unfavorable for our citizen-oriented party. This in contrast to Hamburg, which now has a majority of citizen-party seats. Our very popular mayor is a Social Democrat, so it might result in a Senate coalition where the citizen-group functions as minority.

Father will step out and we are already making plans for the retirement. We can hardly imagine this after such an active life in office. In any event, these last weeks will still be crowded with activities.

Last week we had an "Evangelical week" here in Bremen, a little too noisy for us; cars with loudspeakers were driving around, performances, but also nice concerts and exhibitions of Evangelical art. Everything has to be louder than is used to be, otherwise it doesn't get attention.

If you don't like to write letters, please don't do it. We are used to this from Walter Ernst. But now, since his son is away from home and he exchanges letters with him, it seems that the ice is broken. So Father got two long letters by him, much to his surprise, during last year. Our Christmas package for you will go off in the next few days.

Farewell, all good wishes!
Your Mother-in-law.

From Father.
Best wishes from the heart for you and your family.

Father Hermann.

Book VII
1956-1958

Letter from Father, Bremen, January 1, 1956, (He is now officially retired—at age 80!).

Dear Tita!

Today your letter from December 26 came. Thousand thanks that you wrote so quickly, thanks also to your mother-in-law from whom we also got a letter written the same date. We were indeed quite worried since we had read in the papers about the severe flooding in Oregon and northern California. Sacramento was mentioned specifically. According to your letter, the danger must have been great for you and your new house. We are so thankful that it did not come to that. But your letter was not definite about whether or not the water masses finally receded. Let us know as soon as you can. How unnerving the night from December 23 to 24 must have been for you and the entire city! But the situation is not quite clear for us. How was the connection of city, river, dammed-up basin and lake? Is the river going through the lake? Or is the lake filling up (as Julie sees it) from below from the rising groundwater? Above all, was there or is there still the danger of the reservoir's dam breaking?

Yesterday was the day earmarked for your moving? Did this big event take place? Or did you wait because of the water danger? We are very anxious to hear from you. We thought much about you over Christmas. First, we celebrated with the Kulenkampffs and all the grandchildren, then by ourselves here. Mother is unfortunately feeling low again for the last two weeks and for the last two days extremely bad. In this regard, the new year has begun unpleasantly for us, but we hope that this will change soon.

Tomorrow afternoon we are expecting Tante Mathilde from Dresden. For me this New Year is of special importance. On December 28, our new Senate was voted in to which the two oldest, our friend Spitta and I, now do not belong anymore. Therefore, I am now in the state of retirement. But so far retirement hasn't changed much for me. The flood of letters that have to be answered is immense, almost like your water flood.

Mother has already thanked you for your plentiful gifts. I am very happy with the shirt and can use it well. But the best present is the pictures of the children. How I would have loved to observe Leo, the little man, opening the packages. Too bad that the distance is so great.

Enough for today. This letter has to be sent. Best greetings to all of you. And Mother sends her greetings as well. Write us soon!

Your Father.

Now a citation from Faust II *(Goethe):*

Da rase draußen Flut bis auf zum Rand,
Und wie sie nascht, gewaltsam einzuschließen,
Gemeinsdrang eilt die Lücke zu verschließen.

If outside floods are raving to the rim,
And while they try to gain entrance,
Men band together to fill the break.

Letter from my parents, Bremen, April 15, 1956.
From Father:
Dear Tita!

For your birthday best wishes for you and your family! Recently at a nautical dinner where I participated, they sang the Californian song. I was vividly thinking of "my" Californians. I think that, in a way, you also belong to one of the luckiest gold-seekers in the basin of the Sacramento.

Your Father.

Letter from my parents, Bremen, December 12, 1956 (Christmas letter).
And a few lines from Father:
Dear Tita!

The earth is getting too small for people who have the money to travel. For the others, to which category we belong, the earth is too big and will stay that way for the 10,000 km from here to you. But we still have the advantage of airmail and so these lines with our wishes for a good Christmas and New Years will reach you in time. How I wish I could have peeked into your Christmas room, but that can only happen in our imagination. This year Doris must be able to understand everything better: the celebration, the Christmas tree, and also the presents. We wish all of you, Father, Mother and Children all the best from our heart.

Your old Father, Hermann.

Letter from Father, Bremen, February 2, 1957 (was folded in the *Hermann Apelt* book—an original).
Dear Tita!

You wrote me that you are reading Schopenhauer and that you enjoy it. Schopenhauer belongs to those who wrote the best German, clearly and ingeniously. There was a time (far back) when he was "my" philosopher. This he is not true anymore and hopefully he will not be "yours," because the concusions he reaches are not for people who love life. In spite of that, I still like to read some pages by him. I especially recommend to you the "*Aphorismen zur Lebenskunst*" that contain much truth. He considered himself a pupil of Kant, and in a way, he was. That means he starts with Kant and stays with the nucleus of Kant's teaching: the transcendental identity of space and time. Overall, one can say about the same about the relationship between Kant and Schopenhauer what Goethe says about his own relationship to Schopenhauer in his *Farbenlehre* (science of colors):

"*Träge gern noch länger des Lebens Bürden,*
Wenn Schüler nur nicht gleich Lehrer würden."

"I would like to carry on with life's load
If only pupils wouldn't become teachers."

Or "*Unser Bestgedachtes in fremden Adern*
Wird alsbald mit uns selber hadern."

"Our best thoughts in other's veins
Will soon disagree with our own."

Already Locke and Hume taught that the phenomena of the sensitivities (the colors, the sounds, the odors, the tastes, the feelings) were caused by the organs, and not by the objects. In Goethe's *Farbenlehre* (his *Theory of Colors)* this becomes very clear. An object *is* not red; it *appears* red. These subjective sensitivities were called *secondary* characteristics of objects. In contrast, the special and timely characteristics of objects the British philosopher Hume calls *primary* characteristics. Here Kant does the decisive step by teaching that so-called primary characteristics are not objective characteristics of the real objects: *das Ding an sich,* (the thing itself); surely space and time also are just appearances of the subject, meaning ourselves. And therefore, the objects are not responsible for our sensations but the subject itself is.

(I do not know if I got that right!) I see the objects so-to-speak through colored glasses and hear through so-called sound glasses, sense space and time through space and time glasses. That is the teaching about space and time identity. (The opposite of identity is reality.) If this *Ding an sich,* according to Kant, is real, we'll never know what it really is. It is beyond our understanding. According to him, all we can understand and explain are appearances, meaning those concepts and ideas that we have about the world around us. Whatever is behind those appearances will always be a secret. All this is according to Kant. Here his pupil thinks different. He says, "I, Arthur Schopenhauer, have found what no one has found before (except maybe perhaps the ancient Indians) and what Kant has not been able to find: the will." All appearances are reactions of the will. I believe that if Kant had met Schopenhauer during his lifetime, he would have said, "Dear friend! Also your will, as far as you find it in yourself, is just an appearance. And as far as you think you find it in the things around us, this is not "finding" but "fiction" *(in German "Findung" and "Erfindung")* or maybe a good try to explain things that we mortals can never know. But I only chose the one main point in his teachings. There may be much more to discuss. Our will should not be negative but positive in spite of all the unfortunate happenings in our times.

Your Father

Letter from my parents, Bremen, July 11, 1957 (description of Father's birthday).
And from Father:
Dear Mathilde!

Mother has written about everything so detailed and lively that there is only the opportunity left for me to thank you for your good wishes and the pictures, and for your letter. Mother already wrote that we saw the family Schmidt on our wall in brilliant colors. Thanks to the wonderful technique that makes such a thing is possible now. Still, even these pictures are only *Ersatz* (substitution) for the real thing. The wish to see you all in reality and to hear your sounds will always be our wish. Mother had a few bad weeks, but has gotten over the Californian heat (we felt like we are with you) quite well and is now extraordinarily energetic.

With love, your old father.

Letter from Father, Bremen, December 17, 1957.
My dear Tita!

So you will be five family members this year for Christmas Eve. *(Barbara was born on March 3, 1957.)* Thanks so much for the pretty pictures that came recently. Now we can really see your little folks before us. How big is the boy, how impressive Doris and how cute little Barbara Ann. Of course, how much nicer it would be to see the three little beings face to face and to hear their voices. But it is part of being a human being that one has to be satisfied with his fate.

I am very happy about your wakening interest in Goethe. Among all of those who wrote in "my beloved German," he has remained the greatest. Also it is sad to think that most of our grandchildren will never be able to know much more than his name. But one must accept that.

Mother has, as usual when she is feeling well, done too much, especially now preparing for the coming holidays, and now she is lying in bed for a few days. But she is on the road to recovery and I think she will be much better when Christmas arrives.

For two days now, we have had quite an unusual cold snap. At 4:00 in the morning it is so cold that the birds don't want to leave their nest and while other times they appear in masses to eat our food on the verandah, today not one of them has shown up. So it seems that the need for warmth is greater than the one for food, and so they stay in their nest.

All is well at the Kulenkampffs. Julie was just here, and she wants to go ice skating with friends. Snow and ice, does that exist in the "hot oven"? Or are your children only learning about this through pictures? But I keep forgetting that you are very close to the snow-covered mountains. Aren't they called "Sierra Nevada"?

As cold and frosty as it may be outside and also inside, in rooms that need to be heated, as warm and heartfelt are our greetings and wishes for parents and children!

With constant love, your Father.

Letter from Father, Bremen, July 12, 1958.
Dear Mathilde!

It is a special joy of birthdays that one gets letters from his daughters and even from some granddaughters. And the joy is doubly so when the content is as pleasant as in your dear letter. Thanks a thousand times! How wonderful that Leo is well again.

Nele's letter, unfortunately, brought less good news. I don't know if she already wrote you that Walter had a relapse of nervous tension and he now is in the hospital again. This is a real worry for her. The hospital, a different one than the first time, is very far away and she is visiting him twice daily. He is getting electric shock treatments. Hopefully this will have the hoped-for result.

Mother has had a bad time after a series of very good periods. So she is in bed again and could not come with us on the afternoon of the July 10 to Horstedt (country estate of the Kulenkampffs) where the four little girls had prepared some nice poems for me and had picked a bowlful of forest blueberries. Julie, Christoph, Spitta, and I had a few very nice hours together.

Today we enjoyed the visit of the entire Rohland family here in Bremen. Wulf had business in Bremen. Everything seems to be going smoothly for them. They had some problems with schooling for all the children, but these have also been solved.

Now I have to thank you especially for the photos. It is such joy to look at them and this is only diminished by the knowledge that we will never see them in person.

You write that I should put my memories of my office time onto paper. That is also my own wish, and I have started to gather material together. But though I am now "retired," the "retirement" has not quite kicked in. However, time will improve that.

Please give my greetings to Leo and the three children and many greetings to you as well.

Your father.

Letter from Father, Bremen, October 20, 1958.
Dear Mathilde!

We were very happy about your long letter. Thanks very much! You want to hear about the Spanish adventures of the old man, and I would love to oblige you with that. There really were two magnets that pulled me to the Pyrenean peninsula. When I was young, someone gave me Washington Irwin's book about the "Alhambra." It is very pleasant and even today, one and 1/4 centuries later, very worthwhile reading. Since that time, to see the Moorish castle has been a dream for me, and I became eighty-two years old before I fulfilled this dream of setting my foot onto Spanish soil. The second magnet was a famous picture by Velasquez, called

"*Las Lanzes*," because of the forest of spears that form the background. It depicts the surrender of the fortress Breda (1625) that can be seen in the background on the left side. The center of the picture is the group of victors. The Spanish general Spinole receives from the hand of the besieged, Justin of Nassau, the keys of the fortress that had to be given up after a long siege. Already after World War I, and mainly after World War II, this painting, only familiar from copies and photographs, was expressing the most noble aspect of human relations in history: the relationship between conqueror and conquered that has been repeated thousand-fold. Here it has been captured in a Christian-human sense by the artist, in the most noble deportment of victor and loser, the one in the consciousness of having won, the other of having lost, but standing above his loss and not having lost his human dignity. I had seen some colored copies also and these woke a certain doubt in me as to how true these colors might be. This created the desire to see the original and it became almost a craving.

It would have been next to impossible to make this trip by myself, at my age, not knowing the language and without knowledge of the country. Therefore, I decided to get a seat on one of the travel busses. Such a bus tour has great advantages and unpleasant disadvantages. On the plus side, one does not have to worry about getting lodging and food; all those necessities are included in the price of the transportation. Additional costs are only drinks (*vino, tincto*, and *vino blanca*), postcards, souvenirs and gifts. The disadvantage is that one is practically chained together with the group on the bus, so if one would like to spend more time in Madrid or a few hours more in the Alhambra, he would have to forgo this desire and bend to the itinerary of the tour.

Also left to chance is the composition of the tour group that consists of 35 persons. One has to take the party, so to speak, as *"hazard de la Fouchette."* There might be nothing but losers, or you might be lucky and have some winners. My party consisted mainly of women; there were only twelve men, but 24 women. There was a group of engineers with their wives who thought they were better than the rest and isolated themselves. Another group was consisting of the widows: two happy widows who always were a little drunk and laughed all the time, two serious widows, and finally two very fat widows that I named "the broadsided ones," actually mountains of flesh, but very peaceful souls. If one had to sit next to them or even between them, one had to reduce his own demand for room considerably. But then there were also winners: the work-master Miller who traveled with his wife whom I liked very much, and a nurse in good years who was a refugee from Silesia and had endured many hardships and is now the head nurse of a hospital in Mannheim. She had soon picked me out and took care of me, so that the two of us looked as though we were a couple. Then there were the middle ones between the elegant gentlemen and the lowly folks.

If I should weigh the plus against the minus, the plus definitely overweighs the minus in spite the endless riding on the bus with its bad springs and in intolerable heat, for we saw so many wonderful things!

After two not exactly unpleasant nights in sleeping coaches via Strassburg (where I thought about the time we spent there together) and Avignon (which we unfortunately couldn't see because it was night), we arrived at the Spanish border and there switched to a very classic Spanish train to Barcelona. Here began the real bus tour. First, we went to Mont Serrat (the "sawed-up mountain") with its interesting rock formations and its old cloister that houses the "Black Madonna". Then through the stony desert of Aragon, without trees or bushes, no river or brook, toward Sargasso where we unfortunately arrived in the dark. We had to leave early the next morning, so that my acquaintance with this famous town, situated on the Ebro River, was reduced to an evening stroll with the head nurse.

The next day was a seven-hour ride through the rather boring classical high plateau to Madrid. I did not take advantage of the offered bullfight, partly because I detest such shows, and partly because I wanted more time for the Prado *(art museum).* I took leave of the group, took a taxi to the Prado and entered its holy gates. I had to use my allotted time, two and 1/2 hours, very carefully, just to see what was most important to me. Fortunately, I had studied the catalog before at home and could find my way. I had wanted to see: Velasquez, Goya, Tizian, Dürer and others. "*Las Lanzas*" fulfilled my highest expectations. The modern reproductions are absolutely misleading. The painting is in any respect as subtle in coloratura as any Monet. Actually it is classified as a "historical picture," but it is much more. In the afternoon, we visited Breda.

Next, a long ride to Cordona and Seville. Seville is a lively and pleasant town, the town of Don Juan and Figaro, the birthplace of Velasquez and Murillo, the cathedral houses and the last resting place of Columbus (though some say it is his son who lies in the sarcophagus). Then across the battle field of Turez de la Fontana, where the good sherry grows, to Algeria (unlucky memories); from there across the Strait of Gibraltar to Tangier and Titian; back to Algeria, on to Malaga, and to Granada and the Alhambra, for me just as fulfilling as "*Las Lanzas*," then alongside the coast and the deep blue sea via Valencia back to Barcelona.

In the end, I contracted the so-called "Spanish flu," a severe form of intestinal infection, which made the last two days on the train very uncomfortable. So I arrived in a rather pitiful state at home and had to cure myself by lying in bed for two full days. My first outing was the funeral service for Marie-Luise Ulrich.

I could tell you much more, but the letter would be too heavy. *(I selected two poems in honor of the violinst/friend Marie-Luise in the chapter "My Father, the Poet.")*

So goodbye for today, greetings to all of you and celebrate the birthday of your son in happiness and good health!

Your Father.

Letter from Father, Bremen, November 4, 1958.
Dear Mathilde!

Your parents thank you very much for your dear letter of October 30 and for the two photos. How charming is the little trio, but so far away! I was also happy that you are so interested in my Spanish adventures. Indeed, it was a great event for me, this very late acquaintance with a love from far back that I had never seen. Now as to your questions, I shall try to answer them briefly.

There are four pictures by Dürer in the Prado: The self-portrait of 1498, Adam, Eve, and a picture of an unknown. I saw the first three paintings, the forth I missed.

In Madrid, besides in the Prado, there are paintings in the church St. Antonia with frescos by Goya, then in the Royal Castle and the Royal Academy (mostly Goyas in both of these). Since I had limited time I could only visit the Prado. Even here, I had to be very careful with my time. It is like a blooming meadow; one doesn't know what to pick first. There are many Tizians, more than thirty in the Prado. Among them is the staggering picture of Charles the Fifth on horseback, riding across the battlefield of Mühlberg, in some sense the parallel of "*Las Lanzes*." Here also a victor in whose sadly serious countenance expresses the tragedy of futile fighting and winning. By the way, there is also an "American Museum" in Madrid, but that is mostly containing South American art and I had no time, unfortunately, to look at it.

You are asking why I added the expression "unseligen Angedenkens" (infamous memories) to Algeciras. The conference of Algeciras took place (I believe in 1905) where everyone voted against Germany, and even our *Sekundant* (second in a duel) Austria abandoned us, and so the German Marocco politics broke apart. The visit of the Kaiser in Tangier and the so-called *Panther-Sprung von Agedir* had preceded.

The crossing to Tangier took about two hours and was very pleasant in beautiful weather. The Alhambra, yes, that is a dream come true of beautiful times of form and color. Arches, vaults, walls, and everything tightly decorated with arabesques and verses from the Koran in manifold and wonderfully blended hues. I can easily imagine that in Monreale strong similarities to the Alhambra can be found, only it might be there, as I imagine it, more a mixture of the Moorish with the Norman (as the Spanish Gothic also shows Moorish influence). But the Alhambra (finished during the 15th century) is pure Moorish art.

Finally, you are asking how the climate is. Yes, September had been offered to me as the last chance to do this tour, but for someone from the north of Germany, this was rather hot and I have often thought of you in the "hot oven" of California. It was strange to first cross the battlefield where in 711 the last king of West Gothia, Rodrigo, had to flee after a seven day battle and miserably succumbed, and after that to stand in front of the gate of the Alhambra, through which the last King of Granada, the unfortunate Boabdil, left his beautiful kingdom in 1492. These were two sad royal fates that meant the beginning and the end of the Moorish capital in Spain. *(Father gave a speech about these two kings to the Rotary Club that is included as the last entry in Part II.)*

Mother is feeling well right now, though this morning she had a slight relapse after quite some time. But in spite of that she is now with daughter Julie on the way to Worpswede.

A thousand, or rather five-thousand, greetings to the dear Five of you.

Your Father.

I forgot the animals under the well: Those are lions for which the court is named "Lion Court."

Two notes came from Father before and after Christmas of 1958:

Letter from my parents, Bremen, December 21, 1958.
Now from Father:
I join Mother's good wishes. How charming is your youngest child.
Father, Grandfather Hermann.

Letter from my parents, Bremen, December 30, 1958.
And from Father:
Dear Mathilde!

The contents of your package inside that expert packing in which we recognize Father Leo's skill makes your old father into a happy nutcracker. And in the Californian stockings we will initiate the "Carl Schurz Ball" next January. I am not an admirer of television, but the gift giving at 716 Howard Street I would have loved to see on screen.

1000 thanks and greetings, Father.

Book VIII
1959-1961

Letter from my parents, Bremen, April 15, 1959, (excerpt).
From Mother:

...How nice that you could hear the Matthew Passion. Father went to our *Dom* (cathedral) to hear it. It was so cold that he got the flu from it. That was not so nice. But he is better now. ...

And from Father:
Dear Mathilde!

Your old father joins the motherly wishes for your birthday. The book by Schweitzer, as I can only tell after a little browsing in it, is a well-written book. I believe it is rather hotly controversial. That might be; Schweitzer is a very special person and has occupied himself with many different fields. His style of writing is very pleasant. After you have read the book, please let me hear your opinion.

On May 2 is a meeting of the *Paul Ernst Gesellschaft* (Society) which I will attend with daughter Julie. We shall see a late drama *Childerich.*

Thousand greetings,
Your old Father

Letter from Father, Bremen, June 11, 1959.
Dear Mathilde!

You have not heard from us in a long time. The reason for that was that Mother did not feel well. She asked me to answer your two letters of May 24 and 29 and to thank you, especially for the pictures and the report about the Poolside Fashion Show. This report we enjoyed very much, especially the entrance of "Young Miss Schmidt" with "great aplomb"!

With Mother it went this way: she was relatively lively and sometimes regularly energetic, but had trouble with swelling of the liver. For that reason, Dr. Sommer proposed the treatment in Driburg. Daughter Julie brought her there and I accompanied them. She found everything satisfactory: nice lodging with a nice hostess, a pleasant spa doctor, pretty and well-groomed grounds, very lovely surroundings with forested heights. So Julie and I drove back satisfied about Mother's well-being. Over Pentecost, I visited Mother in Driburg, found Mother happy and in good shape. She could walk better than I could. Her liver had improved according to the doctor's report. Her only complaint was that the baths were too hot for her. Thereupon the doctor, who so far had only prescribed half-baths, now changed this to full baths. This change has not been very good for her. When I visited her again one week ago after the "Wesertagung" in Höxter, she was feeling very low. Now the doctor found it necessary to terminate the treatment, so I took her home with me to Bremen. From then on, she has been feeling differently. Yesterday she had a good day, but last night was bad again. Today before noon she felt miserable, but a little better this afternoon. This could also be connected to the weather that changes every day. Usually these bad times last about three weeks. So I am hoping that her health will even out soon. But the "treatment" was a failure.

Yesterday we had Wulf Rohland with us in the afternoon, a great enjoyment for us. We received sad news in Nele's last letter telling us that Walter is again suffering from depressions and again had to go to the hospital for three weeks. He himself is suffering from this situation, and it is very difficult for Cornelie. And they had intended (according to Nele) to come over for the Golden Wedding by plane! *(This event would take place on August 23, 1959.)* What a wonderful surprise that would have been!

On the place where our *Parzelle* used to be, the city has started to build houses. A sad aspect! But now we are enjoying our garden so much more. Every morning we have an abundance of wonderful roses.

We had bad luck with our new house helper, "Mariechen." She had used our absence to invite her fiancé and celebrate sort of an "engagement" in our house. Therefore, we had to fire her instantly. But we have, with help of Tante Luise, found a girl from the East who helps us now. She seems to be a very pleasant person and proves invaluable for Mother.

To all of you, parents and children, best greetings from Mother and me.

Your Father.

And from Mother:

The next letter I am writing again. Our lovely helper is of your age. Driburg was very pretty, surrounded by forests and fields. But at home it is also wonderful.

Many greetings, Mother.

Letter from Father, Bremen, July 20, 1959.
Dear Mathilde!

Your letter came exactly on my birthday, thanks very much! There was not much family around me this time except Grandmother Julie, who was getting better after a bad week, and only one of the eighteen grandchildren, little Constanze from Düsseldorf *(the youngest of Dorothee's children).* In the evening the Kulenkampffs came, the parents, for an hour, from Horstedt, where they are vacationing. Hedwig is at the Chiemsee where she takes a course in sailing. But several friends came who brought pretty flowers, and for supper my old friend Spitta.

Please tell son Leo thanks for his meaningful picture that now is in a folder among artworks by his cousins Kulenkampff.

The greatest joy was a letter from Nele with the good news that Walter is now definitely better (in the birthday letter she did not mention anything). Now they decided to come after all for the Golden Wedding, and already in two weeks, on August 3, they will land here with a vessel of the SAS and stay until August 25 in Europe. We had almost given up hope that they would be with us this year.

We are having a heatwave here that might be comparable with your tempurature in California. We have, in addition, high humidity so that old people like us feel very tired and limp, and fields and gardens are also longing for rain. The springs of heaven seem to be dried up. But this did not hinder us from spending a nice day yesterday in Fischerhude (Father, Mother, Julie, Wulli, and Constanze). Father Wulf is there now with Julie and Wulli. Dorettchen is visiting us now, as is Constanze.

As I wrote you earlier, I had glanced at the fat Schweitzer book about *Geschichte der Leben-Jesu-Forschung (Quest of the History of Jesus).* I had the feeling that it was written well. He touches on hypotheses that are highly debated. I also don't know much of the mentioned literature, actually only the most important books: *Das Leben Jesu (Life of Jesus)* by David Friedrich Strauss and the *Vie de Jésus* by Ernst Renan. But just the fact that Schweitzer's book gives an overview of the literature seemed to me pleasant and useful. To read everything, be it in any field, is impossible and becomes more impossible every year.

Enough about this for today. Please give my regards to your husband and children and be greeted yourself very much. I wish you could follow Ernst's example!

Your Father.

And from Mother:
Dear Mathilde,

Please pay attention to the pretty Humboldt stamp on the envelope.

We are enjoying our visit with Dorothee (granddaughter) and Constanze very much. That the Ernsts are coming is absolutely wonderful. I lead a good life with the help of Frau Klavitter.

Thousand greetings, Mother.

On August 23, 1959, my parents celebrated their Golden Wedding Anniversary. The party took place in Scheeßel, a small village near Bremen where my mother had met my father and where they had been married. I could not leave my family in Lodi, but I heard all about the big event.

Letter from my parents, Bremen, August 26, 1959.
From Mother:
Dear Mathilde,

The "Golden Wedding Day" was so wonderful. I would have written you earlier, but these days we have so much going on that I did not find the time. On the evening before the festival was a huge thunderstorm; it was a real *Polterabend* (rowdy night before a big event). The Rohlands had come ahead of the storm front to Bremen.

In the morning, Jane (dressed as a young man) and Hedwig (dressed as farmers' girl) came as a young Scheeßeler couple with a large bouquet and congratulated us in lovely verses. Nelchen came had already come for breakfast. Around 10:00, we drove to the Kulos where all were gathered on the large terrace behind the house. We were received with a *Hoch soll'n sie leben.* All the grandchildren were standing behind the new bench in our garden on which we had to sit down. This bench is so beautiful; we needed it and we thank you so much for helping to give it to us. It is supposed to stand on our verandah and still needs a white coat of paint; Julie was not sure what exact shade we wanted.

Then we all went to Scheeßel, with Spitta in our car. At 11:30, the very nice pastor received us at the church door while the bells were ringing. The pastor spoke very well and built his sermon on our Bible verse. The Kulos had brought out a quartet that played a movement by Haydn before and after the service. This church celebration was the highlight of the day. We paused, stayed a while under the old linden tree in front of the church, looked once more carefully at the church, and enjoyed the children and took pictures.

At 1:00, we had our meal in the inn across from the church, a good bouillon with egg and dumplings, for each person half of a young chicken with vegetables, and afterwards ice cream. The pastor came for the meal, sat between Thilda *(my father's cousin, daughter of Gustav Rassow, and my godmother)* and Julie and conversed in a very animated way. I hope he will visit us here in Bremen sometimes. After the meal, we walked over to the Martenshof, now Meyershof, and were received in a friendly manner by the new owners with flowers. The house had been furnished much prettier before, but the children at least saw how their grandparents had lived long ago.

Then followed a rest time and in the evening we all met again at the Kulos on the terrace for a cold dinner. Then the grandchildren performed, all in costumes made of crepe paper as our favorite flowers and sang verses made by Dörte and Julie. The costumes had been made very skillfully, and Charlotte as a snowbell was the hit. You will get the verses. After that, we sat together and talked.

I can't tell you how much we missed you and the children in Dayton. Your telegram and the dear letter were very much appreciated.

That your friend, the pediatrician, had made this trip so unexpectedly and that you suspect that something is very wrong is such a pity. *(She refers to Dr. Kultzen, a friend of ours from Lodi.)* August 23 was a very hot day in spite of the thunderstorm the night before. I could not wear my golden dress during the day and had on the black silk dress from you, with the white lace. Everyone liked this so much. In the evening, it became cooler and I could wear the elegant robe. On the 24th came many visitors and we were rather spoiled. We received pictures, flowers, letters, telegrams, and many other things. It was also mentioned in the newspapers and announced on the radio. Therefore, more people knew about it than we would have liked. Even today, our rooms are very festive with all the flowers we received. Walter took off already on Monday for Frankfurt and had to do business until Friday evening. And on Sunday the Ernsts are already leaving us. Nele has to do a lot of shopping still and wants to see many more people. We are so grateful that both of us were feeling will enough for all of this.

Greetings to all your loved ones,
Mother.

And from Father:
Dear Mathilde!

Yes, it was a very nice day and we couldn't be more grateful. Just two weeks before Mother was so miserable that it was uncertain if we could celebrate at all. But then it turned for the better and Mother became more lively than she had been for a long time. That we celebrated the day in Scheeßel was her only wish. So it was doubly wonderful that all went so well. The only sad part for us was that you and the children from Dayton could not be, but nothing can be absolutely perfect. It was also a thought by Mother that everyone had a Bible verse, a proverb, or famous saying by a poet on his place card at the meal. Every one of these citations had to do somehow with "gold", like *"Morgenstund' hat Gold im Mund"* (the early bird gets the worm) or *"Reden ist Silber, Schweigen ist Gold"* (to talk is silver, to be quiet is gold) or *"Ein Wort geredet zu seiner Zeit ist wie goldene Äpfel in silbernen Schalen"* (a word spoken at the right time is like golden apples in silver bowls). This last one is a verse by Solomon who proved very rich in such wisdom, also a saying by Jesus. I had selected the following verse by Grillparzer for Mother:

Das eben ist der Liebe Zaubermacht,
Daß sie wandelt was ihr Hauch berührt,
Der Sonne ähnlich, deren goldenen Strahlen
Gewitterwolken selbst in Gold verwandelt.

That is the power of love
That it is changing what its breath touches
Like the sun whose golden rays
Are able to change storm clouds into gold.

We have received such an abundance of flowers and more than one hundred telegrams and letters. We were especially happy about the cables from Lodi and Dayton and in the center of the presents stood the beautiful bench with pretty pillows. Also some wonderful art books were among the gifts. And thank you for the great photos, we think they turned out especially well.

On Friday, I plan to go to the theater with Nele and the Kulenkampffs, and we will see *Die Natürliche Tochter* honoring Goethe's birthday and the opening of the fall season. Saturday will be the Ernsts' last day here and on Sunday they will leave us. How fast the time went!

Farewell and greetings to all of you!

Your Father.

Letter to my parents, Lodi, August 31, 1959 (excerpt).

Dear Parents!

Thanks so much for your detailed letter about the G.W. (short for "Golden Wedding") How wonderful that everything was so perfect. The thunderstorm did not seem to have disturbed it; on the contrary, it lent an impressive introduction to the big event. This will make it even more unforgettable. …

Thanks for the two photos of the church in Scheeßel and of Father, all very nice. Will we get more pictures of the G.W.? How come you don't have an awning for the verandah?

Now thousand greetings from all of us,

Your Mathilde

Note from Father, Bremen, December 15, 1959.

Dear Mathilde!

Your Father is joining Mother in her "Five-Greetings." I am not a friend of television, but in spite of that, I thought it would be nice to see what is going on 5000 miles away at your house on the screen. All the ruckus of unwrapping presents! Your Mother had bad days again, but is beginning to feel better. So we look towards Christmas full of hope. After a miserable foggy week, we now have radiant winter weather. Again all our good wishes!

With love, your old Father.

Note from Father, Bremen, December 25, 1959.

Dear Mathilde!

Mother has written so detailed about our double celebration, first at the Kulenkampffs, then at our house, that there is almost nothing to add. We were very blessed that Mother, after having been miserable for two weeks, was up and around and admirably fresh. Then it was with great joy that we had good news from Cornelie about Walter. We shall enjoy all the rich fruit you have sent us. Some of your Californian sun is buried in those! One thousand thanks for all.

With heartfelt thoughts, your
Father.

Note from Father, Bremen, April 9, 1960.
Dear Mathilde!

What you write of your joy about your great-grandfather's book *Die Epochen der Geschichte der Menschheit* is joy for your father, and would have been for your grandfather. Which place your great-grandfather gives to the Baktriens, I don't remember clearly. I have a shady idea that he put emphasis on Egypt. However, you have to consider that he wrote this more than 100 years ago, at a time when the prehistoric was still very young. By the way, you write about two books that your great-grandfather wrote, which second one was in your mind, the "Reports about Astronomy" or the "Metaphysics", or the "Philosophy of Religions"? If we should run across the "Epochs" at the bookshop, we shall think of you.

For now all good wishes, your
Father.

Father was traveling to Greece with daughter Julie Kulenkampff and I was expecting my fourth child in June of 1960. I also had three sick children to care for.

Letter from my parents, Bremen, May 8, 1960.
From Father:
Dear Mathilde!

When I came home last Wednesday, May 4, with intact but tanned skin from Greece (daughter Julie had left the train in Munich to meet her husband), I found Mother in good condition (seems my absence is advantageous for her) and an absolutely radiant house. I also found two letters from you. We are very relieved that the measles are getting better. This must have been quite an additional burden for you. The letters of April 8 and May 2 were here when I came. Mother asked me to thank you for those. Meanwhile, also, the report about Goethe's color theory came back.

Regarding your questions: while the concept of polarity as it appears in electricity and magnetism is not simply applicable to light is most likely correct, one still has to consider; to following:

1. That Goethe took the "pattern of polarity," as he calls it, as a much wider concept, including everything different, contrasting, opposite, etc.

2. That the contrast "all and nothing" fits Newton's theory, but not Goethe's. For Newton (and today's science), light is indeed "all," for it contains all the colors (or color producers). For Goethe, light is indivisible, a solid unit, and the colors are created by impurities of the light. They are created by a mixture of pure light with something opaque; in that way, Goethe thinks that colors are something additional, not subtracted from light. He writes:

> *Sie, die Morgenröte, entwickelte dem Trüben*
> *ein erklingend Farbenspiel!*
>
> She, the dawn, has created from the opaque
> a rich sounding play of colors.

3. In addition, Goethe does not consider darkness as a "nothing," but, like the light a substantial entity, the contrast to light. Between the two is the "opaque matter," developing the colors. He writes:

"Finsternis und Licht stehen einander unumgänglich entgegen, eins dem andern ewig fremd, aber die Materie, die in und zwischen beiden sich stellt, hat, wenn sie körperlich undurchsichtig ist, eine beleuchtete und eine finsterne Seite. Ist diese Materie durchsichtig, so entwickelt sich in ihr, im Helldunklen, Trüben, in Bezug auf's Auge, das, was wir Farbe nennen."

"Darkness and light are basic contrasts, one entirely estranged from the other, and the matter between them, if it is not transparent, has a light side and a dark side. If the matter is transparent, it will develop in the light/dark an "opaque" matter that the human eye perceives as 'color.' "

Maybe there is still a tinge of mystic in Goethe's theory (like in alchemy). Be that as it may, there seems to be the wish to find for light and electricity the same kind of polarity, and Goethe's is the undisputed glory to have felt the possibility of classification of the light into the scale of physical powers. Goethe writes:

"Sie (die Absicht) geht kürzlich dahin, die chromatischen Erscheinung in Verbindung mit allen übrigen physischen Phänomenen zu betrachten, sie besonders mit dem, was uns der Magnet, der Turmalin gelehrt, und Elektrizität, and chemische Processe uns offenbahrt, in eine Reihe zu stellen und so durch Terminologie und Methode eine vollkommene Einheit des physischen Wissens vorzubereiten."

"It (the tendency) is recently pointing to the consideration to classify the chromatic appearances together with other physical phenomena, like what magnetism and electricity, and also chemical processes have taught us, into one system; and that way by means of terminology and method to create unity of the physical knowledge."

If Goethe is then rejecting the, according to his belief, popular opinion about polarity, the now commonly accepted wave theory is also trying to explain physical phenomena as one large entity, only in a different way than Goethe.

But enough of this. Maybe you will express your ideas about what I tried to explain. In Greece we had wonderful days. The abundance of great impressions can only be digested gradually. Anyway, after one has seen the objects with one's own eyes, they look quite different from what was imagined. In this way I had two wishes of my youth fulfilled late in life: only two years ago I saw the Alhambra, and now the Acropolis. What different worlds! Both pinnacles.

I hope my letter finds you all healthy again. Greetings to all your family.

With best wishes, your Father.

And Mother:

Dear Tita,

I just had written to you last night when next morning your dear letter of May 2 arrived. Father feels refreshed. How wonderful that he could do this trip.

Love, Mother.

Telegram to my parents, Lodi, June 11, 1960 (to Mr. and Mrs. Apelt).
Boy arrived, everything fine, Mathilde Schmidt.

Announcement in the Bremen paper, Weser – Kurier, June 23, 1960.

The birth of their fourth child, MARTIN, has been announced in gratefulness and joy:

Mathilde Schmidt, neé Apelt,
Leo W. Schmidt
June 10, Lodi, Kalifornien, 716 Howardstr.

Letter from Father to Doris:
Dear Doris,

Thank you so much for the picture with your own signature. That you can already write your name! I wish I could draw as nicely as you, so I could make a picture of our house for you.

Many greetings, Grandfather.

Letter to Father, Lodi, no date (probably beginning July 1960).
Dear Father!

For your birthday we send you best wishes—and the first pictures of Martin Walter. All six of us are well and all of wish we could be with you on July 10 that falls on a Sunday this year. The Sunday after that will be the baptism of our boy; Leo's parents *(Alice and Waldemar)* will be the godparents.

When Leo Hermann was born, you cited to me from Schiller's *Braut von Messina* from the first act about "The mother and her son." When I read this again right after Martin's birth, I found another citation, about four pages ahead:

Wohl dem, dem die Geburt den Bruder gab;
Mehr kann ihm dann das Glück nicht geben! etc.

Happiness to him who had a brother given to him,
This is more than bliss can give!

That fits for our Leo Hermann who doesn't know what to do with his happiness now that he has a brother. We hope that the connection with the *Bride of Messina* doesn't go any further: that brothers' hate comes between them.

So far our little one looks very much like Doris, but that could change. He had, like the other children, black hair for about two months. It is already thinning on his forehead. Underneath we can detect some wheat-blond down.

Our vacation is very occupied this year. Leo and Doris are taking ballet and baton lessons twice a week, which are given free by the school. Baton is something typical American; it is a metal rod, about as long as an arm with which all kinds of acrobatic movements are executed. For instance, in parades which honor our Lodi Wine and Grape Festival, whole groups of baton twirlers are marching to the rhythm of the bands and show off what they have accomplished. Also at those all-important "football games" baton twirlers are needed. The children love these lessons and exercise diligently. Barbara is still too young for this. Martin is cooperating nicely with all this; he is fast asleep at the time of the lessons.

Now best greetings, your
Mathilde.

Letter from Father, Bremen, July 16, 1960.
Dear Mathilde!

So, tomorrow will be the baptism of Martin Walter! These lines will be too late for this big event, but we will be with you with our thoughts.

The pictures of the little one were gracing my birthday table. Thanks for those and also for your dear letter. The portrait of the young uncle was laying next to the one of his a little older niece Kathleen.

I received other presents too: from Mother a record player, something I had always wished for, and also a chess set and a book about solitaire; all in respect to my upcoming old age and all the leisure time I shall have available. And a special gift from Dayton. Walter is feeling better now and Walt has completed his studies and has received a Fulbright stipend for one year of studying in Germany. We are expecting him in September. He will go to Stuttgart. When will Leo Hermann be so far, or even Martin Walter? I might not live anymore by then.

Unfortunately, I was lame on my birthday. Clever people are going up the stairs; but your not so clever old father fell down. There were no broken ribs, as the doctor suspected at first, but still unpleasant muscle aches. Meanwhile it all healed up and is behind me. It gave me pleasure, though, to be nursed lovingly by your mother who was in an excellent state of health at that time.

To all of you our best wishes! And all the best for the little boy to be baptized.

Your Father.

PS. That you found the citation in the *Braut von Messina* gave me great joy and also the additional complementary verses.

My father was not feeling well during summer of 1960. He, as well as his friend Spitta, had managed to fall and break a few bones. Father also suffered from some infection.

Letter from Mother, Bremen, July 6, 1960 (excerpts).

Dear Mathilde,

… Father had an accident last week. He had gone to the library at the courthouse to look up something. The place for returning his coat was so unfortunately placed in a dark corner close to a stairway leading down that he did see the first step and fell down the stairs. It was a lucky fall, no concussion, but something broke around the ribs. This is very painful for him, but not dangerous. After a short rest, he came home with the streetcar—he does not like taxis—and thought that the fresh air would be good for him. Dr. Sommer came over at once and put a "leucoplast" bandage over the broken rib. He wants to wait with X-rays until the bandage is off again; he had no doubt about the diagnosis. Father is now over the worst part; he even went into the garden already. The most difficult times are the nights since it is hard for him to find a position that does not hurt him. I think that in one week he will be over it completely.

Today two very satisfying letters came from Dayton. Nele writes that Walter is feeling much better. And she also writes so happily about Walt who has finished his studies and has graduated from Harvard at the top of his class with a silver medal! He also received the "Fulbright Scholarship." He comes to Germany in the fall and wants to study in Stuttgart for one year. Walt himself wrote a letter to his grandfather in very good German; he had taken a course in German.

We will celebrate Father's birthday quietly. Christine Kulenkampff will represent her family and will come to the celebration and the first breakfast. The Kulos are on a Dutch island with three of their daughters for about ten days. In the afternoon Spitta will come. Last year, Spitta had suffered a complicated arm fracture; he had fallen in the dark and had to suffer with this for a long time.

On July 16, Frau Toedtman and her son John are coming for a few days. *(John Toedtman's father was the man who was part of the occupying forces in Bremen after the war. He and his family lived in Dayton and became good friends of my sister Cornelie Ernst's family.)*

Many dear greetings from both of us,
Mother.

Letter to Mother, Lodi, July 19, 1960 (excerpt).

... Tell me, what is that with Father and Spitta. What are those elderly gentlemen doing? *(referring to the falls).* Hopefully it is as harmless as you describe it. But what a frightening experience for you! ...

Your Mathilde.

Letter from Mother, Bremen, August 5, 1960 (excerpt).
Dear Mathilde,

I believe I did not write for a long time. Father was ready to go out by himself again by the end of June for a little time before noon and after noon with me for an hour. He still had pain from the fall.

But now, just ten days ago, he all of a sudden he developed a fever and had various pains all over his body. He looked bad and we worried about him. It was difficult to determine what it was. Dr. Sommer consulted another doctor from the Josephstift *(hospital in Bremen).* Both doctors had the same idea about what to do to help him. The fever was initiated by an infection that was attacking him since he was not quite over the trauma of his fall. There are about 40 to 50 different viruses that could have caused the fever. But the main thing is that the fever is gone now. It's only that he is still quite weak.

August 7:

I had to stop writing to be there for Father. Today, Sunday, Father got dressed for the first time and went out on the terrace. He has a better appetite and has slept well for the first time. Tomorrow he wants to go through the garden; we shall see about that. ...

Mrs. Toedtman's visit was different from what I had imagined. *(The Toedtmans were our friends since the time after the war when Americans ruled our city. Mr. Toedtman was in charge of cultural life in Bremen and therefore had to work closely together with my father, the first administrator of the Bremen Art Association.)* They had much too much planned. They came by briefly one morning (Mrs. Toedtman and Johnny), then another time together with an American friend for one hour in the evening. Johnny looked completely exhausted. Their itinerary of an extensive European tour by rail is typical American—I found it painful. Much too much in such a short time. How can they enjoy it?...

Many dear greetings, Mother.

Note from Father, Bremen, August 13, 1960.

Dear Mathilde!

What all can an old man like your father do! I had to regret my "misstep" with several weeks of misery and pain. But Mother has nursed me with such dedication that is it hard to tell what was dominant, the pain of having fallen or the pleasure of being nursed so lovingly.

We are having a rather cool August which is not very conducive to the recuperation. Well, at least you in "Hot Oven Land" don't have to freeze.

Many greetings to all of you!
Father and Grandfather.

Letter from Mother, Bremen, August 28, 1960 (excerpt).

... We are very concerned about the fact that Leo has not yet found a new "job" that satisfies him. For the family it is so important that the father has an occupation he really likes. We had not quite understood the situation. We had assumed that Leo would only temporarily work at Alex's and was still working in Stockton.

Our Father is better, but it is a slow process. He still gets a heart shot every day but the doctor wants to stop with that next week. He has not been downtown in two months, but the two of us go every day on small walks, about 1/2 hour at a time. Unfortunately, he cannot sleep well, only a few hours toward mornings and medications don't seem to help him.

Heavy medication he should not and would not take. *(Though my mother relied heavily on those medications!)* So he always feels tired, but we hope this will get better. The consequences of the fall in addition to the virus infection (without flu, but high fever), and also severe pains wandering through the body, all this is weighing on him. In the case of a steady fever, Dr. Sommer would have prescribed penicillin, but here they are very careful with that because of the side effects. They only give it in case of a known illness like infection of the lung. …

…You ask if I was able to take care of Father. During the first time, I was feeling good and had Frau Klavitter during the day to help me. Nights I could do it alone. But then came a bad time that lasted for two weeks. That, of course, was unpleasant, but then Father had the worst behind him. Frau Klavitter is experienced in nursing and I could learn from her. Dr. Sommer came every day. We can be thankful that Father is so much better …

Mother.

Letter from Mother, Bremen, October 24, 1960 (excerpt).

… Father has suffered quite a bit from his sickness of last summer. He cannot do as many endeavors anymore, especially all those evening activities have to be limited. But how can one go on like that at 84 years of age? It is wonderful that he is still mentally so active, as that gives him much pleasure. …

Mother.

My father died on November 11, 1960.

Letters from My Mother to Me after My Father's Death

Telegram from Lodi, Nov. 11, 1960 (Mother's telegram is lost).
Our thoughts are with you. Leo, Mathilde, and children.

Letter to Mother, Lodi, November 14, 1960.
Dear Mother!

What sad news when your telegram came! This happened so quickly and unexpectedly; we were not at all prepared for this. Do you think that the fall last summer could be connected with the stroke? How did it happen? Did he try to get up? You poor thing, you must have so much to think of now to arrange the funeral and everything, but Julie will help you. Please write us when the funeral will be. At first, we wanted to send a wreath, but changed our minds; it is so frightfully expensive. We shall be with you with our thoughts anyway. What are you doing now? Will you stay alone in the big house, or take someone else in to live with you?

We cannot imagine you without Father, but it would have been harder for Father to be without you. And how is your health? Maybe now you could visit us sometimes. It would be so nice if you could see our children and they could see you; for Father this is too late now. But how would you fare on the airplane? Of course, we would pick you up at the airport in San Francisco. You could make up your mind very quickly; no big preparations would be necessary. Anyway, your garden would not need you during the winter. And Frau Klavitter could take care of the house while you are gone. You would live in our bedroom and have all the rest you need. Good doctors are here too, in case you need them. Well, you have to decide this yourself. We would be so happy if you decide to come.

Did Father hear that Kennedy won the election? What are all of you saying about this? It was a very narrow outcome, and a few Republicans are still hoping that Nixon wins.

We hope to hear more details about Father.

Thousand dear greetings from all of us,
Tita.

Letter from Mother, Bremen, November 15, 1960.
Dear Mathilde.

Your dear telegram came very fast. For Cornelie and all of you it is so much harder than for us here. Christoph wrote you right away, so you know about what was going on here on November 11. *(This letter can be found in the chapter about Father's death.)*

Father was feeling well. You know that he left home on November 10 at 9:00 in the morning to go with Dr. Löbe and Dr. Hanns Meyer to Landesbergen on the Middle Weser to inaugurate the last of the locks. There were many people present. They ate dinner in Nienburg, in a big hall. In the afternoon around 5:00, Father came back, slept a while in the living room, and then got dressed for a celebration with 35 people in the *Rathaus*. This was crowning the day. Father had already worked on this project on the Middle Weser when he was still *Syndicus* (assistant lawyer, trustee) with the *Handelskammer* (Chamber of Commerce). After he was mentioned in several speeches, he spoke himself. Our present trade minister in Bonn, Seebohm, with whom Father got along great, presented him with a beautiful book by Merian. He also had a short meeting at the *Rathaus*. Agatz and Meyer brought him home at 11:00 that night. I was already in bed. He came in very satisfied and told me about his speech when we were together in bed.

During the night he was very restless, but I am used to that. In the morning at 7:00 I woke up from a strange noise; was it a last gasp? I got up and found him on the floor. He must have tried to get up, as Dr. Sommer told me, and then had a stroke. His mouth was a little open, also his eyes, but there was no life in him. I could not feel any pulse. He did not react when I talked to him. Dr. Sommer came right away, checked the heart, but could not detect anything. Then the Kulenkampffs came whom I had phoned at once. Since we could not move him, two men from the funeral institute in the Riensbergstraße helped us to put him onto the bed. This all happened on Friday, November 11th, his death day.

In the evening, they put him into a coffin and we kept him here in our bedroom. His head pointed toward the window and he was surrounded by laurel bushes and chrysanthemums. He looked so peaceful and beautiful. Only yesterday, on November 14, the coffin was closed. We had a memorial here in the afternoon; I had sent for Pastor Besch from the *Liebfrauen Kirche.* There were mainly Bible verses and Psalms, since Father did not want a speech. All the grandchildren with the exception of little Charlotte were present, all the ones who are here, and also Walt who came from Stuttgart. We sang together a few verses of *In allen meinen Taten* and *Nun danket alle Gott.* We had boys from the choir of the Liebfrauen Kirche who sang with us. I shall send you the program. Tante Thilde came from Dresden and was still able to see Father. All the Rohlands came; Dorothee lodges with us. Besides the closest family, the Tiemanns, Tante Lotte, Utta Sanders, Frau Ulrich, Tante Thilda and Ilse, Spitta, Hanns Meyer, and Dr. Busch of the *Kunsthalle* all came. It was such a consolation to have all the children here. Julie, Christoph and Dorothee did all the thinking and organizing for me. It could not have been nicer.

This morning (Tuesday, November 15) we had a memorial in the *Rathaus* in the old hall where the coffin covered with the Bremen flag was surrounded by wreaths. Kaisen spoke and before and after that there was music, a quartet by Mozart and the Octet by Schubert. *(This speech and others can be found in the chapter about Father's death.)*

Frau Klavitter was sick and was in Blumenthal, but she came over on November 11 in the afternoon. It had been Father's wish to be cremated, so after the celebration in the *Rathaus* his body was transferred to the Crematorium. The day after tomorrow the urn will come and be lowered into the same grave where 41 years ago our Friedrich *(my brother who died of encephalitis as a baby)* had been buried. Pastor Besch is accompanying his body and saying a prayer and a blessing.

Dr. Sommer had told us several times that Father's heart was not in good condition, which he could determine with the EKG (Electrical Cardiogram). But Father did not like to take care of himself. I believe that all went well and that we can be thankful that he was with us for so long.

The Rohlands are leaving tomorrow. Dorothee will stay a few days longer. On November 13, we were thinking of Daddy Leo's birthday.

I am always seeing Father by my side. We should be so grateful that he had recuperated after his severe illness this summer; he hardly had any pain and only the heat made him weak.

Julie has everybody at her house today and is showing them the pictures of their trip to Greece. I stayed home to write to you and Nele.

Please greet all your loved ones. For the children this death is hard to understand. Here it is Charlotte who cannot figure out why her grandfather is not there anymore. He is in heaven, but all his clothes and his bed are still here. And her mother is almost always with me, hard to comprehend. I shall write again.

Your dear letter of October 30 came before all this and Father could still enjoy it. Your questions I shall answer another time.

Mother.

Letter from Mother, Bremen, November 27, 1960.
Dear Mathilde,

I have not written to you in so long, so much was going on here. You knew that Father wanted to be cremated. So he was brought directly from the *Rathaus* memorial to the crematorium. Christoph and Julie had selected a simple copper urn. **How little remains of a person!** On the morning of the November 17, we picked up the ashes and lowered them into our small grave where he is joining our Friedrich.

Besides Pastor Besch, who blessed the burial, only Julie, Dorothee, Thilde and Hedwig were present. It was a beautiful autumn day and the birds were singing so beautifully. How pretty is our cemetery! The wreaths were lying far outside our little gravesite. I always have to remember how complete Father's life had been, how grateful we can be that he did not have to end in a hospital. We should not be sad. How few have lived such a life! I still see him before me, how peacefully he was laid out in our bedroom with the last of our pink roses on the blanket. There were not too many flowers in the room, and only occasionally, we burned two candles.

The Rohlands and Walt left us soon after, Tante Thilde a little later. Dorothee was here with me, now Tante Lotte, and the day after tomorrow Julie will be here. I am still sleeping in your room since it is so cheerful and close to the others.

Walt wrote that he is very unhappy; he had loved Father so much, I believe he was closer to him than to his own father. Thank you for your dear letter of November 17. I don't believe that the cause for his death was the fall, but rather the virus infection that he got after the fall and it was a miracle that he recuperated as much from that as he did, so Dr. Sommer says. Yes, it must have happened when he got up, for we found him on the floor next to his side of the bed. Some noise must have wakened him.

Father wanted me to stay here in the house, but somehow I will have to simplify my life. I don't know yet how much pension I will get, maybe 50% of his salary. I was feeling well during the first ten days, but now the fall storms have set in and I feel low. Well, that misery I am used to. A trip to visit you I would not be able to do physically. Yes, Father had learned than Kennedy was elected, but he did not have much to say to that.

Tante Lotte sends her greetings too. It is wonderful to have her here. *(Lotte and Luise were Mother's younger sisters.)*

The Christmas package for you had been packed and ready to send on the day of Father's death, but only left here a few days ago. It contains the silver from the Rassows, otherwise only trifles.

Dear greetings to the six of you,
Mother.

Letter from Mother, Bremen, December 16, 1960 (excerpt).

... We learn from all the letters that I have received how much Father was loved and honored. I am starting to straighten out his desk. Since he was constantly working on some project, his files that came back from his office when he retired in 1956 had never really been put in order. Stacks of files came from the office then. He was very involved with his trip to Spain two years ago and the trip to Greece this year. How wonderful that he could do both those projects and was able to really enjoy them. I shall make many piles: ports, FDR Party (political party), *Carl Schurz Gesellschaft*, *Kunsthalle*, his own productions, verses, memories. Much will be thrown away and for the diverse departments I shall let the responsible gentlemen come here, they are all very understanding....

Mother

Birthday letter to Mother, Lodi, December 30, 1960 (excerpt).

... Barbara says sometimes quite unexpectedly, "Opa Bremen is dead, is he? And Omi Bremen is all by herself now? Can't we go over and see her?" All of them are thinking much about you. Opa is now an angel in heaven with very big wings because he was already so old. Martin was a little angel before he came to be with us. We are talking a lot about heaven, its population, about life after death and before life. The connection between God and Jesus gives them much to think about. Doris especially asks some questions that are hard to answer.

Many greeting from all of us,
Mathilde.

Letter from Mother, Bremen, February 12, 1961 (excerpt).

… Next to Spitta, Hanns Meyer is very close to me, you might remember him. Father always worked with him. He had founded the *Verkehrsverein* (transportation league). Until his death, Father was the chairman of this organization. Hanns Meyer is a pleasant man and had been together with Father until his last day, November 10. I was so affiliated with Father's professional life that I love to be friends with his colleagues still.

I would like to know what pictures you have of Father and me. I am now having copies made of Father's pictures from 1953. He did not change much since then. On March 14 is Walt's wedding, in a tiny church near Horstedt *(the Kulenkampff's vacation home)*. Walt doesn't like those big American weddings. At his sister Barbara's wedding were 100 people! In November, Walt wants to try to find a job in New Orleans. He loves the warm climate. California would attract him too, but that is too far away from Dayton.

A gentleman from Father's office is now managing Father's files for me. There are still big piles since Father was working up to the end. Then there is the State Archive that is interested in many of the files, and finally I have to get through all those speeches, articles, dramatic scripts, and poetry. I always feel that Father's desk and its content are radiating life. *(A few years later, she and their friend Spitta would publish the book containing all those speeches and essays:* Hermann Apelt, Reden und Schriften. *Many of these speeches and essays can be found in Part II of this book.)* …

… Meanwhile you must have received Father's article about Iphigenia, *Zwischen Euripides und Goethe* (between Euripides and Goethe.) It came out after his death. He had not seen it printed. You also should have received the pictures of Father in the coffin here in our house. They are not perfect; I could not be there when they took them.

All best wishes for Martin.
Greetings to all of you, Mother.

In spite of all the common sicknesses and usual household difficulties, our family in Lodi was growing up well. However, our house on Howard Street was getting too small. Leo had lost his job and, after a long search, was now a foreman at another company. It was not certain how much longer that company would last. He also had a bad accident with his hand and a life-threatening lung infection. Having been an addicted cigarette smoker, he quit the habit almost overnight. We were thinking of selling our house and moving to the San Francisco Bay Area.

Letter to Mother, Lodi, July 3, 1961.
Dear Mother!

Now July 10 *(Father's birthday)* is coming soon and we will think of you a lot. Writing letters is very hard for me now since we have again to cope with sicknesses. That's why you hear so little from me. Little Leo had a painful infection in the outer ear that took quite a while to heal; he is not allowed to swim for the time being. The little one had his molars come in and screamed often during the night, and now Barbara comes down with tonsillitis. But all that will go away. Tomorrow is the 4th of July, one of the big holidays here. Leo doesn't have to work and during the day there are boat races on the lake and in the evening big fireworks.

Your Mathilde.

Letter from Mother, Bremen, July 16, 1961 (excerpt).
Dear Mathilde,

Your letter came exactly on July 10. I can imagine that all our four daughters were thinking of us. In the morning, I went to the grave and decorated it with red and white roses from our garden. The gravesite turned out very pretty, only the newly planted ivy has to get thicker. The Transportation Club had sent a big bouquet of red and white carnations; those were standing by the new headstone. In the afternoon, I spent more time with Spitta at the cemetery...

Letter to Mother, Lodi, July 19, 1961 (excerpt).

… On July 10 we thought much about you. The children ask so many questions about Opa Bremen; his existence as a large angel is moving them much. What a pity that grandfather could not live to observe his youngest grandson; he is such a cute fellow. Though right now he is not so cute, since he is pulling all the bobbins out of my sewing machine drawer and is unwinding them!

…Our school children are doing well. Doris is very good; she is a fast learner and is so interested in everything. She has a charming teacher (Mrs. Whitacker); Nele met her also. *(My sister visited us in 1961 for a few weeks.)* Leo is doing fine now. He is now in the top reading group and yesterday he brought home a glowing "report card." Barbara is basking in her "place in the sun" at home and she is also progressing rapidly. She already knows the entire alphabet, can count up to 100 and is always hungry for stories. The little one is in the worst stage, "into everything" all the time. But that will blow over and get better. He is very charming and everybody's darling. …

Greetings, your Mathilde.

Book IX
1962-1965

Letter to Mother, Lodi, January 5, 1962 *(This letter combines past and present of my life).*

Dear Mother!

Today is your birthday and we are all thinking of you very much. You are 78 now, a respectable age. Hopefully you are feeling lively and well like you have been during the last years. I got a letter from Dr. Wagner (director of our Bremen museum) for Christmas that made me especially happy. It was an exceptionally charming letter. He still calls me "My dear Mathilde" and intends to visit us, if possible, during his trip to Mexico *(he never did).* He has resigned from his job in Bremen and will go back to Mexico, his "homeland," in August of this year. He never seemed to belong to Bremen. He felt fenced in there. He expressed his negative feelings about the "*Bremer Staat*" (referring to Bremen as a city-state) in his letter. Our father must have felt this, though he himself was a part of the "Bremer Staat." After his death, several things might have changed.

We are seeing many of the problems in West and East Germany on the TV. Think of this: yesterday there was a surprise for me. There was a program called *Behind the Iron Curtain.* An American reporter had gone to Rostock (East Zone) and had interviewed several people there: students, housewives, workers, children, etc. Then came an interview with a professor at the Rostock university, "Professor Rudolf Schick." He was *my boss* in Neu Buslar, far back in Pommern during the war. Then he was plain "Dr. Schick," now he is "Professor." He still looks exactly the same, a rather unpleasant man. Did you ever meet him? His specialty then was Cytology (science of cells). It was such a weird feeling to recognize, over thousands of miles, an old acquaintance (though not a favorable one). Yes, one has his experiences with bosses. My present one is definitely my favorite one….

Thousand dear greetings,
Mathilde.

Letter from Mother, Bremen, January 12, 1962 (excerpt from Mother's reply to this)

... Dr. Schick I had not met; he was absent from Neu Buslar when I visited you there *(back in 1943)*. Do you remember the sacks of sugar close to your bedroom? Sugar was so limited; you sometimes took some and ate it raw ...

Mother.

Letter from Mother, Bremen, November 1, 1962 (excerpt).

... Tante Thilda *(Father's cousin)* is correcting Father's book, isn't that nice? She has experience in this, from when she was formerly working for the church and did a great deal of correcting. Because of this, I will work together with both Spitta and Tante Thilda quite a lot in the near future because both Spitta and I also read for correction. That will start this week. Did you know that Father did the corrections for Paul Ernst's *Kaiserbuch* besides all his regular work? *(A multi-volume work about all the German emperors, in verse!)* He was often groaning about that. But Else *(his sister)* asked him to do it. *(Paul Ernst, the German poet and writer, was my sister Cornelie's father-in-law. After his children's mother had passed away, he had married my father's sister, Else. Confusing???)*

Very dear greetings, Mother.

The book my mother is referring to, *Hermann Apelt, Reden und Schriften,* is the one that is the basis of this book. I cannot repeat enough that it is the only published book of my father's works, published in 1962 by Hauschild (printing and publishing firm in Bremen) and the most important source for this book that I am writing.

In the beginning of 1963, we found a house in Castro Valley in the Bay Area where Leo was now working. On June 10 of that year (Marty's third birthday), we moved. On November 22, John Kennedy was murdered. There are quite a few references to that.

Letter to Mother, Lodi, June 3, 1963 (excerpt).
Dear Mother!

I am awfully tired, but will quickly write to you. We are moving on June 10, on Martin's birthday, in a week from today! We are going to rent a moving van and packers will come who will do all the packing, loading, and unloading. But there still is a lot of work for us to do …

Now many dear greetings, next time from Castro Valley.

Mathilde.

Letter from Doris to Mother, Castro Valley, June 12, 1963.
Dear Omi Bremen,

We are at our new house now. I got Mommy's desk. We moved with a moving van. We mostly play on hills. We have slept here two nights. My new address is 18218 Walnut Road. I hope you are feeling well. It is so much fun living on a hill. We live right on the other side of Seven Hills Road.

Love, Doris.

Letter to Mother, Castro Valley, November 24, 1963.
Dear Mother!

What terrible events have been happening in the last days! One hardly gets the chance to think. Now Kennedy's murderer, who did not even confess to assassinating Kennedy, has been murdered himself—how will this go on! Here everybody lives with the news; all other activities have stopped. Tomorrow, on Monday, all the schools are closed and all businesses also. Everything is standing still until the funeral. All of us are supposed to go to church. What can all of this mean for the future? Those poor Kennedy children and his unfortunate wife who is so popular with all the Americans! All the things she has done for the "White House" with her energy and her good taste. People seem to be of divided opinion about the successor of Kennedy, Lyndon Johnson. He seems to know a lot about Kennedy's agenda. Isn't it strange that after Lincoln's murder also a Johnson, Andrew, became automatic president because he was the vice president. What do you say to all this and is it as devastating to you as to us?

I still remember when Roosevelt died suddenly in the spring of 1945; only then, there was so much going on in Germany that that faraway event did not hit us as hard as the horrible things around us now. *(I was sick in Traunstein at that time.)* They always tell us, in comparison, that Truman took over the presidency in 1945 completely unprepared, but that Johnson is prepared. Will he now stay alive? Why do they have the expensive agency of "Secret Service" if those assassinations still happen?

One can admire the relative calm with which the United States' government skips over these events and is functioning without interruption. Already two hours after Kennedy's death the new president has been sworn in and is on his way to Washington. All negotiations are still going on, only with a different leader.

Nobody thinks of anything but this!

Many dear greetings, your
Mathilde.

And mother's reaction:

Letter from Mother, Bremen, Dec. 4, 1963 (excerpt).

... Just now your Kennedy letter came and the agitation that also affected all of us is very obvious in it. Now, after the death of his murderer, nobody will ever know for sure what really happened. Poor Jacqueline, what did she have to suffer! But I think it was good that she was with her husband when it happened. That Lincoln's successor also was a Johnson, I did not know. This Johnson will not have it easy. All the festivities were also canceled here and all the public buildings had their flags at half-mast. In the American consulate, I intended to put my name on the list for the fellow grieving people, but it was so crowded that I desisted ...

Life went on through the years up to Mother's death in 1982—the children went through their schooling, started working, married, and had their own lives. We always connected with letters and telephone calls. Several times, I visited my mother and always stayed in contact even after her death with the rest of my ever-growing family. Leo and the children visited Germany. In 1963, I made my first return visit to Germany over the holidays of Christmas and New Years, and my mother's 80th birthday on January 5, 1964. I shall select only a few letters from my correspondence—I never saw my father again after he had ensconced me on the *Magdalene Vinnen* in July of 1952.

Of the last five books (IX-XIII) I will only select excerpts of letters referring to Father. There are less and less of those. Our lives were full of our own events.

Short note from Mother, Bremen, January 10, 1964.
My dear Leo!

All of us are so grateful to you that you let us have Mathilde for these fourteen days. We had two wonderful weeks and the high point was my birthday when I turned 80 years old. All my children and grandchildren have made the day into a wonderful celebration.

In great thankfulness,

Your mother-in-law.

Letter to Mother, Castro Valley, Oct. 31, 1964 (excerpt).
Dear Mother!

Thanks so much for your dear letter with the newspaper clipping about the *Hermann Apelt Straße.* But why not a street downtown on which people can live? Whoever gets to go to a *Hafenzubringer* (connection to the harbor)? Or is that a water way? …

Mother did not answer that letter. Later Spitta, who died in 1969, had a street in Schwachhausen, a prestigious suburb in Bremen, named after him. Well, he was the *Bürgermeister* (mayor), and my father "just" a senator.

Book X
1966-1969

Letter to Mother, Castro Valley, February 3, 1968 (excerpt).

… Your demonstrations and financial difficulties don't seem so enormous to us. Here there are also things going on constantly: the "Hippies," the "anti-war movements," the Black revolution, etc. "Strikes" are a daily occurrence, even the teachers are striking for higher salaries, but not in our area of the county so much since teachers here are paid the highest salaries, but in the East. If I get a teaching position, I will get $6,000 during the first year. The highest salary for any teacher is $12,000 a year. That is as much as Leo is making now.

Thousand dear greetings, your
Tita.

Letter from Mother, Bremen, February 11, 1968 (excerpt)
Dear Mathilde,

I am having a peaceful Sunday morning. The Kulos are in Horstedt. The Rohlands were with me for three days, which was wonderful. Wulf had been invited to the *Schaffermahlzeit. (A Bremen event since 1544, this is a meal for members of a group of ship-owners, captains, and merchants. This city event was still visited by my family after Father's death.)* Both of them are doing well. Dorothee went from here to Bonn by train. There she has a medical course every Saturday about therapeutic medicine. Wulf stayed a few more days with the Darjes in Worpswede and then drove back to Kleve in his car …

Book XI
1970-1973

Letter from Mother, Bremen, April 15, 1970 (excerpt).

... Did I ever send you the *Theory of Induction* by Ernst Friedrich Apelt *(my father's grandfather)*? I have two copies. This little book is the only writing by E. F. Apelt that every now and then becomes available again....

... On April 21 I will do something pleasant and be thinking about you. How happy were we about your birth and how much happiness your Father had with you. You always shared his interests. So often did you speak together about Goethe's color theory. ...

Love, Mother

In the summer of 1970, Leo and I went to Germany to visit both families. It was a wonderful trip. Leo's relatives live in Switzerland, in St. Gallen. Actually, these are his sister Edith husband's relatives, the Deuels.

I also devoured the two books by Albert Speer, *Inside the Third Reich* and *Spandau*, first in English, then in German. This shows what my father might have thought about Speer, the right hand of Hitler:

Letter to Mother, Castro Valley, December 31, 1970 (excerpt).

Dear Mother!

... What did you think about Speer or did you not hear much about him? Father must have known about him. In the end, he saved the lives of many people, which was against Hitler's wishes. He even planned to assassinate Hitler, but this did not work out. The imprisonment in Spandau must have turned him into a wise man. I wonder if he still works as an architect. Do you know what his children are doing? Those are more questions than you can answer! ...

Letter from Mother, Bremen, January 14, 1971 (excerpt).

I know very little about Speer, but occasionally I hear about him. I am suspicious about everyone who was caught into Hitler's net. On the other hand, Speer was a young man and he had high hopes for the new movement; he had those large orders. I read the book by him before I sent it to you. You always have to consider that for us the Hitler time was a period where we had lost and we were very doubtful of the new developments. Think of your time at the *Arbeitsdienst.* That you could do your *Pflichtjahr* (year of duty, for girls during the Hitler era) at Bölkens was a gift from heaven. I called Frau Bölken on the telephone and had asked if she knew any farmers in her surrounding who would take *Pflichtjahr* girls. She needed someone herself and was looking for dependable helpers. So you got the position at their farm. For you that time must be hard to understand, and for us even less. The German people had to expiate dearly for their blind trust in the new movement from which they hoped for all redemption. …

With love, Mother

Letter from Mother, Bremen, June 29, 1971 (excerpt).

… The day before yesterday, Sunday, I had a very interesting visitor, a 40-year-old doctor named Apelt who comes from Zittau and is very interested in the Apelt line. He lives with his mother, also a doctor, in Frankfurt. Those two were visiting a friend of the mother in Rönnebeck and now they want to meet me. I had corresponded with the father shortly after our father died, and meanwhile that gentleman has passed away too. He, the father, had by chance read our father's essay about Iphigenia. He had himself written an essay about Goethe's garden and had published it also in the Goethe Yearbook. He found out Father's address from the Weimar Goethe Club and wrote us. But those two Apelt family lines only met each other 300 years ago with Asmus Apelt. The father and son were both very interested in photos of our father and said, "He has the typical Apelt nose." I shall keep up contact with these Apelts….

Among my books, I found one written by Father's cousin, Willibalt Apelt, his *Lebenserinnerungen* (memoirs). He writes about his and my father's mutual grandfather, Ernst Friedrich

Apelt, the scientist and author. Maybe this young man and his father, who visited Mother, are descendents of Willibalt, whose father's name was Carl Alexander. The picture of Willibalt Apelt shows indeed that he has the "Apelt" nose too. Our family did not have much contact with the Willibalts. Or maybe with another child of Ernst Friedrich. My father's father was Otto Apelt. The name "Apelt" is not found too frequently in northern Germany, maybe more in southern Germany.

Books XII (1974-1977) and XIII (1978-1982) do not contain any references to my father. Also, my mother's handwriting becomes almost illegible. So, this concludes my correspondence with my mother until her death in June of 1982.

Letters from Hermann Apelt before 1900

Copied from the originals by Julie Kulenkampff and Julie Kohlrausch;
Translated by Mathilde Apelt Schmidt

C.M.Bromann (Sweden)	+	Hermann Rassow School Principal (Stettin, Berlin, Weimar) (Must have been "Grandfather") (1819-1907)	Emilie Otto	+	Ernst Friedrich Apelt (1812-1859, he died young) Professor in Jena, and writer

Cornelia (Cora) Rassow (Sister of Gustav Rassow, Senator, Bremen) (1829-1884)	+	Otto Apelt School Principal, Weimar, Eisenach, Dresden. (1845-1932)

Hermann Otto August Ernst Apelt
born July 10, 1876
died November 11, 1960

In the summer of 1890, my father visited Bremen from Weimar and stayed at the house of his uncle, Gustav Rassow. His mother, Cora Apelt, née Rassow, died a few years later in 1892 when my father was barely sixteen years old. Unfortunately we only have my father's letters and only from the years 1890 and 1895. Actually, we are lucky to have those.

Letter from Hermann to his mother, Bremen, July 15, 1890 (14 years old).
Dearest Mama!

It almost seems as if I have brought the good weather to Bremen. Until now, it has been fine every day; yesterday it was quite hot, but a thunderstorm has cooled the air over night. Today the barometer climbed substantially and a beautiful day lies ahead of us. Hopefully you will also get some good weather and don't drown in rain showers. Hopefully, dear Mama, your traveling birthday was not too dismal. I don't even know if you arrived and if you found lodging. How are you and Spüterich? *(I think this was their dog.)*

Everybody is fine here, only the tonsil-less Fritz still persists with his cough that, by the way, has been declared to be a common cold by Dr. Wurm. Also Onkel (Uncle Gustav Rassow) has not quite recuperated yet.

I am indulging in pleasures here and everyone is treating me wonderfully. The little ones are lovely. Fritz has lessons from 8:00 to 9:30 and the twins are in Graves' Garden (restaurant) where I shall follow also. The exhibition is splendid. *(This is the International Industrial Fair held in Bremen in 1890.)* I didn't realize how beautiful it would be. On Sunday Onkel took Fritz and me there. Onkel always has much to do and therefore he let us walk there by ourselves. We concentrated on the trade exhibition that is quite attractive. There one sees oneself transplanted into an indigo plant; then one learns how jute (a strong fiber used to make burlap) and shellac are made and used. Suddenly you are transplanted into a street in Agrar. *(This might be a city in Africa. My father's handwriting was hard to read.)* All around you there is colorful life, the shops are open and carts with interestingly dressed Indians are driving in between. But not everything is in natural size; many are only the size of dolls' houses.

Here I was interrupted, for I had to go into the garden with Fritz. Because of the intermission, this writing paper is a bit crumbled. Please excuse me. Here, also, it is an endeavor to write a letter, for either Leo *(Fritz's younger brother)* is constantly hitting my arm or closing the inkwell with his hand. Just now, he started singing a morning song. Oh, when will I end my letter? Another pause; Leo has just transformed my hands into the hands of Moors. But I shall continue with my narration.

On the same day, I met the Krugs at the exhibition. While the others, the Krugs, Onkel, and Tante (Aunt), had their breakfast, Fritz and I were, for a few moments, in the Marine Hall. But in only a quarter of an hour one cannot see very much and so we only looked briefly at the fishermen's display. In the afternoon, we went to Graves' Garden to eat.

On Monday morning, Tante Langer went shopping and took me along. In the afternoon, we went to Graves' Garden. Later on, I went to the exhibition where I met Onkel, Tante and the Gildemeisters. Onkel intended to take me to the concert of the Meran rifle-brigade band. It took place in the large hall in the *Parkhaus*. And just think how funny this was, that we didn't sit in long rows, but at tables instead, and ate and drank during the show. We were quite a large party: the Wurms, the Sombarts, Herr Rüter and many others joined us. The concert was very nice, but they should have sung more. At times one could have laughed his heart out, especially during the songs that were only accompanied by zither while all the other pieces were performed with trumpets and other brass instruments. And that was a little too loud for this particular hall. There were only six singers. One of them, the main yodeler, was so funny that I cannot describe it. Every time he sang, the entire audience screamed with laughter. We left before the show ended because they were tooting so awfully long. We drove to the Pagoda (a beer hall on Holler Lake) while the electric lights were still on.

Now I have filled my sheet, Leo is bombarding me with questions, and Fritz is reading my letter from behind my shoulder—in short—I have to close.

With many greetings, your son.

Letter from Hermann to his mother, Bremen, July 22, 1890.
Dearest Mama!

Another week has gone by! How fast the beautiful time is passing. I am living such a joyful and pleasurable life here that I hardly notice how long I am here already. Hopefully you experience the same! Until now, I could tell you about good weather, but on Friday the sky changed its face to a less pleasing one. I don't know why it suddenly had to cry so many tears; if it was angry that it could see the exhibition only from top or if it was disappointed that its beautiful starlights had been doused by human flames. For even Tante Christine takes her nice star chart only seldom in hand. But the electric illumination is absolutely magical. On Sunday the entire set blazed with light. Too bad that Tante Maria couldn't experience this anymore. I had not been to the exhibition for several days because of the pouring rain. On Sunday evening, it got lighter and Onkel and Tante took me along. Really—it was intoxicating! All the waters were springing, around each fountain burned many colorful lamps, and the main hall was illuminated with thousands of small lights. One felt like being in a fairyland. The fables of *Thousand and One Nights* seemed to materialize. Can you imagine how enticing this was?

Yesterday, Monday, was a pretty afternoon and it was used accordingly. I believe that they took in as much money as on Sunday. But the last Sunday was much more meager than my first one. On the last Sunday about six or seven thousand Marks were taken in; on the one before about eleven thousand marks. Fritz and I also walked to the festivities. On the stairs, we met with Lottchen and together we strolled about the exhibition. We made the trade show the center of our attention. I could have stayed much longer, but the others started to get bored and I had to go with them after one and one half hours' inspection. We then made one more survey of the entire show.

Today it is pouring rain. Hopeless! Twice I went swimming with both of my cousins. Leo was so funny! He was courageous and determined. He went down the stairs right away, and oops, he glided and lay in the water. Of course, he was a little scared, but soon he was up again and going on. He didn't want to leave the water, while Fritz was a little hesitant. And he didn't want to dive at all. He wanted to leave the water soon.

Tomorrow we are invited by the Krugs for dinner and in the afternoon to the Beckers ... *(Letter ends here.)*

Letter from Hermann to his father, Bremen, August 1, 1890.
Dear Papa!

Thanks for your dear letter about which I was very happy. I wanted to answer it earlier but didn't find the time.

Your quote becomes more and more truth. Though I only sent a letter to Mama last Tuesday, I have a lot more to tell you. Tuesday afternoon Herr Gildemeister took me along to the workshops of the Weser *Aktiengesellschaft*. There was a multitude of things to see. Two large warships were being built; now wasn't that lucky timing? There are huge plants: smithies, foundries, machine halls, carpentry shops, and saw mills. We also observed the casting of several small pieces. This company gives work to about 1200 people. *(I believe that this visit was important for my father's future as the Senator of Ports, Navigation, and Traffic.)*

On the next day, a new pleasure waited for me. Already early in the morning I heard Onkel running back and forth, quite against his usual manner. Already at 6:30, a letter had come from the exhibition. It told him that Vice Chancellor Caprivi and possibly also the Emperor would be at the exhibition at 10:00 to look at it! Of course, Onkel jumped out of bed right away and hurried to the exhibition, and he even bought a new top hat on the way. At 10:00, Caprivi was there all right, but the Emperor, oh, the emperor didn't come! Well, we had to be satisfied with Caprivi, and that we enjoyed thoroughly.

Wednesday afternoon we spent in Graves' Garden. On Thursday Tante Christiane, Tante Agnes, Fritz and I went to Vegesack to visit the Fritzens. They own a summerhouse there, actually a palace. The gorgeous garden, situated on the Weser is a regular park. It was a fine day and today the weather is even nicer.

Hoping that you also have some of this beautiful weather, I am with best greetings,

Your son.

In 1892 my father's mother, Cora, died. And in 1895 my father went to Tübingen to study law. I did a little research through the Eberhard Universität, Tübingen, and came up with a few interesting discoveries that I will insert here:

On the list titled *Strafregister* (punishments for "crimes"):

Apelt, Hermann, jur. stud. von Weimar

Offence	Fine
Den 3. Mai 1895, wegen Nachtstörung Geldstrafe (disturbing the peace in the evening)	*4 Mark*
Den 31. Mai 1895 wegen unbefugtem Laufen über Wiesen (unauthorized running over the meadows)	*1 Mark"*
Den 4. Nov. 1895 wegen Auslöschens einer Gaslaterne unbefügter Weise (extinguishing gas lanterns in an unauthorized way)	*4 Mark"*
Den 2. März 1896 wegen desselben (the same)	*4 Mark"*

This proves that my father was a regular student, going with the flow and having to suffer the consequences from ordinary pranks students did. He never talked about that at the dinner table! A little more serious (so it seems) was the following incident that was even mentioned on his departure certificate:

Note der Königl. Staatsanwaldtschaft Tübingen
An das Königliche akademische Rektoramt hier

Betreffend:

Note from the Royal Legal Government in Tübingen
to the Royal Academic Office here concerning:

Die Strafsache gegen Hermann Ernst August Otto Apelt aus Weimar, stud. jur. hier, wegen Hausfriedensbruchs.

The criminal affair against Hermann Ernst August Otto Apelt from Weimar, a law student here, due to disturbance of the peace.

In nebenbezeichnetem Betreff beehre ich mich ergebens mitzuteilen, daß Apelt durch nunmehr rechtskräftigen Strafbefehl des K. Amtsgerichts Tübingen vom 11. März 1896 wegen eines Vergehens des einfachen Haufriedensbruchs zu der Geldstrafe von fünf Mark und für den Fall der Uneinbringlichkeit zu der Gefängnisstrafe von einem Tag, verurteilt wurde.

Concerning this crime, I am honored to share with you, that Apelt has to pay five Marks because of the royal edict of March 11, 1896, and in the case he does not pay, he must go to jail for one day.

Signature

It is no wonder that none of these offenses were mentioned in any of the letters to his father or grandfather when he was asking for money! What we children did know was about the fencing accident when Father lost his hair. The manager of the university archive in Tübingen did not find any data about that. It must have happened some time before March 5 when Father mentions the head wound in his letter to his father (March 5, 1896).

Letter from Hermann to his father, Tübingen, April 3, 1895 (from school, 18 years old).
My dear Father!

I must thank you from the bottom of my heart that you answered my last letter so fast and in such an indulgent way. I was afraid to hurt you this way, but I could not conceal the truth and actually my guilt was not so great that I—being inexperienced—had been hurt already in spite of all the previous efforts. For you are absolutely correct about the fact that he who introduced me into the circle had nothing but mere fishing of humans in mind. But how could I detect this just by looking at him—he looked just as common as all of us. If I am now attached to these people who call themselves Eberhardiner, this was neither the responsibility of the student association that attracted me, nor the person who hurt me. Though he is a very decent and seemingly honest person, I don't really feel drawn to him. What attracted me were some extremely nice people with whom I befriended right away and who are gaining in my eyes every day I know them. What discouraged me from joining the association was, on the one hand, your and Grandfather's well-known antipathy against official bars and beer drinking places. I can assure you as to your other misgivings.

First to the question of money, there is no problem there. I have looked at the calculations several times. I shall need ten to twelve Marks per month. For that amount one gets twice a week a free beer and—which is more important—the fencing floor for official use. If I mentioned that I am worried about the quick rolling out of the money, this was the shock about a few basic expenses such as lodging, tuition, and fencing gear, and a certain anger that I should need so much while others get along splendidly with hundred twenty Marks even though they belong to the association. But this is how it goes during the first semester. In the second one, the expenses are much less. By then there is no need for fencing gear and many other things. By the way, I was very careful not to mention my situation to others.

Concerning your second point, I can assure you that these are very decent people and half of them are even wonderful, namely the older people. Among the younger ones, regrettably, some are rather boring though respectable. If I will actually join or not, I cannot say for sure. I am almost afraid that I cannot tear myself away. I have met a rather decent fellow during a lecture. He does not belong to any association or club, but even he—as I saw today—visits the Eberhardiner. If he is joining, Hermann Apelt will not remain outside. In any case, I will write you at once when I have decided to join. I am not being forced into this and nobody has uttered a word pressing me, not even close, to join. Only by being very friendly and nice to me have they made themselves indispensable to me.

Since you gave me your friendly concession and I now have a free hand, I am thinking calmly about the situation. At first, it gave me a few days of headache. One thing is certain: my studies will always come first with me. I still like to go to the lectures like in the beginning—partly with great joy and partly with some hesitation. I don't think it is a great sin not to copy Seeger's spongy dictates minutely; this is almost impossible anyway because he speaks so fast. There are two wonderful volumes on my desk, which look like gold pieces. First is Esmanch's *Roman History of Law.* I think this will help me to bridge the holes in my notebook. Then I shall pick up Mommsen from the library. Seeger is supposed to have gotten all his material from him. Second there is Sohm's "Institutions." After having read a few chapters—Wendt only mentioned this book a few days ago—it seems to be a very useful book. Regrettably it is arranged a little differently than Wendt organizes his lectures. Therefore, I shall materialize Grandfather's advice for this course only in a limited way and often read the corresponding quotes later. But I shall get used to this idea when studying history of jurisprudence *(theory and philosophy of law).*

Herr Hugo von Meyer, my encyclopedia specialist, a fat, comfortable fellow, is not by any means of a high-flying spiritual nature, but he is bearable. This afternoon the social class will start with Neumann who is supposed to have a good and interesting reputation. Altogether, I shall now drudge all around and see what is good and what is not so good. Some subjects are highly praised, like Kugler's newest course of history and Spitta's *(no relationship to my father's later friend Theodor Spitta, as far as I know)* logic, among others. Yesterday I heard the initiation speech of the new theological professor, Dr. Häsing, in the big hall. It was a very crowded, musical entrance of the faculty members in violet velvet costumes. There was a speech lasting three quarters of an hour about the importance of systematic theology, and then again music for marching out. Dr. Häsing spoke just as complicated as unintelligibly, and I went home as stupid as I had entered. But all that nonsense couldn't fail to leave some impression. If I had anticipated listening to an interesting medical or scientific lecture, I would have been disappointed. Popular anatomy is only read during the winter semester and botany too, which I would have liked to hear, is scheduled with the law-related subjects.

I wish that my box of books would arrive. I am longing for it very much. Please tell Else that when she sends my wash she should also pack my commentated "Cäsar Gallicum" (on my big red book-shelf). She might also add some coffee, tea, or cocoa.

Letter from Hermann to his father, Tübingen, Bursagasse 2, April 27, 1895.

My dear Father!

There is quite a difference between today and half a week ago. Then one was sitting in the train wagon, subjected to all the tortures of this modern iron virgin and was thinking about the goal of one's dreams, while now, now one is standing at one's comfortable desk and looking over this cozy little room while writing. This is now my home and empire for some time to be. It is not big, but bright and friendly, has nice wallpaper and is equipped with the necessary furniture. Unfortunately, the view is not too splendid. I could have had a room with the most beautiful view onto the Neckar and the Alps—but notwithstanding the cost—I didn't like the decor and I'd rather have a pretty inside than a spectacular outside instead of the other way around. Added to this, there are two very nice people in this house: a medical student and a philologist. Through them, I found a very decent dinner companion and several other good connections.

Most of the students I met so far are studying medicine, at least the nicest ones. My neighbor in the lecture hall is a very decent fellow with whom I can exchange my impressions about the boring lectures by Herrn Professor Seeger and my joy about the excellent ones by Herrn Wendt. This reading of the history of the Roman law by Seeger is very tedious. Not only is this gentleman, with his Schwabish accent, hard to understand, he also has the bad habit of dictating much too fast. This is for me, who has forgotten all about the little shorthand acquired previously and who hates writing anyway, a real torture. Luckily this lecture only lasts for three hours and no less fortunately the six-hour long lecture by Wendt is as interesting as Seeker's is boring. Already the body language of both gentlemen portrays the shadowy side of one and the preferences of the other one. Seeger is an elderly gentleman, sporting gray sideburns, stooped deportment, sitting motionless on his little chair after having put his umbrella into the corner and gotten his manuscript out of his pocket, always with the same gesture. On the other side is Wendt, a slender, still young-looking man, with a blond beard, straight, quick, always standing, his speech always accompanied with lively gestures, never dictating. The lectures are always scheduled between 10:00 and 12:00.

When my father now sighs deeply and thinks to himself, "You mean, this boy doesn't have to be at the university until 10:00? When will he get out of bed in the morning?" (and out of a very good bed!) So I will console him right away and assure him that he does not have to sigh. Because already at 7:00 in the morning, my brave fencing instructor, Herr Hussbaumer, a star in his field, is waiting for his new pupil. And he didn't let him wait, even today, though only yesterday he came home rather late after a pleasant carriage trek (as they call it here) to Reutlingen and back via Achalm. Since everything connected with horses is very expensive here in Tübingen, by taking a carriage with six men and doing the driving ourselves, we get great pleasure for very little money. The weather was interesting, real April weather; first, we got poured on, then we had great illumination. I now hope I narrated to you my beginning in Tübingen in the best light and I hope you are just as satisfied with it as

your son Hermann who thinks
of all of you with love and
gratefulness and sends you best
greetings from Schwaben.

Letter from Hermann to his father, Tübingen, April 29, 1895.
Dear Father!

The check came this morning in due time and has been handed over to the university office. So now this affair has been accomplished in the best way and I thank you many times. But the other things are not as easy to solve. I was torn all day long today by a thousand doubts and mind-changes, but I couldn't arrive at any solution. I wrote you already that I had found very nice connections and that really is the case. Though most of them are medical students and most are older than I, we still have much in common. However, there is a hook. Almost all of them belong to associations and the few that do not belong yet will most likely join too. This particular association is not a fellowship, nor is it a student club, but it still is an association. Though they do not wear colors and do not have any fencing conditions, they only give satisfaction. *(This has something to do with duels.)*

Also, this association does not take much of our time. Twice a week we go to a bar, for this is mandatory. Otherwise, there are no limitations. But the financial question is another problem. Not that they demand great luxury, but everyone is obliged to pay five Mark dues per month besides the expense for the beer. Those are the main points. That such an institution would be best for me, I cannot say. The limitations, small though they are, I don't appreciate at all and a free circle of young people seems to me more desirable by far. On the other hand I must say that the ambiance is very nice—I had been invited to their bar on Saturday. What shall I do now? An unpleasant affair. Either I have to join or my connections will become very loose. In the end, I will get completely away from these friendly people. What shall I do? What should I avoid? I don't want to be completely solitary and it is hard to find social contacts here in Tübingen. I think if one doesn't belong to any association, he is rather isolated. Everything here is either association or club. By the way, I believe that Pfarrer Schmidt in the castle was in the same or a similar association, I forgot the name that he quoted to me.

Would you please be so good and write me your opinion soon? Let me know if you would be angry with me or if you have nothing against my joining. So that I would know, in the one case, what direction to take, and in the other case, if I have a free hand to decide for myself. Neither choice is absolutely agreeable is to me, but the most reasonable choice would be for me to join. The 40 Mark have to be coughed up somehow; it is such a sad experience that life is so terribly expensive. You have been very generous, but if at first I had the impression that I could save quite an bit of money, this hope is dwindling away more and more. There is one expense after the other, always monstrous and unavoidable.

Apart from these setbacks I am very well. Yesterday, Sunday, we made a beautiful excursion to Liechtenstein, a real pleasure and incomparable to anything else. The weather was splendid and the sights terrific. Those old knights had quite good taste. The world looks so different from up there, so free and beautiful. And how bold and courageous this dainty little castle is, rising out of its rock like a flower out of its cup. Though actually the castle is new, but even the most beautiful old ruin couldn't look better up there, the slender birth of our prosaic century. It is most gracious and at the same time impressive. A wonderful tour! All of Tübingen is a marvelous nest. And that there is no rose without its thorns, that's a fact of life.

With best greetings to all at home,
your Hermann.

Letter from Hermann to his father, Tübingen, May 8, 1895.
Dearest Father!

The day before yesterday, Monday, was in every respect a very eventful day. At the breakfast table I was surprised by your dear letter for which I have to thank you especially, because it took away all my doubts of not knowing and unpleasantness. When I then went to the university to fetch a rather stale drink of the spring of science from fat Herrn von Seeger, I beheld right away my name in the new list of matriculated, in the first place! In the afternoon at 3:00, we had to appear in our ceremonial dress suits. Then came the rector, a dignified, a little corpulent gentleman, who welcomed us with a speech that admonished us and praised the many-folded advantages and outstanding characteristics of Tübingen. He then had everyone shake his hand and make a deep bow. There one could make the most wonderful bow-character studies.

After having received finally one's huge placard and one's student card, I went in the direction of Bursagasse and thought, during the walk, once more about the pros and cons regarding the Eberhardiner. And I had just come to my conclusion when, by chance, I met the president and told him I would join.

After having reached my home, the friendly landlady, the wife of a lathe turner, told me from the window that there was a package waiting for me. And so, there was the old box and it woke up early memories of Dorndorf. Now it was no small pleasure to unwrap the well-known volumes quickly and give each of them a deserving place on my little corner shelf. The little room has gained so much in coziness and I am feeling three times more at home in it now.

Books really are almost like living things. They speak to you in a much more eloquent way than most human beings. After having torn myself away from these colorful fellows during the dusk, I strolled along the beautiful Neckar River for a while, and then went to our bar in order to find out about my initiation application. I was told that I had been accepted, and so we started celebrating with all the members by drinking to brotherhood. This led to now having twenty *"Dutz-Brüder"* (people who say "thou" to each other) in this foreign city. All the people are just as friendly to me as before and I hope that this step has brought neither you nor me any misgivings. So now I am an Eberhardiner!

The Derendinger, our sister association, are organized similar to ours and have a good relationship with us. Their center is even in the same house, "In der Linde" on the other side of the Neckar. This gives us the advantage over many other associations, to have permission to sing as long as we want, because there is no police curfew there. So this was a four-fold important day.

I am paying 65 Mark for my apartment, which is a nice low price; most student lodging costs 80 Mark. The meals are not inexpensive, however, at one Mark per day. But the food is good and plentiful, similar to north-German menus.

You don't have to send me the "Mommsen" *(Theodor Mommsen was a German classical scholar and historian)*; I got it today from the library. But please tell Else she should send me the promised Faust commentaries, also the ones on the lecture of Wichesche. If she can't get those, then every now and then an interesting number of "Germany." I don't want to lose contact completely. Also, if someone should write again, please enclose the Horaz preparatory that must be in your Wieland translations, volume two.

Finally I send all of you my best greetings, and wishes that my father would sleep better, also hope that the question of living quarters would be solved satisfactorily, and write in love,

Your son Hermann.

My father had two sisters, Else, a few years older, and Mathilde (Thilde), several years younger.

Letter from Hermann, Tübingen, May 15, 1895 (Must be to Else who had packed the box).

My dear sister!

That was so much joy when the good lathe master came in and put your package on the table. In a second, the knots were opened and all those dear things could be retrieved. Much thanks to all of you, mainly to you, the activator, and no less Tante Maria, who reminds me so lovingly of the tea parties in Unterstadt, as well as the copier. These names, theaters, clubs, and so forth sounded so familiar, but still like coming from a different world, lying far behind and at the same time awakening a little longing. It gave me great pleasure to be allowed to read the newspaper again with all my concentration. It is strange and I can't explain it, though we visit many places, to reach for a newspaper is our last thought. My Tübingen is so peaceful and so far away from the world that one hardly gets reminded of the events and happenings outside and almost loses contact with it. It is hard to comprehend that I only learned one half week ago that Gustav Freytag has passed away. But I would call this seclusion rather an advantage than a deficiency. Over all, can one find a lovelier little town than this heap of stairs, ugly alleys, and ancient gable-houses? The student is king here. There are only students here and whoever does anything else is here for the students. There are a few professors, a few landlords, innkeepers, association clerks, and police-men. Another peculiarity of Tübingen is that of all these students, only a handful are standing on their own feet; everything belongs to the student unions of which there are no less than thirty-six. You can see a whole array of colored caps. Some are living miserably and others are living pompously in palaces. Enough, this Schwaben (southwestern region in Germany) city must be the taste of heaven for any student.

But there are two disadvantages which cannot be pleasing to the spoiled son of the Muses. For one, Tübingen has no museums, nor theaters, nor any stimulating institution as such. How much I long to visit you and have a glimpse of your cultural stimulation. The girls here in Schwaben are so damned prosaic and ugly. I can tell you, it is a boring bunch. For one thing, all of them have their hair in braids, and even if they are quite spindly, they have to bounce, usually two of them at a time. I already saw some old women with hardly any of their white hair left; the inevitable braids are hanging from the back of their heads like two little tails, and on the end each one has as surrogate a long black ribbon tacked on. Also they all have very flat skulls because from early childhood on they carry everything, even the heaviest objects, on their heads. They also seem to be very phlegmatic.

So much livelier and more captivating are my comrades, though not of world-shattering importance, but so sociable and pleasant. Maybe there are a little too many medical students and their interests are often a bit one-sided, as it cannot be helped in their realm of studies. Some of them are downright stupid, but there are four people among them who, had

I had contact with them all my life, I might have become a different person. Well, I might become that person anyway. But for now I am still the same.

With love and friendship I remain with thousand greetings, of course to all, upstairs, downstairs, your girlfriend Pauline and Schönwige,

Your Brother Hermann.

Letter from Hermann, Tübingen, May 27, 1895 (maybe to Thilde?).
My dear Sister!

Your letter gave me the greatest joy and is distributing as much sunshine to my little room as the sun outsides shines on the entire nature. And that was very necessary, for it had rained buckets before and everyone was longing for the sun. We are living here in such a beautiful country. I wish we could sometimes stroll together around here and muse about this living commentary of Uhland and Hauff, Reutlingen, the Achalm, the Liechtenstein, and above all the Wurmlinger Chapel, you know, the one of *"Droben stehet die Kapelle"* (above the chapel is standing) etc. This is the place that has the greatest attraction for me. First one marches for an hour on the crest of a mountain, through deep forest, until suddenly, the path goes down steeply and the view opens up. On the other side of the green, eroded valley, one can see on top of a cone-shaped hill the simple little building, surrounded by green mountains. One understands why so many poets feel their poetic vein pulsing here. And after having climbed up to it, one is overcome by this melancholic mood: the little mountain top is covered with graves and each grave is decked out with a simple poem. One is struck by the perfect beauty of nature and simultaneously by the transference of life.

I also visited the churchyard in Tübingen. It is situated on a lovely spot nestled along a mountainside. Uhland is lying next to his wife underneath green trees.

However, we shall not remain at gravesites, but rather rent a carriage and drive to Reutlingen. That is the most enjoyable ride in the world. Six Eberhardiners are inside the carriage. One is the driver, the other five portrait the *Jux* or, as they say here, the action. Already beforehand, everyone has prepared himself by putting enough small coins in his pocket, and as soon as we come close to one of the long drawn-out villages, the fun begins. We show a copper coin or *pfennig* (penny). "Pfennig" the boys scream from all sides and jump after the carriage. When the entire village is on our heels, the coin flies into the crowd and the most enjoyable fight forms the transition to a repetition of the whole thing. When we cross a bigger town, the youths are more sophisticated and instead of "Pfennig" we hear "Nickel, Nickel"! Such a Schwabish place is the strangest thing one can imagine. It is lovely to look at, but dirty inside and out, where the tailor is named "Uhland" and the shoemaker "Hauff," where often the most ancient and tiniest alley is illuminated with radiant electric light. In this uniquely beautiful and strange world, your brother has already been living for almost five weeks, an independent gentleman and high-ranking student. About the latter, one can draw a picture, more so than of the former one.

I tell you, it is strange when one has to pay for each little thing like buns and coffee beans. Even making the coffee one has to do by himself. I have gotten used to it now and even acquired some skills after several failures. I think of the first morning with horror. Spirit cooker, coffee pot and water kettle had been purchased, and the cup and strainer I got from my dear Frau Karle. (When my roommate asked for a sieve, they brought him a coal shovel.) My class began at 7:00. But now I had the misfortune that during my morning toilet the little lamp under the water kettle had died. When I desperately poured the cold water over the coffee, the grounded coffee swam on top in the form of tiny cherries. You see, it would be more rewarding to observe your brother making coffee than on the fencing floor. There we all look much alike in our fencing helmets. However, the strokes that different people make are causing different results. You could not yet admire me riding a horse because, though horses are inexpensively to rent, I do not have a riding habit yet. My old riding pants are torn and after all, though there is not much luxury here in Tübingen, riders usually dress up in flawless riding pants and radiant high boots. All that is too expensive for me. By the way, riding is very popular here. Some of the associations are riding officially and there you could observe twenty to forty men on horses at the same time. Luckily, our association does not belong to these, but is in no way inferior to others. Although we do not have our own building like some of the other clubs do, our bar is the most ornate, furnished with heavy oaken chairs and tables and very tasteful. Our main advantages are that we do not have any debts and all of us are decent people. Another time I shall describe the people and characterize some of them.

For today, this has to be enough and now farewell, my darling, and be embraced and kissed and please continue to love your brother.

Your Hermann.

Letter from Hermann to his grandfather, Tübingen, June 1, 1895.
My dear Grandfather!

Your letter and the one from my dear father have brought a multitude of news to Tübingen. I can still send my thanks to the old address, but how soon, how very soon must my thoughts go a few houses further down when they want to visit the Rassows. The imagination of this move is still so new and unaccustomed. I only hope that all will turn out for the best.

I hope the same for the production of the new Sappho! This thing has, of course, stirred up my lively interest and the greatest curiosity. I hope very much for a French lecturer since I did not give him the honor to hear him. On the one hand, I was told that his lectures are boring. On the other hand, his hours do not fit into my schedule.

Your "Herr Sohn" *(he is referring to himself)* also has plans for Pentecost in his head. Though he has decided not to join a larger tour—some are going to Switzerland, another group to the Black Forest—he thinks of doing some smaller tours. For instance, today we are going to the *Rossberg.* Next Monday all of us who stayed here are off to the *Nebelhöhle* to have a big party there. If only the weather would cooperate, we shall have lots of fun. A little preview of the pleasures of such a people festival one can get by attending the big children's festival in May. There is always a poetic cloud above this heavenly country and a breath from ancient times is met wherever one goes. I don't know if you remember the parade, where the May Queen was enthroned on the festively decorated coach, dressed in white gown with a train, with crown and decked with May flowers, next to the king, surrounded by knights, everyone in ornate costumes. The son of our landlord proudly portrayed the messenger, and the parents loved to receive compliments.

On Pentecost Monday, I am planning a two day hike into the *Donau* Valley (Danube). We might as far as Lake Constance, but this depends on the weather and our money.

Meanwhile, with me expecting such beautiful things in the near future, you are awaiting greater hopes and expectations farther away. If such plans would really materialize, it would be a gain for the entire life, and I thank you, thank you ahead of time. I shall look for a partner; it won't be easy because I don't like many people. Let's hope for the best.

For now, it is important to continue serving Lady Justitia *(Roman goddess of Justice)* and not forget the seriousness of this over the wonders of life. I am quite industriously at work. I have taken abundant notes at Wendt's lectures. I also considered Rahm. When my pen is following the dictates of Seeger and Reyer only hesitantly, I don't think I am committing a great sin. Mommsen and Esmarch are my witnesses and assessors. If you want to hear about Herrn Heumann, I can assure you that those five Mark are better spent than the thirty for the other two babblers. This gentleman's lectures are as clear and interesting as you can wish for, and having treated the definition and development of the word "socialism," has now transferred to the history of the social ideas. I cannot rave enough about Cuyler. He knows how to inflame everybody with his eloquent style.

Please give my greetings to all of the family, also the ones in Leipzig if they are there already. I remain with best wishes that you are further feeling well, in love and thankfulness.

Your grandson Hermann.

Letter from Hermann to his father, Tübingen, July 4, 1895.
Dear Father!

Real quick, a few lines about a very important thing. My landlady wants to know our decision about the next semester. The time comes close and I need to decide if I am staying here, especially since there is a much better room available two flights up. I think it has a much better view and it has a separate room for sleeping, which would be more advantageous in the winter. It would be feasible to pay a few Marks more. But with the pressing demand that Frau Karle has for her rooms, I, who have first choice in the matter, would have to let her know now. So I would like you to let me know if you might have anything against my staying in Tübingen for another semester. I would prefer this very much. I am ensconced here, found good social contacts, have with Wendt an excellent representative of my faculty and I adore the surroundings. You would give me the best birthday present with your permission. So I am expecting your decision.

The other thing I would like to discuss with you is the summer vacation. With Onkel August and Grandfather's generosity, I have been offered the greatest enjoyment: a trip to Switzerland. Grandfather wrote me that I should select a fellow traveler in due time. Following this advice, I mentally went through the list of my friends, and with a stroke of luck, the one whom I selected was willing to go. But unfortunately, the good fellow got the news that his own wedding, slated for the middle of August, will now take place already on August 1. Now I am in a lurch. So far, I haven't found another companion. I do not want to go on this trip by myself. How would it be if I postponed the trip until next summer? You could send me the 70 Mark that would still be left over from my meal tickets and I would just take a merry boat trip up the Rhein with some friends. I might even spend a few days in Bremen, but that has to be seen. In any event, I would go on the way back over Magdeburg and the *Harz*[6] Mountains; I have good acquaintances in both places. I also could hike across the *Kyffhäuser*, say hello to *Eckstedt* and then have three more hours to go to Weimar. As tempting as Switzerland looks—only nine Mark and one is already in Zürich—there is nothing comparable to the thought of spending a few weeks at home again.

All of these are my thoughts. So far I don't even know how far my money will last. First, I would have to prepare a budget for all of this. But in only four weeks the semester will be over. I should not wait until the last moment with my decisions. Please let me know your opinion about this, and perhaps also talk to Grandfather.

With best greetings, your son
Hermann.

Letter from Hermann to his grandfather, Tübingen, July12, 1895.
My dear Grandfather!

All of you have often given me many presents for July 10, but such a cornucopia as this time has never been showered upon me. Two months in Switzerland! For a long time it had been my wish to better my knowledge of French with such a course, and especially my dear mother whose special day gives me reason to think of her, would like this very much. It was she who awakened my interest for the language of our neighbors and has helped me to acquire knowledge thereof.

If you, as well as the others, have expressed the thought that I might regret to see my own plans thus crossed, I only have to point to the kind of crossing of those plans. Look, I did not dream about such an extended trip, and all misgivings about a missing companion are vanishing. Who would need a German escort in Geneva or Lausanne?

So I can only thank you from the bottom of my heart, my dear Grandfather, and I regret that I cannot find enough words for this.

How good people are, how many have sent me cards of congratulation. Though, even if some were long letters, they could not be substitutes for

6 "*Harz* is the German spelling of "Hartz.")

the real persons. And this gives living so far away a touch of bitterness. Now with your present this separation will last even longer. I shall not see you again until Christmas and that is a long time. I shall not see our old home again. That is a strange feeling. You will already be living in the new home, and as I hear, you are quite satisfied. But for me it still is a strange thought.

How sad that you still suffer from the results of your ugly accident while moving to the new house, and that your Eckstedter visit cannot take place. I can only hope that the sore is healing fast and that the two of you can go as soon as possible to the beautiful "Zwei Eichen."[7] Tante Maria could use some recreation after the strenuous move. She is still at home, while my two sisters, who have surely chosen the easier part, have taken off. I had not heard about Else's big intentions and was amazed. But the joy is so much bigger. The dear sister has made a pretty "block" *(stencil?)* for me. Did you see it? She did this so I could admire the newest branch of her crafts activity.

A few more words about the big main present that I can thank you for, Tante Maria and Onkel August. First according to the recommendations, I can tell you that Tante Christiane has already offered them to me in her letter of congratulation. So, I don't have to do anything but accept with many thanks. Further the pleasure trip through Switzerland, the dessert for the festive meal, yes, that leaves some room for debate. First, if I would use this as first dish or as main dish, and then the route. The way that you are suggesting would be the best and most natural one, and if I am going by myself, I shall follow it. But maybe I still find a companion, but he would have seen Switzerland until Luzern and might not have enough money to repeat the same route, and we would start with Luzern. I don't know if this would be feasible and so all this will have to be cleared. But all this is only secondary; the main point must be decided about the places: Lausanne, Geneva? And which lodging would be the best.

Meanwhile I am occupied with high hopes, going to lectures, happy drinking bouts, climbing mountains (weather permitting), and writing letters. There is always a stack to be answered. Then there are some distractions. Yesterday there was a big party with Professor Wendt in the *Ochsen* in Lustenau. I had recommendations from Frorichs to see him and had paid him a visit. He is a tall, good-looking gentleman, just as sympathetic in private as at the lectern. His better half, or more correct,

7 Zwei Eichen, an estate belonging to Hermann Rassow, my father's maternal grandfather. Its location is unknown.

his better three quarters, is of colossal dimensions, quite a contrast to him, not at all beautiful anymore, so that one has to wonder about their good-looking children. Then on Wednesday we had to go to a big students' gathering in honor of the 50 year office anniversary of the gymnastics teacher, Wüst (rowdy), with rowdy speeches and rowdy drinking.

So I could only answer your dear letter today and thank you for your royal present. I thought I would also write to Tante and also a few lines to Paulinchen who surprised me with such a magnificent "such and such" *Torte* (cake). But dusk is surprising me and I have to continue writing tomorrow.

Meanwhile farewell, dear Grandfather, be embraced and greeted with all my heart.

Your thankful and loyal grandson
Hermann.

PS. Also to T.M. *(Tante Maria)* and whoever else is there of the family, the best greetings.

Letter from Hermann, Rigibahn, August 5, 1895.
Dear Grandfather!

A little frozen by the heavy rain and snow, rather hopeless early morning tour to Rigi-Kulm, we are sitting here in the cold guest room of the hotel *Rigibahn* and are waiting for a break in the weather to be able to descend to Weggis.

Early yesterday at 5:00 we took leave through to Zug. From there we went, in pouring rain, to Innerensee. We had already lost all courage, when suddenly the sun broke through and a rainbow was formed across the lake and we could clearly see the Rigi before us. We had the most beautiful hike through the *"Hohle Gasse"* to Küssnacht, from there up the mountain, always nice, until we arrived about half of the way, then it started again to thunder and rain. But even that is pretty, to observe the clouds chasing each other and every now and then, to see a rock peaking through.

Best greetings to all from your
grandson Hermann.

From Hermann to his grandfather, Lausanne, August 8, 1895 (now in Switzerland).

My dear Grandfather!

You are back in dear old Zwei Eichen and your grandson is sitting on the shore of Lake Geneva. I don't know which is prettier, Leuchtenburg or Lausanne, but where I would prefer to be on Friday that I do know. How much would I love to be on the verandah and congratulate you, together with the others, at the flower-filled coffee table, but this year I have to obey fate by being able to celebrate family birthdays in letters and thoughts only. But whether orally or in writing, the good wishes are no less heartfelt and warm. And so in my mind I accompany you, in the morning, when the children come to you with cries of joy, when the grownups are congratulating you in a more quiet way, when Fritz recites his festive poem—but what am I saying, Fritz is in Norderney!—when you sit down and start to open the stack of letters. I hope that mine will be there too. But a little doubt creeps into my mind that it would make it before evening. I can tell that it will not make it to the mailbox today. After the coffee, you will all take a stroll through the garden, the beautiful garden with its linden trees and its rose bushes, and I hope the sun is smiling upon you just like it is shining here today. Then a game of bowling or something like that and then a big salutation at the dinner table and so forth. I know by experience how wonderful it is to start a new life at Zwei Eichen.

Your grandson will meanwhile listen to the rather flat and controversial utterings of Monsieur André about the classics and the romantics, but in the end, who cares about the contents. The main thing is to hear good French, and <u>that</u> this gentleman provides. He is a rather youngish "salon" professor and does not seem very educated as is the case with many gentlemen I listen to here. Because I am a regular listener of the *cour de vacances,* that, being already more than half over, will last another one and one half weeks. Mondays and Saturdays are free. On the other days, they offer two to three rather worthwhile lessons. For now, this is enough for me. Next week I will look for a private teacher. When the lectures are finished, I will go up to the beacon and enjoy the beautiful view. At 12:30, the bell will ring and we go to the dining hall. There is now the entire company gathered together, the whole family, as far as they are here in Lausanne and the other visitors. And I could describe the singular characters to you, but for this the time is too short and it just occurs to me that I didn't even tell you how I got to Lausanne. If I remember right, it was you to whom I wrote a rather morose card from the Rigi. And that was the correct mood, for the beautiful mountain was shrouded in clouds that day. The descent started well, dry and with rather good view onto the lake, but the last quarter was rainy and poured down on us and completely drenched us again. We were sitting without any hope in the *"Löwen"* at Wegins and thought ....

(Here the letter ends abruptly.)

Letter from Hermann to his father, Lausanne, August 19, 1895.
My dear Father!

Recently I received the letters from both you and Thilde for which I thank both of you very much. You are correct. I have turned into a mute person during the last week in an unpardonable fashion, something that does not become everybody the same way. By the way, if I managed to postpone this letter from day to day—I don't know myself how this happened—so was this lack of wanting to write at least a sign of well-being in a bodily, spiritual and financial way. Referring to the latter point, to speak about the least serious but very important one, right now I am blessed presently abundantly with worldly goods. For of the 170 Mark with which amount I took off from Tübingen, I have only spent on the entire trip to Lausanne, including tickets, not more than fifty Mark. So we can say with satisfaction that we learned to avoid the very high costs of the high season that everybody had raved so much about. We were only seriously overcharged once and that was at the Grindel hostel. Otherwise, we always found the right place with good judgment. I am thinking with fond memories of the last night in Luzern. The nicest landlords, a simple but abundant evening meal, an ideal bed, coffee and breakfast, all together for less money than just the miserable bed at the Grindel in which we froze so our teeth were chattering.

It seems that all of you think that this trip is a great disappointment for me, for you sound less impressed than I am. Of course, the bad weather at the Rigi was disheartening, and, of course, our mood was not the best, but in spite of all the unpleasantness, we have seen so many incomparable things and it would not be overstated to count this trip as the most wonderful experiences of my life.

But I wanted to talk about the money. So my transportation did not cost very much, but my new outfit cost me considerably more because my hat and necktie were completely ruined, and the boots partially ruined. But since Grandfather had sent me already 100 Mark I am now possessing more than 200 Franks. To have any more money would even be unsafe, especially since they want the money for the lodging—150 Franks—only at the end of the month.

I have not paid anything for lectures yet. Those vacation courses that you also mentioned, I had intended to hear, but the price is so high—thirty Franks for three weeks which is only a part of the entire course. When we arrived, the first part had already been over and we were supposed to pay thirty Franks for three weeks even though the others had paid this same amount for the entire seven weeks. In short, I wanted to look at the thing first and went to the classes last week for two to three hours a day. I was not very impressed by those gentlemen, though one hears good French and that is the only advantage. That whole affair is not worth the thirty Franks. I shall go from time to time to more inspiring lectures and not sign up for any courses. Today or tomorrow, I shall look around for a private teacher, which in any case is the more profitable thing to do. My landlady, Frau Gillard, will be able to give me advice; she is a very smart and farseeing woman. A tiny person, not five feet high, mother of nine children, brimming with life and very talkative. It is very advantageous for us visitors since she speaks such flawless French. That woman can tell stories! She never pauses or gets entangled. Her voice flows like a river and before one of us Germans has uttered his thoughts in terrible French, she would have finished it off three times in her beautiful accent.

So you see, we couldn't wish for a better landlady. Also her cooking is very good and abundant. Her husband does not live in Lausanne, since he is a wine merchant in Sion in the Rhone Valley. He is now here for a few days for a visit. He is very pleasant and seems to be a clever gentleman. Of the children two are dead, two not here, and two so little that they are hardly noticed. This leaves a young lady of 18 years, rather good looking, but spiritually only half of what the mother is. Then Robert and Frederick, two handsome but seemingly rather lazy fellows of 11 and 14 years. That is the family. There are presently five visitors, including myself. All of them are Germans; this seems to always happen, as we hear. But it is not as bad as it appears, for within the house they speak only French and Herr Schmidt and Fräulein Kost speak rather fluently already. Herr Schmidt, in his middle thirties, has already been here for five months. He is a teacher and a fairly nice gentleman. Fräulein Kost from Pforzheim is not of distinguished bodily charms, but has a lively mind, acts sometimes almost like a teenager and loves to be teased. As far as I know, she intends to become a teacher. The third visitor is the honest guy from Württemberg,

Herr Eberhardt, who doesn't talk very much, but the little bit he says comes out so funny and with such a hilarious accent that he makes us laugh all the time. He also studies philology. I believe he has passed the first teachers' exam. And about the last one, the crown of the company, is Herr Doctor Schneider, a gentleman of long dimensions, with a tendency for crossed legs, of blond hair and mustache, not handsome, but of pleasant face. He is extraordinary witty and sharp so that he always gets the last word. He even lets Frau Gillard feel the holes in her French logic in a rather pleasant way. He plays the piano tolerably, but better than Monsieur Schmidt, though the latter has monopolized the affection and admiration of the family Gillard. It seems that a person with independent ideas like Herr Schmidt has to impress a younger one with whom this is not the case. But Herr Schneider knows how to express his remarks with such clearness and so cleverly that he can be even rude, but never insulting. If Herr Schneider is thus the most interesting and original one of us, there is also the danger that he leads us more to falling into the German than the others. However, one is not often alone with him, so there is nothing to worry about.

So there are quite a few nice people here in our house, but unfortunately most of them too old for me. I am wishing for a younger companion and now hope that will be Madame Gillard's oldest son. He is expected back next week and is of the same age I am. Then I might see more of this pretty area. Now the gentlemen either want to go on big tours like to Chamounix or Zermatt or they take miniature strolls. And the weather is so nice now, though it's a little hot and the horizon not too clear. When I went yesterday to Morgues to look at the Mont Blanc, this gentleman *(the mountain)* was only very vague in his contours.

With heartfelt greetings, your son.

From Hermann to his grandfather, Lausanne, September 9, 1895.
My dear Grandfather!

With the greatest thanks and the joy, I can inform you of the arrival of your third package and your dear letter. That you are longing for the forest-surrounded Zwei Eichen I can vividly imagine, especially if you are tortured by the same heat as we here in Lausanne. The temperature is getting so unbearable that body and spirit are slacking simultaneously. The little ones in the house have gotten quite sick from the weather. But I was not deterred to accept an invitation by my teacher to go on a little tour in the Alps. There were three of us: two Messieurs Bernus and myself. Of both brothers, one of them strangely is a Swiss, the other a Frenchman. By the way, the French one—also a philology student—*un homme assez cultivé et agréable*. The point of our departure was *Bex*.

On the first day, we hiked on a road, then on a less-frequented, romantic path up to the *Chalets d'Anzeinde*, where we slept on the hay. This was the first time I did this pleasurable thing. The Anzeinde is a beautiful mountain meadow in the *Alpes vaudoises,* the foothills of the Berner highlands. It is situated directly at the foot of the Diablerets, a beautiful strange mountain massive whose highest peak—also the highest point of this entire area—was the goal of our excursion. The evening showed us the bold rocks in the most beautiful alpine glow. The next morning, shortly after 4:00, the moon was our lantern to show us the way for the ascent. The climb was not really dangerous, but for a layman rather difficult. But one of the Bernus brothers made this trip for the fourth time and could thus substitute for the otherwise necessary guide. At two places, the situation got rather embarrassing for me. I could hardly suppress feelings of fright and was very grateful to my creator when we arrived, after five hours, on top of the mountain at 3253 meters above sea level! The view was not entirely clear, but beautiful enough to compensate for the toil of the ascent. The Berner mountain top was covered with fog, but the Mont Blanc mountain range almost visible and the Wallis Alps completely visible. This was important to me, since I saw them for the first time. The descent was the most pleasant and interesting walk of my life: two hours across a pretty, softly declining glacier, roped onto a long chain of nine men, for we had met six more travelers. So I got used to this procedure too, and have taken part in a real mountain ascent, though a small one. A little dirty and ragged, but I got back to Lausanne highly satisfied.

I can hardly decide which of the rapidly following mountain tours I liked best; some provided more spectacular views while others had more interesting ways to walk.

That you had visited the Fle.... *(the name is unreadable)* in 1870 I did not know. But when I crossed the *Col de Balme*, I often thought of the descriptions that my mother gave me. I thought about going there for two days, but had minimized the living standards of the good people at Charmounix, therefore it becomes clear that my money situation was at low tide. But you don't have to worry at all that I am short of money. Besides these small excursions, I have hardly any expenses, especially since tomorrow the last of the other visitors is leaving and therefore I don't have any temptations to spend my capital on social drinking bouts. That I am thus staying here as the only stranger is of course in other prospective unfortunately. However, I am now enjoying the advantage of having only French people around me and naturally it is quite nice to now have all the special attention of my landlords. So this will be favorable for my skills in the French language.

Moreover I have the advantage, as Monsieur Pierre just now mentioned at supper, of celebrating at all the going-away parties of the others, meaning that I will drink better wine, help eat a *torte*, and listen to two toasts, one to the person who is leaving, and one to family Gillard.

This abominable heat! I have to rest a moment and lighten my clothes, since it is so hard to bear. You must understand, if one wants the view of the lake in Lausanne, he must live in a room with southern exposure.

A few things I have to refer to in your letter. You ask me how I was received at the house of the Spiesses? They were as friendly as possible when I visited. But I don't know how to behave with a recommendation in Switzerland. At the Frorichs, I had hardly paid a visit when I was already invited for dinner. I did not hear anything from the Spiesses, and I don't know if I should pay another visit. The affair is a little unpleasant to me because of Tante Christiane; she had recommended me so warmly, and now I am not sure how to behave. Anyway, I don't care too much since I have found enough social contact with the Messieurs, the Bernus, and the Gillards.

All those weddings, that is really funny. Else's honorarium as rose wreath bearer is very interesting to me, as senseless and strange I think about this custom.—I shall not forget to send a telegram on the evening of the wedding. It relieves me to hear that the wedding takes place on the 27th. Else wrote—it might be a *lapsus calami*—it would be the 7th, so that I already thought I had missed the occasion.

Another remark: I sometimes feel guilty about writing my letters in the accustomed German, and not giving you an example of my progress in written French. You might have expected French writings, and rightly so. But there are too many letters to write, partly also to Weimar and Bremen, to old and new friends, so a French correspondence would take too much time. I hope for forgiveness on this point.

With best greetings to all of you in
Weimar
Your thankful grandson.

From Hermann to his grandfather, Lausanne, September 25, 1895.
My dear Grandfather!

Yes, unfortunately already the 25th! It is so very beautiful here and I wish the time would stretch out a bit, though I am also looking forward to seeing Tübingen, the old nest, and all my friends again. Your last package came yesterday evening. You know how much I thank you and Tante Marie that you gave me such a wonderful and useful vacation time. I know it was beautiful and I hope it was useful as well. Mme. Gillard thinks that I made much progress and especially she praises my accent, but that is more luck than effort. Of course, one can hardly master a language in seven weeks and the mistakes that are creeping in and the poorly expressed thoughts are not amiss. But I am now able to converse passably and understand almost everything. Only to follow a reading is still difficult for me since I did not have much opportunity to practice listening. Only every now and then I asked my teacher to read to me. Too bad the fun is over so soon, too, too bad! I am just now in such good form. But longer than the 13th, or14th I cannot wait for my departure. Even though the lectures start a little later—I think on the 16th the official semester begins—I would not want to miss the initiation convention of our association. I also intend to visit Luzern, Zürich, and Ulm on my way back, cities that I don't know yet and that are lying on my route. I hope I will get along with my money. I thank you for your friendly and generous offer, but I really don't need any more money.

So it's two more weeks now. I shall hardly have enough time to answer all the letters that I have received during the last two weeks from all of you. Please give my deepest thanks to Tante Marie and sister Thilde. I shall write today and tomorrow to all the Apelts who probably by now think I forgot all about them. Especially, I thank you, dear Grandfather, for your letters. As much as I am delighted that the Apelts are all well, it saddens me that there is the flu going around at the Rassows. I hope that this letter finds you at a state of recuperation. And if it makes you feel better, I have to report that also the family Gillard had to retire to bed one after the other with a light case of the flu. I have a little cold also. This sickness of my landlords and also an imminent exam that my teacher has to work for are the reasons for a quiet and observant life that I have led during the last 14 days, without bigger excursions. The weather is continuously wonderful, though not quite clear. I would love to climb one of the Savoyan mountains or at least do a smaller hike through the Jura, but don't know if I can find a companion. Meanwhile, by staying more closely at home, there is a greater chance for reading and just now I have finished reading *The Debacle* (by Zola), not without frequent yawning and some self-control. What an awful shocker! My favorite authors now are Lafontaine and J. Lemaitre whose critics give me the most pleasant overview of modern literature. Besides, he is supposed to write the best French at the moment.

I am closing with the best greetings to all, not very much, but at least something.

With love and thankfulness, your
Grandson.

Letter from Hermann, Tübingen, October 13, 1895.
My dear sister!

Now I am back in the old nest! That is, not quite the old one, because I also had a little move and now live two flights up and closer to heaven. This change brings me the advantage of enjoying a pretty view of the green Neckar River. The Neckar right now has very little water and I must think of the endless wet flat area that I was looking at for nine months out of my window. Except for my stuff, everything is here is pretty much the same. Herr Karle still has his curly hair and his reddish nose, also his perpetual laugh, and his wife is still the friendly and sedate matron. Your letter was forwarded to me from Lausanne and I studied it with great interest. I congratulate you for having lived through all that hubbub. The new house seems roomy and comfortable. The only impractical things that I could learn from the plan are that the piano is very close to Father's study and also the great distance between his study and the bedroom. I believe that the direct connection in the old house was much more convenient for him. But I hope to be mistaken and that all of you might get used to the new rooms. That the first time you parted from the familiar rooms makes you a little sad, I can understand well. I also am sad thinking of the changes. By the way, I would like to know your house number, number of stairs and the people across from you. Is this the house in which the Sperlings used to live?

Today the weather is exceptional beautiful, a wonderful Sunday. What a contrast! When I arrived here, I was shivering from the frost and the icy wind that shook loads of leaves from the trees in all the streets creating a real melancholic autumn mood. The weather was like this during my entire trip back. First in the night train from Lausanne to Lucerne, that was a very meager affair, and the on the boat I had to run back and forth for a while just to get warm again. But then I enjoyed myself very much in spite of the gray sky. This lovely Luzern! They really do have beautiful cities, these Swiss people. Also Zürich, yes, especially Zürich, where I spent a night in such a wonderful city. Not only is it situated so beautifully, these stately buildings, the elegant, solid impression everything makes; one is in awe and feels at home at the same time. One can feel as though he is in a large patrician city with a rich past and inspiring life, like a Bremen in Switzerland. Though the *Tannhäuser* that I saw in the small theater was a little strange. Frau Venus looked more like a tragic cook than a temptress, and the noble singer sang convulsively, "Oh, Goddess, let me go!" The Elisabeth seemed to me like your former school-friend; at least she sang like her. Finally the six brave singers, including the elector, pardon me, I want to say Duke, appeared to me more like Eskimos than medieval nobles. But all of that impression might have been the result of my exhaustion that let me continue the habit of speaking French, so that my neighbor asked me rather worried if I understood German!

Your brother

Letter from Hermann, Tübingen, October 14, 1895.

So, in spite of all the hurry, I didn't finish this letter last night. My friends tempted me with a tour to the Reutlinger Mountains and I didn't regret that I went with them. Weather and nature were both wonderful. But I had almost finished. I just wanted to add that I had a much better time at the moderate little theater in Ulm. There they performed *Benedict's Prison* and I had to laugh so much. Though I felt a little embarrassed about my sheer joy about the piece when I later heard a conversation in a café that sounded angry and wise simultaneously about the performance (how untruthful the characters were and the poor choice of the director to give such old-fashioned play instead of some more modern play). But I had enjoyed this comedy so much with its old-fashioned, pleasant awkwardness. It had fit so well into this provincial little theater and the performance was so excellent. But it is possible that I have lost all my theatrical judgment here in the inartistic Tübingen and there in the French Lausanne. That the Münster is beautiful and above fashion, even that the critical and modern people in Ulm have to admit. Though it doesn't top the dome in Cologne <u>that</u> we have to put on a pedestal. And it irritated me that the outside walls are covered with dirty bricks. By the way, they are still building on it. The main tower is incomparable. I have only climbed up to the octagon where the helm begins, though one could climb as high as the flowers without danger. But I didn't have enough time for that.

In Tübingen I only found two of my colleagues; the others might come in tomorrow. Now one more request, last not least. Please ask Father if he might be so good as to send me some money: I am completely broke and have to get several things. Among other things I need a pair of boots. So if you could ask him to send the money fast, real fast. If he could also add about 25 Mark from my own savings, since I would like to take a riding course. So, that's it. It is getting quite dark. Please give my greetings everybody in Weimar whose name is either Rassow or Apelt.

With love, your brother Hermann

Letter from Hermann to his father, Tübingen, January 14, 1896.
My dear Father!

Just a few weeks have passed since Grandma died, and again death has torn another hole in the family. First, you had to lose your mother, and now so soon after that you also lose your sister. I was deeply shocked when I learned the news through Else's letter. I knew that Tante was not well, that she was real sick. But I had not thought about this sad ending. I myself had known Tante Mary only sporadically. I could only remember one visit in Weimar and that was short enough. But even those removed from her will always remember her for being a heroine fighting all during her life against great difficulties, only concerned about others. I will hold her as a great example. I am especially distressed thinking about your poor brother-in-law and their numerous children. Fate can be so cruel. I do not know what else to write. Next to these great tragedies, the little worries of everyday life seem so trivial. Only one more request, please thank Else for her letter and packages. Also the military affair has been settled. The birth certificate was not even necessary.

And now goodbye, your loyal son
Hermann.

Letter from Hermann, Tübingen, February 10, 1896.
Dearest sister!

I am sorry to have not kept my promise about writing yesterday or the day before, but I beg you to forgive me because we have such beautiful summer weather now that one completely forgets about what month we have. Since last Wednesday, nature has completely changed everything here. The dirt on streets and roads has dried up and Tübingen presents itself in its clean beauty. It would have been a sin to miss these wonderful days and we didn't forget to honor *Reutlingen, Bebenhausen*, and *Tutlingen* with our presence, partly by foot, partly by carriage.

Today, on the first of our domestic afternoons, I am finally getting around to thank you for your letter and the pictures. The saddest news in your letter, the horrible death of Rassows' friend, I had already heard in the newspapers.

That one of you always seems to be sick is making me very sad, first Onkel Fritz and now Papa. Hopefully both of them get over this fast.

The affair with Graue is of course interesting me very much. Such a scandal! Without that, you people in Weimar are not doing it anymore since I have left you. If it doesn't happen in the world of theater it must be with the church. By the way—Major Hagen—is that the grandfather of Mimi? But I see right now, this strict gentleman signs his name with "von," that must be somebody else.

That you now participate in society sometimes makes me very happy; with me, it is the opposite. I am avoiding society except my association circle, and they are almost family. But I am visiting the theater more frequently. I consider us very fortunate that Director Heidegger from the court theater in Sigmaringen has been performing here with his troop in the museum hall since New Year's. These people do astonishing things, I assure you of that. Of course, not much can be expected of stage decorations in these cramped conditions. But the director himself, his beautiful daughter, and the other actors are all absolutely passable. They perform the most difficult pieces. Recently they even staged the *Wallenstein*.

In closing, I want to wish you much enjoyment at your various parties. I would love to see the Raphael myself, also the little Hummel table.

With brotherly kisses, your
Hermann

Letter from Hermann, Tübingen, February, 21, 1896.
Dear Father!

The money has arrived, and I thank you a thousand times. It was very necessary since my wardrobe need was in dire need of repair. The news about Grandpapa's health has frightened me. I hope that this attack was not too serious. I hope that Else will let me know in a postcard if there are changes for better or worse. I cannot answer yet as to specific dates of my departure here. The official closing of the semester is, I believe, on March 25. From what I understand, only the do-gooders tarry that long. The lectures are going, as far as I know, until March 14 or 15. I intend to leave between the 10th and the 15th. It depends on how empty the nest here will be; I do not want to live here like a hermit.

And what shall I do next summer? Do I have to get all my belongings together and move to the north with everything? Or could I stay another half year in the beautiful south? And if I cannot come here again, would it be possible to go first for one semester to Berlin or do you want me to go to Leipzig right away? For me this is the order of preference: first Tübingen, second Berlin, third Leipzig or Munich. Please let me know your decision either directly or through Else. Please speak once more with Grandpapa. I talked with him about this during the Christmas holidays. If my letter comes one day late, you have to excuse me. Tuesday was a heavy day and all of Tübingen still felt the consequences of the party night *Fasching* (German Mardi Gras, a carnival following *Fastnacht,* a week of sorrow and deprivation) in its limbs. The celebration started at 5:00 in the afternoon with the whole student body in masks. There were parades with music, fireworks, and cannonades, also floats depicting public peace and brotherhood, and freedom was attained by wearing masks. From 9:00 to 10:00, the overjoyed mood of *Fasching* reached its pinnacle and toward morning everyone that had lasted that long crawled home, being more or less drunk. And all this fun was so cheap since if you wore a mask, you did not have to pay one red cent! The first man in civil clothes that one met was relieved of his beer, food, or wine right in front of him. And the gentleman could be thankful that he did not get molested in other ways.

With the best of greetings to all of you, I am your loyal son or the ex-Turk who knows now what it means to celebrate Fat Tuesday. By the way, I believe that I forgot to mention in my last letter that I finally received the document concerning my temporary rejection *(from the Military)* until the year 1899.

Your Hermann

Letter from Hermann to his father, Tübingen, March 5, 1896.
My dear Father!

Many thanks for your letter and the golden foxes *(money).* That I shall not go back to Tübingen saddens me in many ways, but I understand completely your side of this decision. And so it means goodbye forever. My social circle, as well as the town and the area, have become so familiar to me that I shall miss them dearly. I still cannot tell you the exact date of my departure. My final decision I shall write you on a postcard, or if necessary, in a telegram. When I arrive, please do not be shocked about two things. First, I might bring a friend along. I hope this will not be too unpleasant for you. I wish he could sleep for one night with us. **Second, your son has a few scars on his head. Please don't be too angry, it is all on top of my head, nothing in my face. But since this injury happened rather recently, is still looks pretty raw and seems much more dangerous than it really is.** *(My father lost his hair because of this wound received during a fencing tournament. He was close to being bald forever after.)*

I am very sorry that I cannot see the Rassows anymore, but I am very happy for them that their trip has become a reality. The news of Grandfather's sickness had frightened me some. Recently I received a letter from Willibalt Apelt[8] that inquired about the *Pension Gillard* in Lausanne. I have sent him a long explanation about my best knowledge of the advantages and disadvantages of this house. He did not tell me what he intends to do, though that would have interested me.

Looking forward to embrace you and the sisters soon, I remain in the meantime,

your Hermann.

And so, the letters from Tübingen end and there are no letters from Leipzig. All we know is that my father studied for the next five years in Leipzig and graduated with the title of Doctor in 1901, shortly interrupted by a military service in Erfurt. We also know that he moved to Bremen and passed his second bar exam in Hamburg. In Bremen, he made the acquaintance with his lifelong friend, Theodor Spitta.

8 Willibalt Apelt was my father's cousin. He wrote a book *Willibalt Apelt, Jurist im Wandel der Staatsformen, Lebenserinnerungen, J. C. B. Mohr (Paul Siebeck) Tübingen,* no dates found, no copyright either. He was a hiking companion of my father's in Weimar.

Theodor Spitta[9]

My father's best friend was his colleague in the Senate, Dr. Bürgermeister Theodor Spitta (1872-1969). This friendship goes far back to the year 1904 (or even earlier) when both Spittas, Theodor and his wife Paula, had spent some time at Lake Como and had invited my father to join them.

Letter from Paula Spitta to Father, Tremezzo, 1904 (excerpt).
Hotel Pernion Bazzoni et du lac

Tremezzo (Lac du Como) 1904
Dear Dr. Apelt,

We have not given up hope to see you here where it is really beautiful. We will not be here much longer. If you could manage to get here by coming Sunday or Monday, you'll find us still here and we can be together for a few days. We also thought that maybe we could meet you at the *Vierwaldstättersee.* When the weather is good it is quite nice in Vitzau and Gersau. Next week the fruit trees will be in bloom there. Please, let us know your decision. My husband thinks it's best if you send us a telegram on Saturday, with when, where, and how. …

… See you again, hopefully soon.

Your Paula Spitta

---

9 Letters are translated from *Theodor Spitta, Keine andere Rücksicht als die auf das Gemeine Beste.* Published by Bouvier Verlag, Bonn, 1997, in conjunction with *theTheodor-Spitta-Gesellschaft.* Dr.Spitta was second *Bürgermeister.*

In 1909, my parents married and the friendship with Spittas deepened. Chance had it that the birthdays of my mother and of Herrn Spitta fell on the same day: January 5. My mother must have had a difficult time with the birth of her first child, my oldest sister Cornelie, who was born on May 28, 1910. Already on this day, Paula Spitta wrote to my mother:

Letter from Paula Spitta to Mother, Oberneuland, May 28, 1910.
Dear Frau Apelt,

From the bottom of my heart, I hear with joy that your little daughter was born this night. I have during these days, when you were feeling so poorly, thought of you with empathy. My inner foreboding did not let me guess that you would be over the hurdles by this morning already. I wish all the best of fortune for your little girl.

Five years ago today, our little Theo was born—it was a brilliant Sunday morning when he was brought to me when the bells rang at five o'clock. I thought about that when I came to your door with my bouquet of lilies. Then I heard the good news—

My children said at once, "Now Margarete has a friend." For themselves they had to deny this friendship, as they would be 'much too old' *(and of course they were boys).*

I hope you will recuperate fast. With wishes for you and your little child, I remain

Yours, Paula Spitta.

Frau Spitta also wrote to my father on the day of Cornelie's birth.

Letter from Paula Spitta to Father, Bremen, May 28, 1910.
Dear Apelt,

I was very happy when I heard from Maria *(wife of Gustav Rassow)* that the expected hard hours are over and your little daughter had made her appearance. The purest and most untroubled joys of life are brought to us by our children—we often felt this. We are happy that this source of joy will also flow for you now. From the bottom of our hearts, we wish that you will also enjoy the development of your children.

I heard from Anna Stemmermann that she weighs 6 ½ pounds, that is a good start. Today is also the birthday of our Theodor and he is my most promising child. So maybe this is a good omen.

I am inclosing this quote (proving that I didn't abandon children together with the so-called German upbringing):

Wirk, soviel du willst, du stehest doch ewig allein da,
Bis an das All die Natur dich, die gewaltige, knüpft.

Though always doing your best, you will always stand alone,
Until powerful nature connects you with the universe.

To you and the baby all our best wishes.

Your Paula Spitta

And two weeks later Spitta writes:

Letter from Theodor Spitta to Mother, Bremen, June 17, 1910.
Dear Frau Apelt!

I would have liked to visit to greet you in your new role as mother and to express my well-wishing in person. But regrettably your recuperation hasn't progressed enough yet to do so. So let me congratulate you this way and send this token of the beautiful summer that has been denied to you until now.

Wishing that you could enjoy this summer yourself soon and also your child without the unpleasant side effects, I remain with heartfelt greetings,

Your Th. Spitta.

From these letters—unfortunately I have none of my parents' replies—I learned that my mother's later frequent illnesses must have started with the complicated birth of my oldest sister. Evidently, this followed her through all her life. I also learned that the friendship between those two couples deepened over the years. Still, they addressed each other with the formal "Sie." Though in another letter by Spitta, still before the war, it's "Apelt and Spitta"—never "Hermann and Theodor." (Though the wives addressed each other later as "Julie and Sie—Paula and Sie.")

Letter from Spitta to Father, Bremen, July 16, 1913 (excerpt).
Lieber Apelt,

I would like to express my happiness about the wonderful days that we spent together at the *Burgstall* (an estate in the Alps that belonged to my father's uncle, Gustav Rassow). Wonderful nature, wonderful discussions. Also hiking with you in the snow was an experience. In order to keep in shape, I climbed the steps of the dome in Constance. The way down was harder than ours from the snow. *(Evidently, the Spittas left before my parents to do some more traveling at Lake Constance.)* We recommend this area to you. Also the *Schwarzwaldbahn* (Black Forest train) that leads through no less than 38 tunnels, but when above ground it has many beautiful sights.

On my way back to Bremen, I found everyone well, ours as well as your children included. We wish you a pleasant stay with good weather and happy hiking. Again, thanks for the lovely time.

Your Spitta

When World War I started on August 1, 1914, my father became a soldier instantly. Whether he was drafted or enlisted voluntarily, I could not find out. Most likely, he enlisted to help his country. He joined our army as *Feldartillerist* (a field gunner) at the West Front. He fought in the Battle of Verdun. He achieved the rank of Lieutenant. We have a picture of him at the front. I also remember him telling us at the dinner table about his valet. Fortunately, he was not wounded. He had stayed with the German troops for three years when he was called back by the Bremen government to serve as a senator. Spitta himself could not serve as a soldier because he was needed in the Senate in 1914. He was instrumental in my father's election as senator in 1917. My father and Spitta had kept up the correspondence throughout the war years and also later when one of them was away on vacation.

Letter from Spitta to Father, Bremen, February 1, 1915 (excerpt).
Dear Apelt!

You gave me much pleasure with your letter of January 1. Words of friendship found in me a lively echo. Thank you so much for both, the friendship and your words. Don't feel obliged to answer this letter—you have more pressing obligations now, standing at the front as lieutenant. You should limit your correspondence to that with your wife, since she can tell us here what is happening with you at the front. We who are not allowed to fight for our country are happy to be able to write to you.

Instead of going to war as soldiers, soldiers come to our house. So now we have one of them staying with us and I hope that our boys and girls (Spittas had six sons and three daughters) don't molest the man too much with questions. Tomorrow we will also have three of the Eggers children moving in—Frau Eggers had a nervous breakdown and Dr. Eggers is fighting in the war. Others are also hurt by the war. Senator Barkhausen is severely sick and might not live much longer. We would miss him very much.

Come back to Bremen in good health, we need able men, not to mention good friends.

Your Spitta

In 1921, both families had their last child: the Spittas had a little girl, Paula; my parents had me. It was so perfect. The three Spitta girls were almost exactly the same ages of three of us: Margarete was born in 1909, Cornelie in 1910; Eva in 1913, Dorothee in 1912; and Paula and I both in

1921. Only Julie, born in 1915, did not have a female Spitta companion. We visited each other often and their spacious house and garden was almost like a second home. Later all these friendships faded and other ties were bound.

In 1917, Senator Barkhausen actually died from his afflictions. My father received a long letter in November of 1916 with the following paragraph that was most important to my father:

Letter from Spitta to Father, Bremen, November 13, 1916 (exerpt).
Dear Apelt!

… Compared to world historical problems ours here in Bremen seem small. So what is new with the coming election of the new Senate? Right after the death of Senator Stadtländer, the question came up, "Isn't it possible to get Apelt into the Senate?" However, there is the law that senators can only be elected if they were not related to other members of the Senate. *(This is the Nepoten-Klausel that would—unless the law was changed—prohibit my father from joining the Senate because he was a relative of Senator Rassow – our Onkel Gustav.)* It would have been too much to ask the *Bürgerschaft* (League of Bremen Citizens) after having me elected to join the Senate by changing the law to the *lex Spitta* (the law that only ten senators could be lawyers and had to be changed for Spitta who was the eleventh) now to also change the law to *lex Apelt.* So the time is not ripe yet. I personally could not think of a better choice in case our Barkhausen would resign. …

With heartfelt greetings,
Your *(Ihr)* Spitta

Well, Senator Barkhausen died before the election of the new Senate and my father was elected in his stead, *lex Apelt* having been adopted. He came home from the front to join the Senate in the summer of 1917. Spitta and he must have sealed their friendship by offering the informal "Du" to each other because this is an excerpt from his next letter to my father's birthday:

Letter from Spitta to Father, Bremen, July 9, 1918 (excerpt).
Dear Apelt!

Unfortunately, I can't come to bring you my heartfelt greetings for your birthday. *(He cites words from Molière.)* May the ghost of Molière bring my greetings.

All the best for your new year of life, outside in world happenings and inside at home.

Heartfelt greetings, D. Spitta

The "D" stands for "*Dein*", meaning they are now *Dutzfreunde,* officially close friends.

So, between the years 1916 and 1918 the friends changed from the formal "Sie" to the colloquial "Du" in their letters. In 1917, my father was recommended for the Senate.

The friendship continued, and probably so did the correspondence whenever the families were not together. The last written document I have from Spitta in relationship to my father while he was still alive is a speech, held on July 9, 1956, to a circle of close friends:

July 9, 1956.

For the 80th Birthday of Herrn Senator Dr. Apelt

(It is not mentioned where the speech was held)

It is an old German tradition to start celebrations of important events the evening before. Therefore, we start here the evening before the big day and thank our friends for inviting us. We thank you for your warm welcome and feel united with you in our friendship.

Just as we looked back onto the year passed on New Year's Eve and recalled all the good and the bad it has brought us, so we recall tonight the past eighty years that our friend has given to us and to Bremen's advantage.

You were, my dear Apelt, born and raised in a city that was also part of our youth and upbringing:

Oh, Weimar, Dir fiel ein besonderes Los,
wie Bethlehem in Juda, klein und groß.

O Weimar, you have received a special gift,
like Bethlehem, small and great.

And when we think with sadness and hurt about the present situation of Weimar *(it was in the East Zone, beyond the Iron Curtain)*, so we bless the day that brought you to us from Weimar, to Bremen so much more.

Wen die Götter lieben,
den führen sie zur Stätte,
wo man seiner bedarf.

Whom the gods love,
they lead to the place
where he is needed.

And indeed, Bremen needed you: state, city, trade, and navigation; the spiritual and the cultural life in Bremen needed you.

I will not speak about your public activities now. All pertaining places are praising your work and our Bürgermeister Kaisen has repeatedly praised you in gratefulness and admiration.

Instead, tonight we want to testify how much your friends appreciated your coming to Bremen. We did not know you then. But when you turned to us in friendship, we learned what we were missing much in spiritual treasures, inner motivation, human empathy, and real friendship. We experienced that we ourselves needed you. Then you and your family became for us the embodiment of the spirit from Weimar with the best of Bremen. Your house became for us—to paraphrase Gottfried Keller—*a homeland of all good things.*

For all this we thank you, not only for the past, but also for the present and the future.

How much we are able to rely on your thorough knowledge and your rich experience in public affairs, no one knows. I guess that you will be asked again and again to advise and help.

Maybe the same thing that happened to Francois Ponçet when he retired will happen to you. He was asked by the Goethe Institute to hold a speech in honor to Goethe, but he declined, explaining that he would have done so, had he still been working. But now, being retired, he was too busy to do this extra chore.

Be that as it may, we know that you will still, as *pater familias,* as father and grandfather, as friend of your friends, as promoter of art and science, never have the feeling of being useless.

And one more thing: When the German Empire was founded in 1870/71 and Bismark and Moltke met socially once, Bismark asked Moltke, "What other great events can we still expect?" Moltke answered, "To watch a tree grow!"

I don't need to explain in this circle that Moltke has touched upon something very deep and everlasting. You, dear friend, will continue to stay active and give us strength and motivation. We wish for health and strength to you and especially to your wife so she can assist and help you.

Please, let's have a toast for our 80-year-old!

After my father's death, Spitta and my mother became closer and worked together on his unpublished documents and put together my father's legacy: *Hermann Apelt, Reden und Schriften,* edited and published by H. M. Hauschild, 1962, Bremen. I used much of this for the second part of this book, my contribution to the legacy of my father. I find it fitting to put the following *Gedenkworte* (eulogy) by Bremen Bürgermeister Hans Koschnick at Spitta's memorial on January 28, 1969. This speech is the last part of Spitta's memoirs[10]. I only translate the parts pertaining to my father.

10 Theodor Spitta, *Aus meinem Leben, Bürger und Bürgermeister in Bremen,* 1969, Paul List Verlag, K.G. München (page 387).

Speech by Bremen Bürgermeister Hans Koschnick at Spitta's memorial, 1969.

Highly esteemed mourners!

Again we have congregated in this ancient hall in order to take leave from a man who gave the citizens and Senate in Bremen decades of invaluable service, in his office as well as in his free time. Bürgermeister Dr. Theodor Spitta has left us at the age of 96 years.

Unfortunately, he had an accident shortly after a visit with me on January 9. A heavy door at the *Rathaus*, where he had his office, hit him and caused him to fall. He never recuperated. I still remember that on the same morning we had discussed many problems of the present time. We talked about the times before 1915, the years between 1919 and 1933, and about the difficult mandate that confronted us after 1945. We were debating the future and the need to pave the way for the younger generation. He was called to the Senate in 1911 and served here—interrupted only by the time between 1933 and 1945—first as a senator, then as the Second *Bürgermeister,* until he retired in 1955. He and Dr. Apelt received the *Bremer Ehrenmedaille in Gold* (Bremen Gold Medallion). Even then he did not stop working. He did not know the meaning of the word "retirement." Every day he went to the *Rathaus,* wrote a commentary to the Bremen constitution, wrote, together with Julie Apelt, a book about his friend's writings and speeches, and produced his memoir. His professional and political life was so closely connected to the *Rathaus* that it almost seemed to be a consequence of fate that he also spent the last hours of his life here. He also managed to lead a wonderful family life. Blessed with a happy marriage to his wife and leaving six out of nine children behind—having lost three sons and two sons-in-law in the war—connecting to his children, and many grandchildren and great-grandchildren he spent his time away from the office at home.

We say goodbye to him and mourn a great man. The Senate of the Free City-State Bremen is honoring its Bürgermeister Dr. Theodor Spitta by renaming the street *In der Vahr* from the *Kurfürstenallee* to the *Schwachhauser Heerstraße* to now be named *Bürgermeister-Spitta-Allee.*

And now a few words about Rudolf Alexander Schröder. He was a man of many talents and a mutual friend of both

Spitta and my father. He was also a loyal citizen of Bremen. I select a description of this interesting man from Spitta's memoirs. On page 108 he writes, "Rudolf Alexander Schröder has brought to life the image and essence of his (and our) Bremen." He also refers to a speech that my father held on Schröder's 70th birthday, on January 26, 1948, in a hall in the old *Rathaus.* A small part of that speech has been translated in Part II of this book. I had the chance to live with Schröder and his sister Dora for about three months in his summer home in Bavaria after the war. (See my letter dated June 7, 1945, from Bergen, earlier in this book for a description of this visit.)

He spent this time in Bergen to escape from the bombing of Bremen.

The Book of the Bremen Ports[11]

Published by the Bremer Lagerhausgesellschaft M.B.H.
1952

Introduction by Dr. Hermann Apelt

The book, handsomely linen bound is a so-called dual language edition—all even pages are in English, all odd pages in German. I copied the translated text. (If the Latin quotes were not translated, I did not change them. My father explained the meaning clearly.)

Zur Einführung

Introduction

The origins of this book are twofold. 1952 marks a double anniversary for the ports of Bremen. 125 years ago this year, in 1827, the construction of the oldest harbor-basin in Bremerhaven was begun, and 75 years ago, in 1877, the *Bremer Lagerhaus-Gesellschaft* (Bremen Warehousing Company) was established. The two events differ in time and kind. But not only does each of the two form a link in the development of the Bremen ports; each stands in a significant relationship to the other.

Bremen owes nothing to Fortune. Its history is a history of struggle—the struggle to establish its right of existence, the struggle with *nature* and with *man*. But the dominant theme of this struggle is Freedom, whether freedom of trade and navigation, freedom of belief, or, most important of all, freedom for the community.

---

11 Das Buch der Bremischen Häfen, Herausgeber: Lagerhaus-Gesellschaft und Gesellschaft für Wirtschaftsförderung. Bremen. Copyright by Internationale Verlagsgesellschaft M.B.H., Bremen, 1952.

"Navigare necesse—vivere non necesse est."
To navigate is necessary—to live is not.

This saying of the ancient Romans, which was inscribed over one of the gates of the *Haus Seefahrt,* has become widely known and is, in fact, almost a household word as the motto of the city itself. The saying, in a sense in which Bremen has adopted it, and shown at its paradoxical refinement, means no more than that no overseas trading center can exist without shipping, that to exist it must of necessity maintain shipping services.

The maintenance of shipping services requires navigable access to the sea. Throughout the centuries, indeed up to the present existence, Bremen has had to fight the adequacy and freedom of its shipping approach, the River Weser. One of the most important turning points in this struggle was the founding of Bremerhaven by Bürgermeister Johann Smidt. The new port built at the point where the Lower Weser opens into the sea safeguarded the ability of Bremen ships to sail in and out unimpeded by the caprices of the river or by manmade difficulties.

This, however, solved only half the problem. Just as shipping is vital to overseas commerce, so overseas commerce is vital to shipping. But even after Bremerhaven was founded, the base of Bremen's overseas commerce remained in the city. This was shown once again when the Bremen cotton trade brought the Bremen *Lagerhaus-Gesellschaft* into existence in 1877. It was a requirement of any solution, which should give promise of durability that seagoing ships should once more have access to Bremen itself. It fell to Ludwig Franzius to achieve what had eluded the efforts of two centuries. About a decade after it was established, the Bremen *Lagerhaus-Gesellschaft* was able to take over the management of transshipment and storage in the free port newly opened on the *Stephanikirchenweide* (meadow near the Stephany Church). From that time on Bremen could count on two complementary port systems.

It is a characteristic common to the Baltic and North Sea coasts, from Pillau to the Hook of Holland, that the main ports are linked to a subsidiary port nearer the sea. The relationship between Bremen City and Bremerhaven has, however, features of its own. A glance at the story of the construction of both groups in the last half-century is sufficient to show that here it is not, as elsewhere, a question merely of the auxiliary status to a main port, but that both ports, in Bremerhaven and the City, are equal contributors to Bremen's importance as a sea port. Bremen needs Bremerhaven—for instance think of the large passenger ships—and

Bremerhaven needs Bremen, in spite of the independent position it has made for itself as a community, particularly through its importance as a fishing port. It is only natural that difficulties in the field of division of competence should emerge from the special nature of this relationship, and both parts must therefore bear constantly in mind that they form one economic whole, and that each needs the other. This book with its twofold starting point attempts to give expression to this necessity.

"Conserva Domine hospitium ecclesiae tuae"

So read the inscription over the gatehouse at the old *Große Weserbrücke (Big Weser Bridge, destroyed in the war but built up again under the lead of Bürgermeisters Kaisen and Spitta)*. If Bremen became what the inscription proclaimed, an asylum for the church, a refuge of religious freedom, this too came about only through constant struggle, not indeed with external powers, since the disputes with the Archbishops were of a political, not a religious nature, but in repeated and bitter conflict within its own walls. Thus, though the city had adhered to the Reformed Faith from the time of the Dordrecht Synod, while the secularized arch-diocese and with it the Cathedral had remained Lutheran, the incorporation of the latter in the City precincts (by the Imperial Commission of 1803) now broke down the exclusiveness of the Calvinists. The Bremen Church could, as a result of this restless development, boast of a greater degree of freedom than any other German provincial church. Many a minister of the church has found refuge and a new home in Bremen, who had elsewhere had to yield to the stricter ordinances of his ecclesiastical authorities. If recently the Bremen Church Assembly decided in favor of accession to the German Evangelical Church, one may understand the declaration to the effect that it is not a question of surrendering inherited freedom, but solely of a recognition that bounds must be set to the most widely extended freedom where it might lead to abuse and distortion of the essence of the matter.

Vryheit do ik ju openbar …
(Freedom I proclaim to you)

This inscription on the shield of the Roland Statue, the symbol of our city, may originally have referred to the market rights conferred by the Emperor, but became in its broader sense the expression of the striving for independence from the temporal overlordship of the Archbishop or in other words of the striving for immediate access to the Imperial Crown. Bremen sought recognition as a free Imperial city, owing allegiance to the Emperor and the Empire alone. Step by step in the centuries-long struggle with the archbishop it had approached this goal, until in 1646 it won formal recognition of its status from Ferdinand III in the Decree of Linz. If now Bremen guards its hard-earned freedom as a sacred jewel, it is not for the sake of boasting of a historic right, not from vanity or megalomania, but from the unshakable conviction, reached and ever confirmed anew by experience, that only thus can it hope to fulfill its vocation as a sea port in the service of all Germany.

Storck reports about the legend that so long as the Roland Statue stands, Bremen's freedom will be secure. The Roland Statue has survived the First and also the Second World War. May it come through future dangers as well. On one side of it stands the Schütting, the home of commerce and navigation, restored after the war, opposite of it the Cathedral, symbol of the spiritual power, and on its other side the Town Hall of the Free Hanseatic City—and from all three of them Roland calls to us, today as throughout the centuries:

"Vryheit do ik ju openbar,
De Karl und menich vorst vorwar,
Desser stede ghegheven hat,
Des danket Gode, is min radt."

Freedom I publicly proclaim unto you
I, Charles (the Great) and verily many other lords,
In this city have given,
Thank God for that, that is my advice.

Apelt (signature)

Dr. Hermann Apelt
Senator of Ports, Shipping,
and Transport, Bremen

My Father, the Poet

My father always lived with words. He never published a book written by himself but, especially while on vacation, he wrote poems. He always knew how to put his beloved translations from Greek, Latin, English, or French into German meters and rhymes. My mother collected all those poems and most of them are beautiful. Many of his poems were for his children. Some are riddles and we children had to solve them. I selected some of these poems and translated them roughly into English.

Zeit

Unaufhaltsam rinnt der Strom der Zeit
Rinnt und rinnt ins Meer der Ewigkeit.
Uns zwar scheint es manchmal still zu stehen,
Manchmal schnell in Wirbeln dann zu gehen.
Und doch ist es stets dieselbe Zeit,
Die beständig mit derselben Schnelle, Well' auf Welle,
Rinnt ins Meer der Ewigkeit.

Impetuously flows the stream of time
Runs and runs into the ocean of eternity.
Though sometimes it seems to stand still,
Sometimes it seems to whirl fast.
But still it's the same time
That flows with the same speed,
Wave upon wave,
Into the ocean of eternity.

An Julie, 1910

Wenn Schönheit war in meinem Leben,
So nur durch dich.
Wenn Reinheit war in meinem Streben,
Du führtest mich.
Und wurde Friede mir gegeben,
geschah's durch dich.

To Julie
When beauty came into my life,
It was because of you,
When I strove for purity,
You led me.
And when I obtained peace,
It happened because of you.

When my father worked as an assistant attorney for the Chamber of Commerce in Bremen, he had to travel frequently. In 1910, he was sent to Berlin where he attended a dinner at the Savoy Hotel.

So vornehm man sich nicht alle Tage erweist!
Hab' mit dem Kanzler zu Nacht gespeist,
Nur freilich, wir schüttelten uns nicht die Hände,
Er saß am obern, ich am untern Ende.

Such elegance does not happen every day!
I dined with the chancellor at night.
Well, unfortunately we did not shake hands.
He sat at the top and I at the lower end.

On April 21 (my birthday) in 1926 my father had to go to Berlin for business and he sent me this poem from the Continental Hotel:

Zum 21sten April 1926
Heute wird fünf Jahre meine kleine Teite
Und derweilen fahre ich im Lande weite!
Ach, wie ist's mir schmerzlich, daß ich fortgemußt,
Hätte gern so herzlich heute dich geküßt.
Hätte all die Lichte gar so gern geschaut
Und dein Festgesichte, deine Jubellaut'.
Zusehn tät mit Wonn' ich, wie ihr spielt so schön,
Paula, Julie, Jonny, Klara, Hilde Hähn.
Wie gar wohl gelungen wird das Ganze sein,
Denn die bösen Jungen läd man garnicht ein.
Wenn zu euren Spielen sie herüber schaun,
Laß sie neidisch schielen über ihren Zaun.
Sanft und lieb und milde, eitel Mondenschein
Zeigt sich heut Mathilde, ganz wie Perlen fein.
Mückchen nur, nicht Mädchen heut' auf jeden Fall,
und kein einz'ges Böckchen darf nur aus dem Stall.
Meine kleine süße, gute, liebe Teite
Hunderttausend Grüße schickt dir Vater heute.

Today my little Teite *(pet name, actually "Tita", but it had to rhyme)* will be five years old
And I am traveling in the wide world!
Oh, it hurts me so much that I had to leave,
Would have loved so much to kiss you today.
Would have loved to see all the candles
And your party face, your squeals of delight.
Seen you all play so nicely,
Paula, Julie, Johnny, Klara, Hilde Hähn *(friends)*
How well everything will have gone,
Because the bad boys were not invited *(our neighbor's twins boys)*
When they watch you play your games,

Let them look enviously across their fence.
Be very nice and gentle. Like a moonbeam
Should be today Mathilde, pretty like fine pearls.
Only a little mosquito, not a little mite (wordplay,
Made=mite, *Mädchen*= little mite)
And not a one little goat (wordplay, *Böckchen*=temper
tantrum) shall leave the stall.
My little, sweet, good, dear Teite,
Hundred thousand greetings your father sends you today.

My father always loved music and though he never played an instrument nor did he sing, he fully appreciated this art.

Was ist Musik? Tönende Mathematik.
Was ist Mathematik? Tonlose Musik.

What is music? Sounding mathematics.
What is mathematics? Soundless music.

Wem der Töne Macht gegeben,
Zweifach lebet er sein Leben.
Schon als Mensch in Sternensphären
Darf, begnadet er verkehren.
Und den Klang der Himmelsbahnen
Darf hinieden er schon ahnen.

Whoever has the gift of expressing musical sounds,
Lives his life twice.
Already such a man is permitted
To converse in heavenly surroundings.
He already has a foreboding of heaven
While still here on earth.

Our good friends and neighbors on Richard-Strauß-Platz in Bremen, the Ulrichs, were a family blessed with musical talent. Both parents played piano and the daughter, Marie-Luise, was a gifted violinist. Nothing would make my father happier than Marie-Luise playing Mozart for him. When she died of a painful disease in 1958, barely over 40 years old, he was heartbroken. He dedicated two poems to her memory, one when she was still alive, but very sick, and the other after her death.

Marie-Luise,
Der Frühvollendeten.

Nun liegst du krank, es will der Schmerz nicht rasten,
Die Geige liegt, die Freundin, still im Kasten
Und schweigt—die uns zur Lust so oft erklungen,
Mit ihrem Wohllaut Sinn und Herz bezwungen.
Sie schweigt, da deiner liebgewordnen Hand—
Der völlig sie gehorcht—die Kraft entschwand.
O! ließest über die vertrauten Saiten
Du einmal, einmal noch den Bogen gleiten,
Wie würden dann, von Dankbarkeit getragen,
Die Herzen alle dir entgegenschlagen.

Marie-Luise,
To the early perfected

Now you lie sick, we all feel pain
The violin, your friend, lies in its case.
And is quiet—who so often created joy for us
And with its sounds has conquered our mind and heart.
It is quiet since the skill of your beloved hand—
fully in control of you—has lost its power.
O, if only you could have your bow glide
Across those well-known strings,
How would all our hearts, filled with gratitude,
Then beat for you.

Eulogy at Marie-Luise's Memorial

Nun schweigt der Schmerz wie deine Geige schweigt,
Uns lastest's schwer, dir aber ist nun leicht.
Das Ird'sche ließ'st du hinter dir zurück,
Uns läßt du der Erinn'rung Leid und Glück.

Now rests the sorrow as your violin is resting,
We are hurting, but you are bare of hurt.
You left this earth behind, and leave
For us the memory of suffering and happiness.

1945

Natur ersteht im Frülingsschimmer.
Mein Volk vergeht für immer.
Der Krieg wird eng und enger,
Der würgend uns umschließt,
Das Herz schlägt bang und bänger,
Der letzte Wein zerfließt.

Wohin, wohin uns retten
In dieser Not und Qual?
Nur zwischen Tod und Ketten
Bleibt uns die letzte Wahl.

Nature awakens in Spring,
My country dies forever.
The war gets tight and tighter
It surrounds us choking,
The heart beats anxiously,
Last hope is waning.

Where, where can we flee
In this sorrow and pain,
Our only choice
Is between death and chains.

1946

Oh Zeit, du hohes Gut,
Oh Zeit, du großes Weh,
Ach gib mir Kraft und Mut,
Daß ich den Kampf besteh'.

O time, you great treasure,
O time, you great pain,
Ah, give me strength and courage,
That I may last through the battle.

1948

Mögen sie's mit unsrer Währung bunt und immer bunter treiben,
Bremer Thaler, Bremer Mädchen werden wertbeständig bleiben.

They may make mayhem with our currency,
Bremen money, Bremen girls will always keep their value.

When my father retired in 1955, he had even more time for poetry. Even a trip to the dentist pricked his poetic vein:

To Dr. Eickermann

Ihr habt gar manchem wehgetan!
Doch durch den Schmerz von Schmerzen ihn befreit.
Gezogen habt Ihr manchen Zahn.
Wie wär's, Ihr grifft als Meisterstück, es an
Und zieht den Zahn der Zeit?

You have hurt so many people!
But by hurting them you relieved them from their pain.
You have pulled many a tooth.
How about to do your masterpiece
And pull the tooth of time?

Adages

Wenn doch vor seiner Tür ein jeder kehren wollte,
Wie sauber dann hinfür die Stadt sich zeigen sollte!

If only everyone would clean before his own house,
How neat would then the city be!

Dein Wirkungsfeld, sei's groß, sei's klein,
Gleichviel—nur mußt du Meister sein.

Your work, may it be great or small,
No matter, only you must be the master.

Play with Words

Das Leben ist und bleibt ein Wagnis!
Das Leben ist und bleibt ein Fragnis
in Zeugnis, Klagnis, und Unsagnis!
Nie wird das leben zur Behagnis.
Und doch nur selten ein Untragnis.
(All these words are made up to rhyme
with *Wagnis,* which exists.)

Life is and stays a risk!
Life is and stays a question!
In proof, complaint and the unspeakable!
Never life will be sheer comfort.
And seldom unbearable

Das Glück

Nah, ganz nah ging das Glück
Heut' an dir vorüber
Aber weder Gruß noch Blick
Gabst du ihm, mein Lieber.

Voll Verdrusses klagst du nun
Daß das Gück dich meide.
Brauchst dein Aug' nur aufzutun,
Und du hast's zur Seite.

Luck, Happiness

Close, quite closely Luck
passed you today
But, neither nod nor glance
Did you give it, my dear.

Full of grievance you now complain
That Luck is voiding you.
You just need to open your eyes
And you'll see happiness beside you.

Beware of what you say

Ein jedes Tun, ob leicht, ob schwer—
Ob gut, ob bös', ein jedes Wort—
Du rufst zurück es nimmermehr,
In Ewigkeiten wirkt es fort.

Every deed, whether easy, whether hard—
Whether good, whether bad, every word—
You can't ever call back,
It will exist forever.

Living vs. Dead

Was lebt—muß werden—sich verändern und vergehn
Nur das, was leblos ist—kann dauern und bestehn.
Drum sollst des Lebens Bild du unverändert schaun,
So mußt im Kunstwerk du's dem toten Stein vertraun.

What lives—has to keep growing—changing and dying
Only what is without life—can last and stay.
Therefore if you want to see life's image unchanged,
You must trust the work of art made of dead stone.

My father loved nature and all that had to do with the natural flow of things. Before World War II broke out on September 1, 1939, he mused about mankind in general.

Das—Menschlein—was du gut vollbracht,
Dein Lebelang wird's dich beglücken.
Das aber, was du schlecht gemacht,
Dein Lebelang wird's dich bedrücken.
So als dein eigenes Gericht
Wanderst du in des Tages Licht.
Wenn dann des Todes Nacht herniedersinkt—
Geheimnis bleibt, was sie dir bringt:
Ob du verwesest, zu nichts vergehest?
Ob vor dem ew'gen Richter stehest?
Doch ob es so ob so sich schickt,
Das, was geschah—so Tat wie Worte
Du rufst es nie ins Nichts zurück,
In alle Ewigkeiten wirkt es fort.

That—little man—what you did well,
Will always make you happy.
That, however, what you did not do well,
Will always make you depressed.
Therefore as your own judge
You'll wander in the light of day.
But when the dark night of death sinks down upon you—
It is a secret what it brings:
Whether you disintegrate into nothing?
Whether you are standing before the eternal judge?
However, whether it is this or that way,
Whatever happened—deeds as words,
You can never recall them into the nothing,
They live on in eternity.

And in 1948 when his work reconstructing the port seemed futile, he wrote this prayer to time:

O Zeit, du hohes Gut,
O Zeit, du großes Weh,
Ach, gib mir Kraft und Mut,
Daß ich den Kampf besteh.

O time, you precious treasure, o time, you great sorrow,
Ah, give me strength and courage that I get through this ordeal.

He loved our garden and helped my mother harvest the various fruits and vegetables. A dying quince bush stimulated his muse. We cannot grow oranges in Bremen. For that, one had to go south, to Italy. But the quince rivals the orange in beauty.

Abschied von der Quitte

Vier Jahrzehnte hast du Frucht getragen,
Jahr um Jahr in immer größrer Fülle—
Treuer Freund, nun wirst du abgeschlagen,
denn so ist's des hohen Rates Wille
Golden, goldener, so will mich deuchten
Kann im Süd' die Goldorange nicht
Zwischen ihrem dunklen Laube leuchten.

Als im herblich späten Sonnenlicht
Deine Frucht erglänzt—als fühltest du,
Daß es Abschied gibt—und noch einmal:
Überfülle! Früchte ohne Zahl!
Goldenen Scheidegruß strahlst du mir zu.

Farewell to the Quince

Four decades you bore fruit
Year after year more of it—
Dear friend, now you will be hewn down,
For this the high council has willed *(my mother)*
More golden, it seems to me,
Can't be the golden orange in sunny Italy
Glow between its dark foliage.

When in the late sunlight
Your fruit is glowing—as if you feel
That farewell is near—and once more
Overflow! Fruit uncountable!
Golden farewell you radiate to me.

My father also tried the art of translating. I selected one sample of this, maybe from the French to German:

Peace

Und wo ich stand und wo ich ging,
Ein Buchfink und ein Schmetterling
Die waren mir zur Seite
Als freundliches Geleite

Und wo ich ging und wo ich stand,
Der Schmetterling, der Buchfink fand
gar pünktlich sich und schnelle
Zur Stelle.
Ei sieh! Ei sieh! Das liebe Ding
Der kleine, ziere Schmetterling,
der schwarzpunktierte Gelbe.
Ei horch,! Ei horch! Des Friedens Sang
Der altgewohnte liebe Klang,
von Adam her derselbe.

Es starb das Volk, doch seine Dichter leben
Der Leib ist tot, lebendig bleibt das Leben.

And where I stood and where I went,
A finch and a butterfly
They were on time and quickly
At my side.
Look! Look! The lovely thing,
The tiny, graceful butterfly,
The one with black-yellow spots.
Listen! Listen! The song of peace,
The lovely sound, familiar from old,
Known to us from Adam's time.

The nation is dead but its poets are alive;
The body is dead, but the spirit lives.

From the Latin (Aeneid, Book V)
Der Ruderwettkampf

… Draußen weit im Meere ein Fels, der umbrandeten Küste
Seitab, wo sich die Sterne in Wintersturmzeit verbergen
Wird er von schäumenden Wogen gepeitscht und rings überflutet.
Doch bei beruhigter See entsteigt seine Kuppe dem stillen
Wasser—erfreulichster Nistort dem sonnenliebeden Tauchern.
Hier errichtet Aeneas aus laubigen Zweigen der Eiche
Grünend ein Mal den Schiffern zum Zeighen, wo sie zu kehren
Hätten, im Bogen herum den Lauf des Schiffes zu steuern.
Nach dem Los bestimmt sich der Platz: im schmucke von Golde
Und von Purpur zeigen am Heck sich strahlend die Führer.
Doch von der Pappel Laub ist die übrige Mannschaft bekränzt,
Und von Öl überströmt erglänzen die nackenden Schultern.
Nieder sitzen sie bankweis', gespannt die Arme am Ruder,
Warten gespannt des Zeichens und an den klopfenden Herzen
Reißt Erregung und reißt des Ruhms geschwellte Begierde …

I do not know enough Latin to be able to check this passage, but I do own a copy of the Aeneid, translated by John Dryden (1631-1700) who worked at the time of Shakespeare. I have included his translation:

The Rowing Contest

… Far in the sea, against the foaming shore
There stands a rock: the raging billows roar
Above his head in storms; but when 'tis clear,
Uncurl their furrowed backs, and at his foot appear.
In peace, blow, the gentle waters run;
The cormorant, above, lie basking in the sun.
On this the hero fixed an oak in sight,
The mark to guide the mariners aright.
To bear with this, the seamen stretch their oars;
Then round the rock they steer,
And seek the former shores.

The lots decide their place. Above the rest
Each leader shining in his Tyrean vest:
The common crew, with wreaths of poplar boughs
Their temples crown, and shade their sweaty brows:
Besmeared with oil, their naked shoulders shine
All take their seats and wait the sounding sounds.
They grip their oars; and every panting breast
Is raised by turns with hope, by turns with fear depressed …

As one can see, both translators did a different kind of translating. While Dryson made a poem in pentameters that rhyme, my father tried to give us the original hexameters, but without rhyming.

One of my favorite poems is the one about cows grazing on a meadow. My parents used to stay overnight in a small village close to Bremen and stroll along a path close to a wide pasture where one could see forever. Only the light evening breeze and the lowing sounds of the cattle would break up the stillness and tranquility. It was away from the hustle of the city. Utter peace!

Beim Anblick des weidenden Viehs

Ihr braucht euch nicht zu sorgen
Um gestern und um morgen.
Für euch gibt's nur ein Heut;
Nur Gegenwärt'gem offen,
Erinnern nicht noch Hoffen,
Ein Dasein ohne Zeit.

Zwar ihr auch werdet älter,
Auch euer Blut wird kälter,
Doch bleibt's euch unbewußt'
Daß Zukunft sei, ihr wißt's nicht,
Vergangenes—vergißt's nicht,
So ist es kein Verlust.

Looking at the Grazing Cattle

You do not have to worry
About yesterday and tomorrow.
For you there is only today;
Only the present is open
Neither remembering nor hoping,
To be without time.

Although you also get older,
Your blood also gets colder,
But you are not conscious of that,
That there is a future, you don't know,
The past—that's forgotten,
Therefore it is no loss.

I only selected one of the many riddles he made for us children since most of them are plays on words and are hard to translate. However, this one makes sense in both languages:

Arme hab' ich vielleicht—
Doch Beine hab' ich gewißlich keine,
Auch findest du mich stets in meinem Bett,
Bei Tag und Nacht, so früh wie spät.
Und dennoch lauf' ich von Ort zu Ort,
Bei Tag und Nacht, in einem fort.

Arms I have perhaps—
but legs I don't have any
Also: you always find me in my bed,
Day and night, early and late.
And still I am running from place to place,
Day and night, on and on.

Can you guess the answer? Hint in Germen: *Fluß*

Approaching Death

After an accidental fall in summer of 1960, which was followed by a severe flu, my father never fully recuperated. The following three poems are foreshadowing his death toward the end of the year.

Nimm mich auf in deine Schatten
Göttliche Gerechtigkeit,
Auf die ewig grünen Matten,
Wo sich Lamm und Tiger gatten,
Sei auch mir ein Platz bereit.
Unter deinen sel'gen Schatten,
Ohne Falschheit, ohne Neid,
Ewige Barmherzigkeit!
Sei auch mir ein Platz bereit.

Receive me into your shadows,
Divine justice,
On to the eternally green meadows,
Where lamb and tiger are side by side,
Have also for me a place.
Under your blessed shadows,
Without deceit, without envy
Everlasting compassion!
Be there also a place for me.

Müde lehnte er sein Haupt rückwwärts in die Kissen.
'Alles habt ihr mir geraubt, nicht mein gut' Gewissen.
Starb ich drum in Schmerzen gleich,
Starb ich doch in Frieden—
Denn ich weiß, daß Himmelreich
Ist auch mir beschieden'.

Tired he reclines his head backwards into the pillows.
'All you have taken away from me, but my clear conscience.
Although I had to die in pain,
I died peacefully—
Because I know that Heaven
Will also be mine.'

Vor des Todes Angesicht,
Seiner stillen Majestät,
Mißgunst wird und Neid zunichte,
Alle Hadersucht vergeht.
Lüge und Verleumdung schweigen,
Und ihr reines Antlitz mag
Ohne Furcht die Wahrheit zeigen
Unverhüllt dem hellen Tag.

Facing death
His quiet majesty,
All feelings of grudge and envy disappear.
Lies and slander are quiet
And their cleansed face may
Show truth without fear
Unveiled in the light of day.

Father's Death

On November 11, 1960, my father passed away at the age of 84. I was not in Germany at that time, having just given birth to my fourth child. My brother-in-law, Christoph Kulenkampff—the only one of my in-laws living in Bremen at that time—wrote a detailed letter dated November 12, 1960, to my father's sister (my godmother), my sister Cornelie in Dayton Ohio, and me. I have included the translation of this letter.

Christoph Kulenkampff

Bremen, November 12, 1960
Beethovenstr. 16

My dear Aunt Thilde!
Dear Cornelie!
Dear Tita!

Please forgive me that I write to all of you at the same time. Just as unexpected as our telegram of yesterday *(which is lost)* had to hit you, we were devastated when Mother called us yesterday that Father had suffered a heart attack.

We had seen Father frequently during the last few weeks and had always been happy to find him so healthy and obviously recovered from his recent fall at the justice hall as well as the following an attack of the flu. Though he seemed a little older, his bodily as well as his spiritual constitution was admirable. He was highly interested in all phases of life, on the home front, in political, economical, and spiritual happenings. Briefly, he still was his good old self and lived a full life.

On Thursday of this week, the last lock of the Middle Weser was inaugurated for regulation of the waterway between Bremen and Minden. This was the culminating event of a plan that had been worked on since my father *(Christoph referred to my father in this manner)* became a trustee of the Chamber of Commerce in 1906. He had been elected to the Senate in 1917 and he had given this project all of his loving energy. The regulation of the Weser that now makes it possible for more than thousand ships to navigate directly to the Midland Canal is for Bremen, as well as all of Germany, a very important event. Our father was able to participate in the inauguration in his best physical condition. He was also fully able to attend a celebration at City Hall in the evening where the minister of traffic Seeboom held a speech honoring him. Our father spoke briefly and interestingly about the decades of Weser regulation.

After all of that—in a way the zenith of his long life and career—he naturally was a little tired when he arrived late at home at the Richard-Strauss-Platz. But otherwise he was very alert and shared all the events of the day with Mother.

On Friday morning, about 7:30, Father must have suddenly and without any struggle suffered a heart attack that killed him instantly.

In the meantime, Father has been laid out in the bedroom of the parents, very festively and honorably surrounded by laurel wreaths and huge chrysanthemum bouquets. Peacefully and with relaxed expression he lies there after a perfect, much fulfilled life.

For Mother, of course, these days are extremely difficult. But, at least until now, she has found the strength to do all the necessary things. Julie *(Christoph's wife, my sister)* spends most of her time with her and tries to relieve Mother as much as possible. Unfortunately, Frau Bräntle *(house helper)* was absent, but came as soon as possible to help Mother with the daily work. Dorothee Rohland *(my other sister)* will be coming today from Kleve and Walt Ernst *(Cornelie's son)* will arrive on Sunday from Stuttgart.

How wonderful, dear Cornelie, that your son was able to spend three weeks in Bremen. This gave him the opportunity to be with Father and work with him intensively. I believe that the two have become very close. Walt has been coached by his grandfather in the German language. Maybe examples of Goethe and Schiller—as it was unavoidable in the classical atmosphere—were not the easiest examples for learning the language.

The memorial will take place on Monday afternoon at 5:00 in the afternoon. Pastor Besch from the *Liebfrauenkirche* (Our Lady of Grace Church) will officiate the event at the Richard-Strauss-Platz home. Only the closest family and friends will attend. I think that we will gather in the living room of the parents while Father will rest peacefully next door in the bedroom. Mother has moved upstairs to Tita's room for the time being.

On Tuesday at 10:00 (November 15), an official state celebration will take place, in our beautiful old upper City Hall room. Bürgermeister Kaisen will then take the official leave at Father's coffin, surrounded by music. All people, even those who do not belong to Father's closest circle, will be invited. Immediately after, the cremation will follow and on Thursday of the coming week will be the internment at the Riensberg Cemetery.

Though this sudden event has hit all of us unexpectedly and severely, all of us here in Bremen as well as all of you in America will experience a feeling of gratefulness—in spite of the mourning—that Father was allowed to leave this world after a long life without any pain and suffering. It surely was godsend that he could partake in the Weser canalization, a project that was so close to him. This project was one of his goals and it has been achieved.

The local newspapers are full of praise for Father. There were announcements by the family of Bürgermeister Kaisen and all the establishments that Father had belonged to, as well as the art museum and the *Deutsche Gesellschaft Zur Rettung Schiffsbrüchiger* (German Society to Rescue Shipwrecked People). The *Carl Schurz Gesellschaft* (Society) to whom Father felt especially connected also had words of praise for him.

We think of you often, so far away, who have to take leave of your brother and father. We here in Bremen were so fortunate to have his uniquely special personality with us daily. Father's modesty and frugality, his spirit, his culture, and steadily widening horizon will be a model for all of us and a part of our lives forever.

Hopefully Mother will keep the strength and health necessary for the big change in her life. We shall help her as much as we can.

With heartfelt greetings, your
Christoph.

The following speeches in honor of my father were held a few days after his death. My cousin Niels Rodewald had made voice recordings of these speeches and sent these to me from Bremen. I listened to them and transcribed them into English.

I do not know who the speaker of the first speech was or where it was held. The second speech was by First Bürgermeister Kaisen, most likely at the Bremen City Hall.

MEMORIAL SPEECHES FOR SENATOR DR. HERMANN APELT

Bremen, November 12, 1960

Introduction

The former Bremen Senator for Ports, Navigation, and Traffic, Dr. Hermann Apelt, has unexpectedly passed away last night in his 85th year of life.

Speech

(I do not know by whom, but it could be by Senator Theil)

Just a few hours ago, the 84-year-old had been welcomed by a circle of prominent men who were gathering yesterday on behalf of the opening of the navigation canal of the Middle Weser at the double lock to lower and raise ships in the province of Bergen. For this project was part of the life works of our senator who was so extraordinarily involved in our common well-being. Even after he retired in 1956, he was still interested in the promotion of these works, just like during the decennia of his active collaboration. Once more, he was in the center of public honorarium and we were all happy about his presence. Today he is not among us anymore; however, his personality will never cease to affect us. Whoever brings the portrait of Hermann Apelt to his memory will always see the friendly and kind face of this man before him. He was the embodiment of a Bremen senator.

He also, like so many other men meritorious for Bremen, came from outside of our *Hansestadt* (city-state), for he was born in Weimar on July 10, 1876 as the son of a high school principal. So he grew up in a house where science and arts were fostered. Humanities stood at the cradle of Hermann Apelt. He had a classical education and studied the law. In 1900, he came to Bremen and settled here as a young attorney. He could also be seen as an example of the immigrants formed by the power of assimilation that our *Hansestadt* asserted, and that became finally the prototype of the Bremen citizens, so much more after he was elected into the Senate in 1917. Already in 1908, he had been chosen to belong to the city council and soon thereafter, he was elected to become a member of the deputation for ports and railroads. Politically the young senator stood out because of his collaboration in founding the national-liberal syndicate where he became the chairman right away. Until 1933, Dr. Apelt was a member of the Senate without interruption and in 1945, the Americans called him back into the government of the *Hansestadt*. In 1946, he joined the Bremen Democratic Citizens' Party, which later on became the FDP *(the "F" stands for "free")*. Not until he reached the age of eighty did he retire from the Senate.

His many-faceted merits are mostly related to the development of Bremen into one of the most modern and efficient seaports on the North Sea. After the First World War, he helped create the *Columbuskaje* (quay, wharf) that made Bremerhaven become the foremost important passenger port for Germany. After the last world war, Senator Dr. Apelt was confronted with the heavy task of reconstructing the demolished ports and reactivating the completely destroyed port economy. The outstanding characteristic of his life's work is that he had to do this gigantic task twice after both world wars were lost. Therefore, his works are part of Hanseatic and German history.

However, his life's work did not only consist of pure technical achievements. The cultural life in Bremen, the art museum, the lecturers, the theater, the philharmonic society, they all found a passionate promoter in Senator Apelt. These affections deepen the lifelines to Hermann Apelt and transfer his personality from the official realm, as important as his performance herein is, into the universe. How many pleasurable hours has he given to so many people during relaxed sessions after meetings and also at festive occasions in mutual conversation? Again and again one was surprised by the extent of his interests, the fullness of his knowledge, and the thorough understanding for the basic questions of philosophy and history.

He was by nature a fully liberal man, in the best meaning of the word, always inclined to comprehend the position of the other side. His whole affection was given to, besides his work, to point this out once more, the *Kunsthalle* (art museum). It was a matter of the heart for him and as honorable chairman of the art society he proved himself to be—in spite of the generational distance—quite open to works of modern art. With great sorrow he will also be missed in the Carl Schurz Society, whose active president he has been until the very end. His personal obliging manner was profiting this society with their tasks over the entire world again and again. Without interruption, Dr. Apelt was also until now chairman of the *Verkehrsverein* (Traffic Association). His friends in the FDP will especially miss his intelligent advice. The president of the Bremen town council, Hagedorn, has proclaimed today in his eulogy, "Not in vain, Senator Dr. Apelt has been declared the father of the Bremen ports."

Twice after the world wars, he succeeded in giving back world status to these institutions so important to Bremen. The history of Bremen during the last three decades is therefore indivisibly connected with him. Therefore he received—when he retired from the Senate four years ago—the highest distinction that our *Hansestadt* has to give, the Bremen Gold Medal. The president of the Bremen Senate, Bürgermeister Kaisen, declared then, "He was active in the public life for forty years, only interrupted by the National Socialists from 1933 to 1945. All of Bremen knows how closely the activities of Dr. Apelt are connected with ports, navigation, and traffic in Bremen."

For the reconstruction, the rebuilding of the ports, and the upkeep of the navigation of the Weser, immense sums of money were needed which Senator Dr. Apelt had to request. But again and again, the judgment that it was necessary to give utmost consideration to keep the foundation of our city prevailed and his plans were accepted with willingness. His opinion and judgment was always considered valuable since he had wide experience and knowledge. Captain Stede said to me once, "He is a man who gives trust since he can also expect to receive trust."

One can say that hardly any of his predecessors during the time of their office has ever been confronted with such difficult tasks as Dr. Apelt. It has now been 600 years since Bremen joined the League of the Hansa (hence it called itself "*Hansestadt*") and soon became its most prominent assistant. In the course of these 600 years, many a senator for ports and navigation has been confronted with great and vital tasks for Bremen's existence. From the ranks of these men several are standing out who had part in preventing the fact that Bremen might have to suffer the fate of Brügge (another port that never had a chance to grow). One of these great men is also Senator Dr. Apelt. Without Dr. Apelt's far-reaching knowledge, we would not have overcome the utter destruction through the two world wars and would never have arrived again at what we have today.

But with this indication, his importance for Bremen has not been exhausted. His humanistic scholarship, his deep understanding for the basis of human society, his knowledge in the areas of literature, history, philosophy and art gave him as well as Bürgermeister Spitta a very special position in the Senate, in the city council, and finally in the Bremen population.

It is difficult for me to find the right words for Senator Dr. Apelt at this moment. I am still entirely under the influence of the sad news about his so rapid parting from this earth. His sudden death was first inconceivable for his family and inexplicable for all who knew him, for just hours before, on Thursday evening, a group of his friends had been listening attentively to him when he gave a short speech at the *Rathaus* pertaining to the successful completion of his works on the Middle Weser. He spoke with as much animation as ever before and was so happy so be able to relate to us that these works that had occupied him for decades have now been crowned with success. None of the participants could have had the slightest inkling that this would be the last speech they would ever heard from him and that only a few hours later his death would cause such deep grief among us.

Now this man, whose life is fulfilled, is not among us anymore. He has done much for Bremen during the hard times after the two world wars. He has been in public office for more than five decades, three of them in the Bremen Senate. Every Bremen citizen knows how closely his activities were connected to the construction of ports, navigation, and traffic. He has rendered important services in these areas. He belongs to the line of great men who contributed to the ongoing renewal of the basic existence of our free city. Dr. Hermann Apelt is one of these great men. Therefore, he received the greatest honor Bremen can bestow on anyone, the Gold Medal. The Senate will take the opportunity to dignify the deeds of the man we honor so much.

Before his death, he was able to see that his last effort—the navigation of the Weser—has been completed. His uncountable negotiations, speeches, and articles have again and again called us to assist in helping the cause of the Weser, so that this river could serve all of the population of our nation. And the most beautiful reward was given to him when, still alive and in full capacity of his mental abilities, he witnessed the success crowning his endeavors. Now his eyes have closed and all of us have been thrown into deep mourning. Our heartfelt condolences go especially to his family and his close friends, mainly the well-advanced in years retired Bürgermeister Dr. Theodor Spitta. Also, in the Senate, this exceptional man will be missed, as well as in numerous organizations in which the deceased has been active. With him, a man of bright spirit and high sense of honor is leaving us and what remains of him is his legacy, and a testament for the living and coming generation to continue helping Bremen to sustain its common sense of working together. In the fulfillment of this legacy, we follow Senator Dr. Hermann Apelt, who will be unforgettable for his never-tiring striving for Bremen's well-being.

Here ends this informative speech by one of Bremen's dignitaries on the day after my father died. A few days later the citizens of Bremen were invited to a *Staatsakt* (state proceeding) at the *Rathaushalle.*

Bürgermeister Kaisen's Speech

November 15, 1960

Introduction

With a memorial celebration in the upper hall of our old *Rathaus* (city hall) that also is attended by representatives of the cabinet of the *Bund* (German government) as well as several ministers of the German lands, Bremen took leave of his long-working senator of ports, Dr. Hermann Apelt, this morning. The president of the Bremen Senate, Bürgermeister Kaisen, will describe, once more at this state function, the life of this so very deserving man for our city. Please listen to his speech.

Kaisen's Speech

We have gathered here in this old hall around the pier of a man renowned by all of us, Senator Dr. Apelt in order to say goodbye to him forever. In this very hall he has often spoken to us in serious and in happy times. Today he is surrounded by much honest mourning. Senator Dr. Apelt had been in full control of his mental and physical capacities until the last moment. In my opinion, he has found a merciful death. Only a few hours ago we experienced him in the *Rathaus* on the occasion of state proceedings. We were privileged to hear him when, in the end, he clarified the situation with a few anecdotes that were his forte, how it had been and how it is today and we all were happy to hear him speak so lively. *(Unfortunatel,y I do not have that speech. It must have been one of those unrecorded "off the cuff" addresses that do not exist in the vast mountains of papers left in his office.)* So we were, of course, very much surprised when just a short time afterwards the news came that he had succumbed to a sudden heart attack. Just one more smile on his face, one more look around him, and so he left this world to go over into another one. Was it an easy parting for him or not? We think that he departed gracefully in accordance with his entire lifestyle and the way he shared with us his political inclination. Though his bodily elasticity had somewhat diminished with increasing age, he could compete in mental capacity with anyone else. And his great talent of expressing his thoughts clearly was just as admirable as his power of memory. He stood by his friends in good and in bad times and he relished the esteem and respect of his co-workers for whom he had honest empathy, which was returned to him in same fashion. Here the key to the secret of all his successes is to be found. He knew how to surround himself with able men who would help him, each one according to his ability, to fulfill the gigantic task, the reconstruction of the situation of the Weser, successfully.

Here his work begins to become visible, which we are so thankful to him for. Not only once, but twice, he had to shoulder the colossal labor to build up again the destroyed ports. After 1918 and 1945, he was confronted with a completely new beginning for which at that moment all material funds seemed to be lacking. But Senator Dr. Apelt was a through-and-through realistic, reasonable person who did not give in to illusions about the difficulties that rose up against him. But one thing distinguished him here: whatever he confronted and did was always well thought through and was backed by a will that shrank from no difficulty whatsoever.

During the years I was working with him, I have always admired the ease with which he expressed his plans and how—even in times when there were roadblocks and when absolutely no funds were to be had for all the things he demanded—his composed serenity never left him; it remained with him on good and on bad days. I am fully convinced of the fact—this is my personal view—that Senator Apelt was in possession of real political abilities that helped him with his decisions. These abilities allowed him to establish high goals and to succeed with the reconstruction of our ports after two severe catastrophes. This is not the hour to go into details since all of us know about this. Only one thing may be said: The work of Dr. Apelt is closely connected to this reconstruction. Even if distress of the past is often forgotten too fast or seems to be self-understanding, there is still the memory alive of this man who warrants the renown that Bremen, even after the Second World War, was again enabled to take its position as world trade center.

After he was allowed to enjoy a few years of life outside his office, he has now left us. He departed from us after a richly fulfilled life. While he was still alive, the Senate honored him with bestowing upon him the greatest honor possible to give to a Bremen citizen: the Gold Medal. The last men who had received this honor were Ludwig Franzius and Bürgermeister Smith. The list is short—in my opinion there are still two representatives of the generation that Senator Dr. Apelt belonged to among us. *(He does not say whom he is thinking of. I believe Dr. Spitta was one of them.)* This old hall has seen them all of them alive. They are living on in this hall and when we are gathered together here, we are thinking of them. They are, for us living, the crown witnesses of the historical tradition of our old free state. Here Dr. Hermann Apelt is still among them.

I have tried to bring to you some characteristics of this man. However, it is impossible to give a complete picture of his personality; in this moment it has to be piecework. The double task of reconstruction of our ports is not the only task he confronted; he also solved the problem of the situation of the navigation of the Lower and Upper Weser, the entire river. What our great port builders had to struggle against daily in and on the river, Dr. Apelt solved politically by a series of negotiations. He created the basis to enable the port engineers to shape our ports. So it is not only impossible to divide his work from Bremen, but also from the Weser.

In order to compare his achievements with his work, his work was fulfilled with success. He left a legacy that enables his successors to build on. Measuring his inner life, it also yields fulfillment in the sense that beginning and end are harmonically united. This also meant much for the cultural life of our city. Testimony for this is the *Kunsthalle* and many charitable organizations. He has represented the cultural spirit of Bremen in these humanistic institutions.

So may I ask you now to stand. We have to say good-bye to our deceased. We will remember him and this memory will lead us to the legacy for the coming generation. This legacy is as follows:

"To act in the same spirit and to live the same righteous and duty-bound life and to serve our old free *Hansestadt* Bremen with the same courage and farsightedness as did Senator Dr. Apelt."

The references to the Gold Medal is best described by Bürgermeister Spitta in the previously mentioned collection of letters and speeches by the *Theodor-Spitta-Gesellschaft*, published in 1997, on page 102:

The Gold Medal of the Free *Hansestadt* Bremen was created 110 years ago to honor Bürgermeister Johann Smidt (1773-1857) and later water engineer Ludwig Franzius (1832-1903) for their lifelong efforts to establish Bremen as a seaport. The Gold Medal given to Smidt and Franzius had been created in a time that, compared with the time of both world wars, had been relatively quiet and sure. We three senators (Spitta, Apelt, and Theil (who was given the 'Reconstruction Medal')) are conscious of the importance of the qualities of our colleagues in the Senate. In accepting this high honor, we feel that the entire body of the Senate has been honored.

And now, a few newspaper items:

In the *Bremer Nachrichten*, November 12, 1960 (by my mother).

After a blessed life, my dear husband passed away early this morning, unexpectedly and without any struggle. He was in his 85th year of life.

Dr. Hermann Apelt

Senator, retired.

Julie Apelt, neeé Nielsen
Walter Ernst and wife Cornelie, née Apelt
Wulf Rohland and wife Dorothee, née Apelt
Christoph Kulenkampff and wife Julie, née Apelt
Leo W. Schmidt and wife Mathilde, née Apelt
Dr. Mathilde Apelt *(my Aunt Thilde)*
19 grandchildren and one great grandchild

Bremen, the November 11, 1960, Richard Strauß Platz 15
The interment will take place quietly
Please do not visit

Two articles (authors unknown, newspapers either *Bremer Nachrichten or Weserzeitung*):

Five Centuries Work for Bremen

Retired Senator Dr. Hermann Apelt died.
State memorial in the *Rathaus*.

Senator Dr. Hermann Apelt has died suddenly in the night sometime between Thursday and Friday. He was 84 years old. This news was especially devastating, as he had just the evening before had been allowed to witness the fulfillment of one of his life's goals. He had been invited as the guest of honor to the celebration of christening the *Weserstaustufe Landesbergen* that finished the *Mittelweserkanalizierung* (the last lock finishing the connection to the Midland Canal). On Thursday evening, he held a short spirited speech about the work on the Middle Weser at the *Rathaus*.

Hermann Apelt had dedicated more than half a century to the city-state of Bremen. His merits are extraordinary. We have this man to thank for the fact that Bremen has now reached its historical world reputation.

Hardly any of his predecessors had to confront as many difficult tasks as Dr. Apelt. Once, after W.W.I, he stood before a port without navigation and trade. A second time, after 1945, he confronted a destroyed port, seemingly without hope of winning back world navigation or trade.

What had been recreated in peacetime by Senator Apelt, through of organization, management, and repair of the harbor—in Bremen City the *Europahafen* and the *Überseehafen*, the grain trade and mass trade facilities, in Bremerhaven the construction of the *Columbuskaje*, the rail station on the Sea, and the *Nordschleuse*—had been laid lame by the two World Wars. Unfazed by the difficulties, Dr. Apelt was available again in 1945 and what he has done under the worst conditions economically and politically, is a masterpiece of a special kind.

Because of his all embracing experience and knowledge about all problems of traffic, he was consulted by all agencies involved in reconstruction all over Germany. The network of canals, the construction of freeways that had access to Bremen, the organization of railroads serving import and export and handling of tariffs, are mostly his legacy. Bürgermeister Kaisen, a long-term colleague of his in the Senate, told the audience about Apelt's receipt of the Bremen Gold Medal, the highest honor a Bremen citizen could earn. *(Kaisen's speech can be found immediately preceding this one. Also, the other speech mentioned here is the one whose speaker I did not know that is immediately preceding Kaisen's. First I thought that it was by August Hagedorn, the* Bürgerschaftspräsident. *My father had been elected in 1909 into the* Bürgerschaft *(the body of outstanding citizens), elected by the second rank, the merchants. But after examining the speech closely, I believe it was Senator Theil.)*

His legacy is not only limited to his knowledge pertaining to his job. The magic of his personality results from his humanistic education, and his deep understanding for the basics of human co-existence. Again and again we are surprised by his broad interests, the fullness of his knowledge, and not least his love of Fine Arts, effected by long years of working with the *Bremer Kunstverein* (Art Association). For 47 years, he belonged to this organization. Then the *Carl Schurz Gesellschaft*, the *Verkehrsverein*, the *Deutsche Gesellschaft zur Rettung Schiffsbrüchiger*, and numerous other organizations were served by his wealth of experience and expert advice.

Senator Dr. Apelt was born in Weimar on July 10, 1876. He studied law in Tübingen and Leipzig, and in 1900 moved to Bremen, where he opened an attorney's practice in 1904. One year later, he was called to work at the Chamber of Commerce as *Syndikus* (trustee, assistant attorney). Herewith his public work began. It would last for half a century. In 1909, he became a member of the *Bremen Bürgerschaft* (Citizen Organization).

In 1917, he was called from the front into the Senate where he took over the department of navigation, trade, and traffic. He was replaced by a Nazi in 1933, but was called back to his job as Senator for Ports, Navigation, and Traffic in 1945.

In 1945, the American military called him again to serve in the Senate. He took care again of his previous departments. He worked for the next nine years. In 1955, he decided not to run for reelection, mostly because of old age.

The Senate will honor Dr. Apelt with a state action at the *Rathaus.*

This article stresses, besides the job-related work of my father, his free time interests, and endeavors as well.

In Memory of Retired Senator Hermann Apelt

Willst du dich deines Wertes freuen,
So mußt der Welt du Wert verleihen.

If you want to enjoy your own value,
You have to give value to the world.

Bremen has lost her most important citizen. What retired Senator Dr. Hermann Apelt has done for our city, our ports and navigation, and for the traffic, is the work of a lifetime that few can demonstrate when their hour comes. It seemed to be divine providence that on the day before his demise he could participate in the crowning of his most important project: the finishing of the regulation of the Middle Weser and the connection between Bremen and the Midland Canal.

There were more high points in Hermann Apelt's life besides this one. After both World Wars, he was confronted with the severe destruction in Bremen's ports and he not only repaired the damages, but built new facilities so Bremen is now back to her high standards and even better. And this man was not even born in Bremen. His cradle stood in Weimar, a city that surrounded him from early on with the high values of German culture in all spheres of Fine Arts. Apelt's successor in the Senate, Dr. George Borttscheller, wrote that Hermann Apelt treated his job as a work of art. The ports, actually instruments of trade and traffic, became in his hands instruments of art. This was a rare synthesis of the realistic and the idealistic that made every meeting with him a joyful event. In conversations with him one did not only learn about factual items, about freight volume and tariffs, he also liked to talk about science, poetry, music, and the Fine Arts.

His humanistic thinking and feeling instilled so much "good will" in Bremen as well as other places in Germany during the terrible years after the wars. The friendly connections that he initiated, not only for Bremen with other parts of Germany, but also abroad, are still solid. They will not tear even after he is not among us anymore. But we will miss him, his advice, stemming from deep wisdom and endless experience.

We bow in honor before one of our greatest.

PART II

Excerpts from

Hermann Apelt, Reden und Schriften

Preface by Theodor Spitta[12]

Double Purpose of the Book

This book shall serve the memory of the Bremen's Senator Dr. Hermann Apelt by emphasizing the merits of this outstanding, richly talented person, and his various activities.

Furthermore, this book shall demonstrate what has been accomplished in Bremen in the era of Apelt's public activity (from about 1910 to 1960) in cooperation with state and citizenship politically, economically, socially, and culturally, especially after backlashes and devastating destruction in both world wars and under the crippling burdens and limitations that Germany had to suffer after the wars.

This double purpose shall be accomplished by rendering articles, memoranda, and speeches, word for word, without explanations. Therewith will be created a picture of what Bremen has to thank Apelt for these fifty years and what kind of person he was. At the same time, it will demonstrate an essential part of the fight and struggle Bremen had to endure and the reply to the constant question: stay with the old ways or dare the new in order to survive? "*To be or not to be,*" that was often the question whose answer had to be decided.

The great wealth of material forced us to choose.

Unfortunately, many of the unique personal addresses and poems meant for family and special friends had to be left out; though it is regrettable to miss such speeches and verses that demonstrate the spirit and heart of the man, Hermann Apelt.

But also in the area that this book is earmarked for—the realm of public life—choices had to be made. That was not always easy because valuable works had to be excluded. The decision as to what to include

12 Hermann Apelt, Reden und Schriften, page 5. *(Spitta and my mother published this book together.)*

and what to omit will always be done by subjective weighing. Some other person might have chosen another speech or memorandum. However, the final composition is fulfilling the intended objective.

An historical sketch of Apelt's life is not necessary for this book. Let his writings and speeches speak for themselves. Historically, Apelt's works have to be put into the framework of the Senate. The activities of the other members of the Senate in their entity have an influence on those of Apelt and vice versa; Apelt's activities had influence on decisions of the Senate, even outside the public domain.

Bremen, August 23, 1962.
Theodor Spitta.

To this preface, I would like to add that I also had to make decisions as to what to select from this book, the most important publication documenting his legacy, since he never published his memoir nor any compendium of his writings. Others did this for him. I selected those writings and speeches that emphasize my father's admiration for my second homeland, The United States of America, where I have lived for two thirds of my life. In addition, my own personal love for Greek mythology and love of books guided my choices. Otherwise, why would I have chosen Father's treatments of Iphigenia and Alcestis? The speeches in honor of Carl Schurz motivated me to read the *Lebenserinnerungen (*memoirs) of this remarkable German American and I included excerpts of my father's speeches about him at different occasions, in order to awaken interest in others who lived full lives on two continents. Other speeches about famous German people might also be of common interest.

Two other speeches were very tempting for me to add to this collection. My father and I shared a love for Goethe and Schiller. However, both speeches he gave about them are very long. I decided to shorten them by selecting those parts that interest me most. The two speeches are: (1) The Color Theory from the viewpoint of both Goethe and Newton and (2) the description of the dramas in Father's talk about Schiller.

The publishing house of H.M. Hauschild that printed and edited Spitta's book still exists in Bremen today.

Memories of His Youth[13]

Als ich noch ein Knabe war ...
When I Was a Boy ...

Before the horrors of the Hitler times began and before my father was encumbered by bugs and devices to discover some resistance to our *Führer* that might land him in Auschwitz or other selective places, he often shared stories about his youth with us at the dinner table. Being the only boy in the family, he had a special relationship with his father, the high school principle and teacher, who translated Greek classics and frequently sent him to the nearby library to retrieve and return books. But none of these stories are as complete or as lively told as the first entry titled *Jugenderinnerungen an Weimar* in this book of my father's speeches and writings —a speech presented to the Rotary Club in Bremen in 1932:

Honored Rotary members,

My predecessor has predicted a speech concerning the inner self, but has elevated his presentation to a higher level. I—for my part—beg for permission to delve into my personal self, into the realm of earliest remembrances. My reasons for this are that I am at a disadvantage for not being a "real" Bremer, but have the advantage of being a native Weimaraner.

---

13 Hermann Apelt, Reden und Schriften, page 13. Speech, Rotary Club, 1932. This heading is my memory of Father's telling us stories about his youth.

O Weimar, Dir fiel ein besonderes Los
Wie Bethlehem in Juda klein und groß.

Oh Weimar, you received a blessed fate
Like Bethlehem, you are small and great.

Weimar is the city of Goethe, though he was born and raised in Frankfurt am Main. There stands the house of his birth, and everyone who visits Frankfurt, visits it. But in his later years Goethe had avoided the city of his youth. Though the old German town impressed the boy, he was too young for it to make this impression permanent. Neither did the places of his higher education, Leipzig, Straßburg, and Wetzlar, leave a permanent imprint on his soul. Even Rome, the goal of his yearning and fulfillment, was not the place where he spent most of his life. It was a powerful world, but passed quickly. Only Weimar was his real home. He spent two thirds of his life here and was put to rest in the vault of his sovereign. It was he who made this little Weimar great and gave it his character.

How much Weimar is still the city of Goethe, I realized when, after several years of absence, I returned there and looked at my old home with the eyes of a visitor. I had spent the first eighteen years of my life there and it had been quite natural for my sisters and me to breathe the air filled with classical memories. Goethe's and Schiller's homes belonged to our concept of the hometown like the City Church and City Hall. And if Old Master Goethe had met us alive in the park, we would not have been surprised.

Indeed, wherever we went, we met traces and reminders of Goethe's time. I was born *An der Ackerwand* and may rightly say that my first sight was that of Goethe's garden. Our house was standing opposite of the wall that bordered Goethe's city garden. About thirty years earlier a passionate war broke out to save this very wall. *(This must have been the revolution in 1848, so vividly described in the memoirs of Carl Schurz.)*

Later we moved to the *Schillerstraße,* called *Esplanade* in Goethe's time. Here we could look—from our kitchen window—into the little garden of the *Schillerhaus.* There lived then an old respectful policeman with a long, white beard by the name of Blei. I remember quite vividly how one day our cook pointed out Old Blei to me and asked whether it was true what the people said: that Blei was Schiller's grandson. Though still quite young, I could honestly tell her that those rumors were not correct. But let me turn back to the *Ackerwand.* From there, around the corner, stands the *Goethehaus*—in a way, the spiritual castle of Weimar—on the former

Frauenplan, now *Goetheplatz*. During my early youth I did not know about all those treasures that were hidden here since the grandchildren of Goethe were still living in the upper story. The hallowed lower rooms were still not open to the public. Across from the *Goethehaus* stands the restaurant *Zum Schwan*. Between the *Schwan* and the *Goethehaus* is a narrow alley, called *Seifengasse*. Rumor has it that there was once a fire and Goethe and the night guard had the following conversation *(Goethe style)*:

Sage mir Wächter der Nacht, wo ist die Stätte des Brandes?
Mann im Rocke des Schlafes, es brennt in der Gasse der Seife

Tell me, guard of the night, where is the location of the fire?
Man in the coat of the sleep, it burns in the alley of the soap.

When we were children, we connected the *Seifengasse* with the image of great poverty and foul air. In spite of that, Goethe had lived there for a while, though in a garden house away from the alley, close to Frau von Stein who played such an important role in his life. That peculiar long house of Frau von Stein had several stone platforms in front on which every spring orange trees stood. In our time, the Greek-Catholic community had their band in this house. This building was for us children as familiar as the *Goethehaus*. Then around the corner to the library, the so-called *Red Castle,* where we were allowed to enter from early on because the librarian, Reinhold Köhler, the famous researcher of fairy tales, was our fatherly friend and always showed us around when we brought or picked up books our father needed. There was a lot to see: the large picture of Karl August with his dogs, the busts of Schiller and Goethe, and other treasures like Schiller's scull, which was later declared not genuine. Anyway, it served Goethe to express his wonderful observations.

Then on to the *Fürstenplatz.* past the Karl August statue to the castle that showed definite influences of Goethe before it was ruined by adding the fourth wing. Then across the beautiful castle bridge to the *Stern* that, at the time when Goethe came to Weimar, belonged to the duchy of Weimar. Behind this garden was Goethe's own garden and his *Gartenhaus* with whose image most Germans are familiar.

Übermütig sieht's nicht aus,
Hohes Dach und niedr'ges Haus.

It doesn't look exactly extravagant,
High roof and low house.

In front of it the lovely valley of the Ilm, "*Das liebe Tal*", as Goethe called it. We find it mentioned in the *Poem to the Moon:*

Füllest wieder's liebe Tal
Still mit Nebelglanz.

You fill the lovely valley
Quietly with shining fog.

Not only in this famous song but almost everywhere where in Goethe's poetry the landscape speaks, one who was born in that region can feel the soft touches of the land Thüringen. Then we go across the natural bridge to the *Borkenhaus,* called the *Eremitage* in Goethe's days. Here great parties were celebrated by the circles around the Duke. Further on to the grave of Karl August where a beautiful linden tree marks the resting place of the Duke. The entire park is a creation by Goethe.

Also the surrounding areas, near and far: Belvedere, Tiefurt, Ettersburg with their parks, outdoor theaters, and their cornucopia of memories.

Donnerstag nach Belvedere,
Freitag geht's nach Jena fort,
Denn das ist bei meiner Ehre,
Doch ein allerliebster Ort.
Samstag ist's worauf wir zielen,
Sonntag rutscht man auf das Land
Zwäzen, Burgen, Schneidemühlen,
Sind uns alle wohl bekannt.

Thursdays to Belvedere,
Fridays on to Jena
For that's honestly
A most delightful place.
Saturday is our goal,
Sundays we roll to the country,
Zwätzen, Burgen, Schneidemühlen,
We are well familiar with.

Well, we also knew them well: Jena, Zwäzen, the beautiful Dornburg, etc.

But not only places, personal relationships also created bridges to the past. I remember clearly the gaunt, grey-haired figure of Walter von Goethe, the last surviving grandson. Once I saw him getting out of his coach and disappearing in the secretive *Goethehaus.* He was a sad man who experienced the tragic fate of an infamous descendant of a famous man. He wrote the devastating verse:

Ich trete stets daneben,
Ich trete niemals ein,
Ich möchte einmal leben,
Ich möchte einmal sein.

I always step besides,
I never step inside,
I wish I could live once
I wish I could exist once.

Several friends of ours were descendants of great personalities such as Schiller and Herder. Of course, Policeman Blei, living in Schiller's house, was not really his grandson, but there were some true relatives around. Two elderly ladies, Sophie and Lottchen Krakow, lived in an old house that we children knew well. We had access to every little nook and cranny of the old angled house that has now become a museum. The sisters stayed in contact with us and 90-year-old Aunt Lottchen even sent me self-knitted knee warmers to the front in 1915. Then there was Knebel, a good friend of my father's, who was suspected to be a natural son of the Duke.

In my time, it was Duke Karl Alexander, grandson of Duke Karl August, who was governing the country. Under him, Weimar had what they called the Silver Era. That was the time when Liszt and his circles ruled the salons. We children often met Liszt strolling in the park in his strange coat, with long hair and big warts. Karl Alexander was the founder and protector of the Goethe Society, whose yearly meeting represented one of the high points of Weimar's social life. However, this did not sit well with the higher authority, the Grand Duke Karl Friedrich, who had different priorities. Sometimes after a long speech he would say, "*Na, Gethe is mer bis dahin*" ("Well, that's too much Goethe for me"), adding a descriptive hand motion. With his son Wilhelm Ernst and his brother

Bernhard—both deceased now—I had occasional times together since the parents were looking for decent citizen youths for the boys to play with. They considered me as such a one. Therefore, I had the high honor of being allowed to measure my skill against theirs in a wrestling match. *(According to my sister Julie, he got angry at one of the boys and trashed him. He never was invited again.)*

But enough of that. Let me close with the verses that Goethe has written to express his gratefulness to his Prince and that demonstrate the beautiful relationship between sovereign and poet. I think that Goethe's verses are greater –in my opinion—than even Horace's praises of August and Maecen.

Klein ist unter den Fürsten Germaniens freilich der meine.
Kurz und schmal ist sein Land, mäßig nur, was er vermag,
Aber so wende nach innen, so wende nach außen die Kräfte
Jeder; da wär es ein Fest, Deutscher mit Deutschen zu sein.
Niemals frug ein Kaiser nach mir, es hat tsich kein König
Um mich gekümmert und Er war mir August und Maecen.

Though unimportant among the princes of Germany is my sovereign.
Small is his country, limited in what he can do,
But if everyone would turn his powers inwards or outwards,
Then it would be great to be German among Germans.
Never an Emperor asked for me, nor a king showed interest.
But He was August and Maecen for me.

To understand this poem that my father chose for his speech, I refreshed my memory about Augustus. Augustus was Rome's leader following Caesar, who was murdered by Brutus and Cassius in 44 B.C. Horace, a young poet of great promise—his father had scrimped his meager assets to give this son a great education in Rome—was introduced by the renowned writers Virgil and Varius to Maecenus, a rich man who took Horace under his wing. Maecenus was a good friend of Emperor Augustus. This in turn led to the relationship between Augustus and Horace, which made Horace a successful man. Their mutual interest in Maecenus (or Maecen) created the classical friendship between Augustus and Maecenus, made famous through poems by Horace. Maecenus' name became a symbol for rich people helping talented poor people to become famous. Because of Horace's success to become one of the greatest men of his time, Augustus showered Maecenus with favors; they might even have been lovers. My father thought that the closeness of Goethe to Karl Alexander even surpassed the friendship between August and Maecenus (evidently every person in Weimar knew enough about Roman history to appreciate Goethe's poem. I am not so sure if every person in Bremen did likewise. But many might have done what I did: study up on Roman history!)

Be that as it may, the *Goethegesellschft in Weimar* is still the center of all other such societies and eventually led to the founding of *Goetheinstituts* (Goethe Institutes) all over the world. Here the German language is taught and German heritage promoted. People like my father might still profit from the diligent work of Duke Karl Alexander.

Trip to America in 1912[14]

By Hermann Apelt

This is an excerpt from a report about a trip my father made to America in 1912. My daughter, Doris Schmidt Michaels, and I translated this article together. Her interest in this report actually gave me the idea that my father's writings might be interesting to our family and friends in America.

I would like to limit myself to a few short comments about the impressions I had from the land and the people. Here I bear in mind, at first the powerful impression the entrance to the harbor and the harbor of New York offers. However, this impression of true beauty was revealed at a later visit since fog covered the city skyline during our first visit. Nevertheless, the blurred outlines were enough to recognize the wonderful water-surface nature presented and the enormous stone mountains that American architecture has erected upon the small tip of the island of Manhattan. The gigantic extravagance, though having outgrown the European measure, of the American way of life is heralding here at the entrance of the country in the most characteristic manner.

Whether one finds the gigantic structures beautiful or ugly is a second question. However, no one who sees them for the first time will deny a unique impression. Especially from the distance, one gets the impression of a medieval castle city, grown atrociously. In each case, the limitation of available space forced towering building styles reaching toward the sky. And when the fog softens the prosaic rows of lattice-like rows of windows, the amazed observer may imagine beholding an earthly Walhalla.

The buildings discussed here are best presented by the fact that the newest building, the just completed Woolworth Building, has no less than

14 Hermann Apelt, Reden und Schriften, Bericht über eine Amerikareise, 1912. page 31

fifty-six stories and is over 200 meters high, i.e. substantially higher than the Cologne Cathedral. The huge ocean liners and the gigantic skyscrapers seem to stimulate growth reciprocally. Amazed, one asks where and when the final limit will be reached.

For myself, I can only say that I have returned home as a definite supporter of skyscrapers. One may think about the aesthetic side as one pleases; in any event, they are unique and practical and actually so in three ways: they save space, save commute time, and they are healthy. Space saving, since the smallest space is used to maximal capacity. Offices of related firms are often in the same building, which also saves commute time, sometimes just a lift ride away. Healthy, because during summer time in large cities like New York the height of the top floors offers more cool air and other advantages.

In addition, the interior of the buildings is not only practical (namely via the installation of superior lifts or elevators), but also certainly demonstrate good taste in the relative simple style of the interior structure designed by the American architects and usually made of the best materials. Even the outside is not always insipid and tasteless, but in some cases, as for instance the town hall in Chicago, the architectural solution of the giant wall surfaces was attempted with success.

Indeed, I have come to the conclusion that the ideal version of a large, modern business city should be presented as follows: the center of the business life should take place in tall, room-efficient skyscrapers and the living quarters in low-built, widely spread out dwellings, surrounded by gardens. This seems to be the idea whether conscious or not, which is the basis for the modern development of American cities, even though it has not yet been implemented in too many instances. Reluctantly, New York has realized part of this plan: the business section with tightly compressed, high-towered buildings; however, the other part: the low-built, gardenlike residences are only just beginning around the borders of the inner city. Essentially the huge ocean of houses of the living quarters of New York offers the sad picture of countless parallel rows of gardenless apartment buildings. Also, the parks of New York are giving, compared to other cities, a sorrowful impression.

Fortunately, other cities have kept, as we have in our town Bremen, the low-styled buildings for one and two families in their suburbs like Philadelphia and especially Baltimore. But also in these cities, the city plan, at least in the older parts, is frightfully prosaic with its block system. This is mostly the case in Philadelphia, where the sad impression of the inner city oppresses one's soul like a nightmare. This negative feeling is added to by the checkered collection of architectural mishmash of different styles and the absolute scandalous condition of the street pavement.

The most enjoyable of the American city landscapes are the enormous and particularly beautiful parks, found in many cities, namely in Boston, Buffalo, and Cleveland. One can hardly comprehend the extension of these parks that one can drive through for hours, using the fastest speed.

Some cities have succeeded, with great skill and much taste, to fuse parks into garden cities, namely Buffalo. Streets like Delaware Avenue in Buffalo or Euclid Avenue in Cleveland are the well-earned pride of these cities. What impresses one mostly is the absence of fences between lots or toward the streets. The single dwellings stand on green lawns, which fact contributes to the impression of being in a park. Admittedly, modern American cities had the advantage of having an abundance of low-priced land available. This does not take away from the foresight with which this advantage has been recognized and used extensively.

Overall, one may say that in spite of the hopelessness of the inner city conditions, living in America is in general more favorable than in our country. Moreover, it could be added to the description of cities that naturally the difference between new and old isn't as obvious in a relatively young country. In our country the new has to develop from the old, must link with it, while across the ocean it starts from the beginning.

In addition to the above outlined ideal of a high-towered business town surrounded by a low-built suburb, it should be noted that two essential premises have to be fulfilled. There has to be stable ground that is able to carry the high buildings without danger, and there has to be good connection to the business center. Naturally, it presents growing difficulties to organize the daily traffic congestion in the morning into the workplace and in the evening from the business to the home. Both these suppositions, the natural one and the artificial one, have been fulfilled splendidly in New York. Because Manhattan is a granite island and has a subway (comparable to our *Straßenbahnen* or *S-bahnen*) that connects the lower business part with the suburbs, it is perhaps the most excellent traffic system ever created. The street trains are moving constantly in three stories: under the street, on the street, and above. Especially helpful is the scheduling of express as well as local trains side by side—only a few of the former that stop seldom and many of the latter that stop at every station—so that the greatest distances are also covered with exemplary speed. Also servicing and controlling traffic are so fortunately organized and on the other side the public is so well trained that the mammoth traffic is handled by only a few personnel. Supervision on the platforms and in the coaches is unnecessary with the subway. If in spite of this, only few cases of overcrowding or accidents happen, so it is not only the good behavior of the users responsible for this, but also the clever way the stairs are constructed. They only let the exact amount of people down to the platforms as the trains can hold at one time. In order to understand the brilliant solution to the traffic difficulties, one has to consider the complicated situation of New York. Here the business center is not, as in London, in the middle of the town, but on the lower end of a small, sack-like island. Therefore, trains cannot arrive and depart from all sides, but the entire traffic has to flow through a narrow opening in the sack, into the work area in the morning and home again in the evening.

If I am allowed to switch from the city train system to the railroad, I can mention some good, but also some not-so-good facts. Certainly, the wagons, especially the Pullman wagons, are well aired and comfortable; but if one would prefer these, no sectioned wagons, over ours with separated compartments, is a matter that in the end is up to the taste of the traveler. Each one has its advantages and its disadvantages. In respect to the sleeping coaches, I am definitely a follower of our compartment system. Those three washbasins that about twenty to thirty gentlemen have to share, I consider rather primitive, if not barbaric. The fact that traveling on American trains is considerably higher than on ours has been proven by statistics. Fortunately, I did not have any experience with this. But I found the bumping sensation very annoying, especially when the trains started. The reason for this is the simple clutch system and the absence of buffers. Another problem is the frequent delays, sometimes of grotesque length. Very well regulated, on the other hand, is the handling of the luggage. All considered, I believe that our German trains are faring well in comparison to the American trains.

If the statement that America has great advantages by nature, this also rings true with its seaports. If one looks at harbors like New York and Boston, where nature did almost everything and there was not much that men had to do, and if one compares that to the conditions on our German coast and considers how much trouble and costs it takes to keep our harbors open for sea traffic, it might seem warranted if a little envy is added to the admiration. This feeling of envy becomes intensified when the comparison regards the Hanseatic cities (Bremen, Hamburg, and for a while, Lübeck). If the Hanseat hears that the little cost the Americans have to spend on using the ports is not even due to the cities or states, but to the federal government, he considers the fact that Bremen and Hamburg are city-states and have to pay those millions to keep the Weser and the Elbe rivers open for sea vessels out of their own coffers. Further considerations leading to justified embitterment are that instead of gratification about Bremen's effort to shoulder all the expenses to keep the port open, there are constant malicious contradiction and the will of the federal government not to help but to hinder us in the struggle to keep our ports functioning.

As the upkeep of the sea traffic is a federal issue, so the construction of the ports is partly the business of the states, as in Massachusetts, and partly of the cities, as in New York. But it is important to mention that until relatively recently, private companies, like ship owner companies and railroads, have paid for the construction of ports, especially the piers. Therefore, in general, the construction of American seaports is lagging behind the European ones, especially the German ones. What strikes people from Hamburg and Bremen first is the lack of direct connection between railroad and port as well as mechanical loading gadgets such as cranes. This is mostly prominent in New York. However, it is not only the trade that suffers thus, but also the railroads. With regards to competition among themselves, as also to the others ports, the railroads have to pay for the relatively steep costs of trading in New York without the benefit of levying freight tariffs. A sense of pride must the man from Bremen feel when he sees that the Lloyd piers are the most beautiful among the others. Only the Busch piers are comparable, however, they are situated in distant Brooklyn.

Montreal's harbor has been constructed more like the European ports, in contrast to the American ports. Actually, cranes are missing here also, but there is always direct connection between railroads and ships.

In contrast to the seaports are the Great Lakes ports. There one finds loading and unloading equipment of extreme perfection. I think primarily of the great trade systems for ore and coal traffic, perhaps incomparable to all other ports in the world. The four recently installed giant cranes are capable of unloading a freight of 10,000 tons in four to six hours. The sight of these monsters is one of the most remarkable sights I had experienced in America. In their characteristic robot-like form and in their manifold flexibility, they stimulate automatically the impression of living beings. One feels as if he is part of a society of giant dinosaurs of the past. Especially splendid is the connection in Cleveland between coal unloading and ore loading. The wagons loaded with coal coming from Pittsburg, with capacity of mostly thirty to fifty tons, are being turned over by a mechanical tilter and emptied into a steam ship. This process takes, considering no delay, about 2 ¼ minutes. The returning empty wagons run automatically up a slanted plane, change position, and roll on to the above mentioned cranes in order to be loaded with ore and sent back to Pittsburg.

It is said that the loading systems for ore in Duluth are even more spectacular. But unfortunately I had no time to see them.

Actually, one has to add that those systems are only possible due to the unique traffic conditions and in their way only possible in the Lake District. Mass traffic as it happens here is unheard of and without parallel. It is sufficient if I mention some numbers. The strait close to Detroit had traffic of about 66 million tons of our weight in the year 1910. Compared to this, the entire traffic in Emmerich on the Rhine came only up to 40 million tons. In Duluth there was traffic of about 32 million tons in 1910 and in Duisburg, the largest inside port in Europe, not quite of 20 million tons.

There are three main commodities prevailing in the Lake District: first ore, then coal, and third grain. That it is feasible to erect costly and refined loading systems is understandable. The conditions here are so unique that they cannot be duplicated in European situations, especially in Bremen.

Therefore, it is not feasible to become motivated to duplicate the American systems pertaining to ports. Seaports are too backwards and the Great Lake ports too unique.

Nowhere, not even in the harbor of New York, is the natural wealth of the country as obvious as here in the Great Lake District. Facing these inexhaustible treasures and this giant traffic, the citizen of little Europe may be overcome by a certain worry. At some point the day will come when the Holy Iliad and the lance-toting Priam will sink down, not before the sword, but before the economic weight of America, the land of the future.

Hansa and City-State[15]

In the celebration issue of *Niederdeutsche Woche,* 1922

Self-willed segregation and voluntary congregation may be considered two poles of the German essence. Good and bad manners, virtue and vice pertaining to Germans, become manifest to them. On the one hand, there is defiant urge of the individual for uniqueness, for development of its own characteristic, on the other hand a deep-rooted feeling for organic community. As long as that urge, reined in by common thinking, was held in its own limits, Germany was great and strong. But it was small and weak when the self will conquered the common will, whether it was individuals or communities: small or large, tribes or royals, cities or states, ranks or political parties. This play of changes between contrasts explains how wealth as well as poverty in German history affects fullness of life, and the power to start again after all is lost as well as the inability to grasp tightly what has been conquered, and to avoid repeated catastrophic falls into the abyss. To gain unity and to keep it without giving up the wealth of inherited, manifold uniqueness, is the basic problem in German state law and a main problem of German history. The model of the old empire had looked for a solution to this problem when the new German league was founded, but still today we are wrestling to find such a solution in pain and sorrow.

As a typical example of such German manner in good and bad ways, we could look at the medieval city leagues. What fullness of lively and unique communities that congregated in these leagues without giving up their independence, powerful when united, powerless when split by strife. And by themselves these leagues could cause either bliss or danger within the larger unions.

By far outstanding among the city leagues is the Hansa, whose name is involuntarily associated with the German prestige at sea. But the Hansa

15 Hermann Apelt, Reden und Schriften, page 36

was by no means exclusively a league of seafaring cities; its influence was reaching far into the interior of the country. However, coast, ocean, and sea wind gave it individuality and character and only three maritime cities have remained Hansa cities in name and nature (Hamburg, Bremen, and Lübeck). The Hansa, in its prime, shows us an example of unique and impressive development of power, a magnificent part of German history. The British, now the near single commanders of the oceans, do not like to hear that others before them had control over the seas. "The Germans may plow the earth, sail with the clouds, or built castles in the air, but never since the beginning of time had they the genius to measure the ocean or the high seas or even coastal waters." Thus proclaimed Palmerston in the English Parliament. The proud Lord did not know from his limited vantage point of being an islander, nor did he want to know in his insular arrogance that, long before England had developed into a seafaring nation, trade and navigation was conducted by defiant German citizens. The British pound sterling, this token of English sovereignty of world commerce, that only after the war sank to second place behind the dollar, is an involuntary witness for German influence in Hansa times. From its origin it is an Eastern coin. *(The word "sterling" comes from "Easterling.")*

The Hansa was a league, a merger of indispensible civic communities, and by itself again an indispensible part within the empire. Being such a part of the whole it became the organ-hood (center) for the medieval German navigation. *(In order to use a better English word for this Organschaft (the word my father used), I choose the word "cooperative.")* The Hansa bequeathed this cooperative to the three German cities that still remain as Hansa cities and city-states.

That a cooperative like this (the taking over of several, necessary to the whole functions by parts of the whole) coupled with specific adaptation of these parts to its special purpose, has never been developed to such degree as in Germany, is understandable. One has to consider the unique basic drive of the German character, which is at the same time healing and destructive. Also, the diversity of the German land that stretches from the sea to the Alps, from the valley of the Weichsel River to the Maas River, presents a dangerous position in the middle of other countries without closed borders. Germany, the natural connection between north and south, east and west; the neighbor of so many nations, looked at many more problems than any of the other nations around whose geographical position allowed much more compactness and unity. The abundance of tasks—either political, economical, or cultural ones—was too big to be solved centrally; the life too diverse, in order to be handled centrally. Not even a more powerful position such as the emperors knew to assert against the overgrowth of unique spirits, would have been enough here.

Therefore, perhaps the only possible government form to foster development of the wealth of the German essence was the developing organic division of labor. Its value must not be denied because the egotistic urge of the members and the inadequacy of the central powers must lead to deteriorating of the whole. Also the power grip of the central force became duties that the parts had to take over, though they were actually tasks that the Empire should have handled. This is mostly true for Prussia that had to fulfill so many tasks that it had to transfer these to others. One should consider what the smaller principalities in Germany did for the cultural life because the empire could not do so. For instance, Weimar in the cultural realm or the Hansa cities on the Weser and the Elbe that knew how to become leaders of ocean navigation and world trade in spite of unfavorable natural conditions. Because of this, Prussia, besides its important continental tasks of political and economical kind that it solved with assured instinct, could not have become the center of German literature or create the basis for the German oversea trade. For that it had neither sufficient strength nor inner calling.

Without the Hansa in the old times for the development of German navigation, the rebirth of German prestige at sea would not have been possible. The descendants of the old Hanseaten *(plural of Hanseat, which means a person belonging to the Hansa)* had guarded the seafaring tradition through all the miserable times in German history as their valued inheritance. Germany was lucky that it had kept the three Hanseatic republics as organs for developing its navigation and its oversea trade. As it had been formed geographically and historically it needed such special organs to confirm the calling to navigation, the instinct to sea faring since old times. Otherwise it had to forego the connection with the oceans. And now, since we have to rebuild again, the same is true. *(This was after World War I.)*

Quite different was and is the situation in England. After the decline of the German Hansa and the ascent of their own country, the island nation found itself naturally inclined to become a seafaring nation. The Merchant Adventurers, the trade companies, were characteristic for the entire nation, not single communities. It was a nation of Hanseaten not needing any Hansa cities.

Germany, on the other hand, being a continental country, will never become one entire seafaring organism and therefore it needs its special organs in order to have ports that not only serve foreign ships (like Antwerp), but are also designed for domestic navigation.

However, if Germany wants this, it also has to decide the form of those organs.

It is important to the concept of any organ that it fits into the whole as a member. Nonetheless, it is mandatory that it remains within the whole in its unique form—only form—that only this uniqueness makes it an organ and creates the premise for concentration and specification of powers on which the essence and the value of cooperative is based. One should never forget that the Hanseaten are one of a kind and that this kind can only prevail if it possesses its own unique organization or form. If you break this form, you also break the Hansa. And this form is the city-state.

But one should not, not even only partly, think of outer appearances, of the importance of the flag, the good reputation that the name of the old Haseatic free cities has still preserved in foreign countries even today. The importance is the Haseatic way itself that could not persist without the traditional form.

The Hanseaten are not a special race, neither by origin nor by all means nowadays; but the Hansa cities are historically developed communities. Surely there are many more families today in Bremen that have immigrated than those that have been here from the beginning of time. And the same is true about Hamburg and Lübeck. But the historically engraved, naturally developed form is like a retort in which foreign bodies are molten and changed and amalgamated with the grass roots. Or one could think of sourdough that has be carefully kept and transferred so it may work for new breads forever.

So one may understand, the Hanseaten did not want to give up their independence as a city-states. This is not defiance or self-conceit, but the strong conviction that they could only thus fulfill their given task and that they would be able to serve the whole in the best way.

It would be fallacy to believe that Hanseaten would remain Hanseaten if they would meld into a greater community; that the main reason for becoming Hanseats was perhaps the geographical conditions which were advantageous. Surely, the Bremer *(citizens of Bremen)* would not have become Bremer if they had not chosen to dwell at the mouth of a river. But other people had dwelled at mouths of rivers and did not become citizens like the Bremer. And if one would argue that Bremen had been the ideal place (to become a harbor), since it was situated at the natural crossroad of sea and inland navigation, they were wrong. And not the least advantage: it was the last place where the river still allowed a bridge. But then it could be argued that other cities had the very same advantages and did not develop into a Hansa city-state. More than that, soon the advantage of Bremen's site turned into a disadvantage. The river became choked with sand and for centuries the city became cut off from ocean traffic. First it helped itself by constructing the port of Vegesack, where the Weser was still navigable, then it became the guest of Brake in Oldenburg, then it built its own port in Bremerhaven, and also spent much energy and money for correction and dredging that made the Hansa city again to a seafaring town. Nature did not do much for Bremen. Most of it was done by the citizens of Bremen. In fact, that Bremen became what it is now is due to what might be called the "Haseatic Spirit." Rightfully so, we may quote the old Roman adage:

Navigare necesse est, vivere non est necesse.

Seafaring is necessary, life is not.

Trade, Navigation, and Construction of Harbors[16]

The Years Between the Two World Wars

Article for technicians for building ports, May 7, 1926.

Trade and navigation are, at least for the *Hanseat* (citizens of a Hanse town), not to imagine without each other. Though the dominant form of combination—that for instance the merchant was also the owner of the ship, the owner of the ship also merchant, that the merchant fitted out his own ship and the owner transported his own goods; when also this old form of union of trade and navigation merged into one person had become a rare exception under the influence of the development of the economy and the rising division of labor, still for the Hanseat this old tradition remains. Even if the ship's owner and trader are not the same person, at least both should be in the same community, in the port city with its harbors. And the harbors need the technician, namely the builder of ports. Therefore, three people are necessary: the port builder now joins the league of merchants and ship-owner.

Certainly it was the natural situation that decided the construction of the port in the beginning, be it the mouth of a river or a secured bay and for a long time these given circumstances were enough for the budding harbors. However, in modern times, the increase of traffic, the gradual growth of ships, and the progress of technique led to the necessity of employing engineers who were specialists in building and maintaining harbors. Even the ports that had the best natural conditions needed such specialists. This is especially true for the ports of North West Europe, the ports on the North Sea that had not only to create their port areas artificially, but also had to constantly fight to keep up the connection to the

16 Hermann Apelt, Reden und Schriften, page 140

sea with the help of water engineers because the natural waters of the rivers were not sufficient after a while and had to be extended and deepened. The connections to the open sea would have been completely cut off and sand bound without the help of water specialists.

Therefore, no North Sea port exists that can depend on nature alone. All of them, more or less, are nowadays the creation of technique and are deeply indebted to it. At least Bremen has to recognize this commitment gratefully. Though Bremen does not, as the large Dutch harbors, Rotterdam and Amsterdam, have to rely on technique completely to create connection with the sea. It has the old Weser River that carries the ships not only to the daughter town Bremerhaven, but also to the mother town Bremen itself. But here the case is different because Bremen had actually lost the direct connection to the sea more than 200 years ago and was still able to turn its fate around. By using the technique of correction of the lower Weser, it has connected the name of Franzius forever with the history of water engineering.

The important and courageous work of correction was the necessary premise for the leading position Bremen asserted on other North Sea ports. The competition escalated constantly. If Bremen wanted to prevail, it was not enough to rely on Bremerhaven alone. The work of Bürgermeister Smidt had to be reinforced by the work of water engineer Franzius. Especially after the war *(World War I)*, Bremen, which had been robbed of its trade fleet, would not have prevailed without these supplementary additions. Only through the correction of the Lower Weser, was it possible for Bremen to use its favorable connection to railroads and attract foreign ships to its harbor. This was also connected to the recently disbanded tariffs for goods in the times of devaluation of money. *(The tariffs had meant an income for Bremen and before new tariffs for the railroad had been levied, Bremen had to suffer financially.)*

Bremen's Ports[17]

From the Time after World War II

The following are excerpts from the book *Schaffendes Bremen,* 2nd edition, pg. 109-134.

Never in its thousand-year history had Bremen been in such a difficult, almost devastating position as in the spring of 1945 after the end of the war and the occupation of the victorious powers. However, it had experienced enough during Napoleon's times of what it meant to lose one's freedom and live under foreign occupation. Bremen had lost its trade fleet after World War I, also all of its financial assets abroad and its colonial properties. But city and ports were left intact even then and the fleet was reconstructed, having no other setbacks than financially because the wharfs were not destroyed and there were no prohibitions. The Second World War not only brought the loss of the trade fleet, but Germany was also absolutely forbidden to construct new ships as well as being disconnected from the sea. In addition, half of the city was destroyed by bombs, many of its ports and wharfs were destroyed and not only was all foreign capital gone, but the right to found new business abroad and even to travel there was taken away. Therefore, Germany had almost no way to renew relationships that were torn away by the war.

This essay falls into four parts:

a) The Ports, Their Destruction, and Their Reconstruction
b) The Trading Fleet, Its Loss and the Beginning of Building it Up Again
c) Trade and Navigation
d) The Traffic to the Inland

17 Hermann Apelt, Reden und Schriften, page 146

I shall only give the essentials of these four parts.

(a) The Ports, Their Destruction, and Their Reconstruction

There are two groups of the ports in Bremen: The ports in Bremen-City and the ones in Bremerhaven, 65 kilometers down the Weser. After the war also the former "Fischereihafen Wesermünde," now "Fischereihafen Bremerhaven," was added. During WWII almost 9/10 of the sheds and warehouses were destroyed, of the cranes 2/3, of the bridges more than a half, also of the floating facilities. Luckily, the quays were only slightly hit. The grain facility was still usable, but severely damaged in parts. About 200 shipwrecks clogged the port and part of the waterways inland. In addition, there were a great number of mines that rendered any navigation impossible.

> **"Whoever was trying to find his way through the wreckage of piled up and thrown asunder pieces of the *Überseehafen* (oversea port) and the *Europahafen* (European port) had to ask himself if it would be possible to ever again create a useful instrument serving trade and navigation out of this chaos. Indeed, in the beginning, it was very uncertain if this would ever happen."**

I find this passage the most impressive in the book. I remember my father saying during *Mittagessen* (dinner at midday), when I was in Bremen between studies in Hamburg, that we should feel like ants after the destruction of their hill and start all over right away. And that is exactly what he did!

This was a decision that had vital impact on the existence of Bremen. The port was the most important base for the Bremen economy. Credit must be given to the American garrison that the decision fell in favor of reconstruction. This decision was partly in their own interest to make it possible for their troops to use the ports of Bremerhaven and the City of Bremen. The very difficult removal of mines was accomplished by the British Marines and was done in four months. The removal of the shipwrecked vessels was done by Germans under the command of the A.G. Weser company (*Aktienggesellschaft,* an investment company, founded in 1843). This laborious process took four and a half years. The most difficult task was the lifting of the fully loaded steamer *Philipp Heineken,* a ship of 2300 BRT (gross tons). Work at the quays and cranes was done right away. Working with the American officer in charge was not always easy, but he attacked the difficult job with abundant energy. Already in September of 1945, the first trader—a ship from Poland—was able to get into the Bremen City port. The Americans were especially helpful in providing the necessary materials for the reconstruction. By 1950 the ships from abroad were able to do trade with Germany through Bremen again.

Within five years the first part of reconstruction of the *Überseehafen* had been accomplished. Now it was time to start reconstructing the *Europahafen* as well. This was partly done during the next five years, from 1950 to 1955.

Fortunately, in contrast to the ports in Bremen City, the ports in Bremerhaven had suffered little damage. Most damage was done to the Fischereihafen where more than 50% of the warehouses were destroyed. In spite of that, the big passenger steamers could continue their services and by 1955, the Fischereihafen was also back to full capacity.

(b) The Trading Fleet, Its Loss and the Beginning of Building it Up Again

The worst consequence of the war was again the loss of the trade fleet. Bremen has always been a city of ship-owners. A century ago when sailing vessels still ruled world navigation, Bremen was at the top of all continental ports. The first postal connection between Europe and the United States of America took place in 1847. Though this connection ran under the American flag, Bremen's initiative and financial help made this possible. Ten years later the Norddeutsche Lloyd company was founded. The names of this shipbuilding company and also the A.G. Weser prove the importance of Bremen for being leaders in European navigation. There was always the competition with other seaports, especially Hamburg.

Here I would like to insert a few remarks. At this time I was working on my thesis for the state exam for teaching Geography in Hamburg or Bremen and had chosen the title *The Importance of Cotton for Bremen* for this thesis. In the chapter that I titled "The development of the cotton trade after World War II," I point out that, though Hamburg has larger trade figures (about 300% more), Bremen's cotton trade is also about 300% larger than Hamburg's. This fact—cotton being the Number One commodity of Bremen trade—shows the importance of reconstructing the Bremen *Überseehafen* as fast as possible.

Hamburg always had more ships, but after the wars all European ports had had great losses. Bremen had lost most of its ships after WWI and nearly all of them after WWII. The complete trade fleet was gone. Difficulties for a German oversea trade were created by many limitations of the federal government, according the "Potsdamer Vereinbarungen" of August 2, 1945. Finally, in 1950, these restrictions were partially lifted during conferences in Petersberg (Florida, U.S.A.) and the purchase of ships by America was permitted again by the Washington agreement. In 1948 Germany was again allowed to take part in world trade, first only between European ports, and a year later also to the Mediterranean Sea and to Canada. Finally, the Petersberg Program of 1950/51 and later of 1951/52 brought further possibilities to rebuild the German fleet and with this Bremen again had a "home" fleet. Financing all of this was a major stumbling block. Statistics show that in the time from 1951 to 1958, the number of BRT (gross tons) had risen from 271 in Bremen to 1122, in Hamburg from 636 to 2446, and in all of West Germany from 1185 to 4292.

In 1957, the Bremen trade fleet had risen to 4/5 of the volume it had in 1939. Bremen always had more emphasis of *Fahrgastverkehr* (passenger traffic) than the other German ports.

(c) Trade and Navigation

Of all imported goods in the Bremen ports, the most important commodity was cotton. Even before WWII, Bremen was the most important cotton market on the continent. The Bremen Cotton Exchange even rivaled the Cotton Exchange in Liverpool. Bremen exported cotton not only to Germany but also to Switzerland, Austria, Hungary, the area around Lodz, and the Scandinavian countries. Besides cotton, Bremen traded sheep wool, grains, furs, also wine, lumber, jute (a natural plant fiber commonly used for making rope and sacks), and, in growing measure, coffee. After WWI, Rotterdam tried to capture the cotton trade but did not succeed. In 1927, Bremen even topped the Liverpool trade. 1928 was a record year for import and export. The following years showed the tendency of raising import and export quantities but lowering values.

After WWII, trade in Germany was all but dead. Not only that—similar to after WWI—it had lost all its assets abroad; its wings were also cropped by the control the victorious powers had over any possible freedom of movement. Trade was only used sparingly to help in certain situations. The Iron Curtain had Germany sharply divided. Bremen fared better than Hamburg.

In regards to conquering powers, both were declared enclaves: Bremen under the Americans, Hamburg under the British. Therefore, Bremen was able to redevelop its cotton and other trade sooner. Already in 1946, its trade rose to four million tons and in 1948 to over six million tons. The total trade figures of the six North Sea ports from 1936 to 1958 show that they not only rose back to the volumes of the years before the war, but surpassed them.

Still my father dwells on comparison with Hamburg and finds that our rival is not only bigger, but also more advantaged. Although Bremen had also been at a disadvantage by the erection of the Iron Curtain in 1945, it still had geographical and financial advantages. Bremen will never surpass Hamburg in overall trading, however, it stood again (in 1960) in first place in raw textile trading: cotton, wool, and jute.

The numbers for passenger traffic also look good. In 1960, almost 6 million NRT (net tons) of passenger weight has been carried under the German flag, more than twice that has been carried under the American flag. The Norddeutsche Lloyd is again as active as ever after an almost complete standstill during the war years. The *Fischereihafen* (fishing port) in Bremerhaven is also coming back to its leading position.

(d) The Traffic to the Inland

Every seaport has its Janus head, one face is turned toward the sea, the other toward the inland. As far as the seaports developed at the mouths of large streams, and that was the rule, the meeting of seafaring and inland shipping was the result. The goods brought in by the seagoing vessels went up the stream with riverboats and reverse. Besides the up and down navigation on the river, there were crossroads or canals. Those ships used to be built out of wood. On sea the rudder and later the sail was used. Inland the boats were towed up stream, but were carried by the water downstream. The last 150 years brought great changes: steam engines and gas powered motors. Instead of wood, steel was used. And on land, cars, trucks, and railroads changed the transport from sea to land completely.

In our century, the airplane began influencing traffic of goods and passengers. Especially after the First World War, navigation on sea and land lost more or less all mail service, transport of many perishable goods, as well as most of such passengers who wanted to save time, such as the business travelers. Airplanes did not need seaports. However, the importance of trucks soon surpassed that of railroads. Now railroads have (for transport of goods) three competitors: inland vessels, airplanes, and trucks. So far, the railroads have still managed to keep up with this struggle.

For Bremen, the railroad has proven to be advantageous. Inland waterway connections, especially the Weser, were not keeping up with other ports, like Hamburg or Rotterdam. The Elbe and the Rhein were more powerful waterways than the easily sand-choked Weser. Senator Arnold Duckwitz, the grandfather of Theodor Spitta, saw the advantage of developing the railroad system. Bremen became a typical railroad port, more so than Hamburg and the Rhein ports that used inland waterways for the greater part of their traffic of goods. However, transport of goods on inland waterways is cheaper than through railroads and Bremen had to pay the price for this.

Therefore Bremen always wanted to keep up the inland waterways by fostering the construction of canals. A new network of canals had been created before the great wars and Bremen strove to be connected to this system. **A connection to the *Mittellandkanal* (Midland Canal) would be especially helpful to compete with the other sea and inland ports.** In 1935, between the two wars, the *Küstenkanal,* a connection to the *Dortmund-Ems-Kanal* and with that to the Rhein, had been opened. This canal is connected to the *Eisenbahnhafen* (railroad port) within the Port of Bremen City. Still, a direct connection the Midland Canal would be a possible goal. The A.G. Weser has started its work on the middle part on the Weser again and of seven necessary locks, five have now been completed.

I have to add here that my father's dream of a direct connection to the Midland Canal was fulfilled on November 10, 1960, the day before he died in the early morning hours. It was the zenith of his career and he was allowed to conduct the christening of the seventh lock at Minden on the Middle Weser. My father ends the above article by mentioning the creation of the Bremen *Flughafen* (airport). Already in 1964, I had the opportunity to get acquainted with this new addition that slowly grew over the years from its timid beginnings after WWI. He ends this article with the following words:

> Everything flows and development never stops. This is true for all earthly things, especially the traffic. The history of the Hansa cities shows how their self-governing constitution makes it possible to adjust to ever occurring changes. What influences for the traffic the European Economic Union *(already debated in 1960!)* have, and what for it the use of atomic power will have, nobody can predict, just like what the contrast between East and West will bring.

Bremer Baumwollbörse[18]

The Bremen Cotton Exchange

Speech to Celebrate 75 Years of Existence (excerpts)

Given in 1947

Because I chose to write my thesis for the *Staatsexamen* (state exam, necessary to become a teacher in Germany) about cotton, calling it *Die Bedeutung der Baumwolle für Bremen* (The Importance of Cotton for Bremen), I worked for a while at this prestigious establishment, founded in the year 1872. I learned all about the intricacies of *klassieren* (judging cotton for its length and quality) and I met with the famous Bremen specialists who helped make Bremen the Number One cotton port in the world. After WWII, my father spoke at the 75th year celebration of the Bremen Cotton Exchange. I could not hear his speech because I was busy studying in Hamburg, but now I am proud to present his long speech in this book.

Mr. Bürgermeister, Gentlemen from the Cotton Exchange, honored guests.

A memorial for the Bremen Cotton Exchange will always be a memorial for the Bremen ports and navigation system.

Among the raw materials in world trade respective to value (not weight), cotton stands in the front row. Bremen's growth in trading cotton starts with the second half of the 19th century. While by 1801 only about 1,000 bales of cotton went via Bremen, by 1950, the number climbed to

18 Hermann Apelt, Reden und Schriften, page 170

30,000, and by 1870 to 70,000 bales. The decisive step for the expanse of the Bremen cotton market was the founding of the *Komittee für den Bremer Baumwollhandel* or, as the name changed later, the *Bremer Baumwollbörse,* in 1872, modeled after the then leading cotton exchange in Liverpool. Keywords for the newly erected facility were *Klassierung* (measuring the value of the fiber), *Arbitrage* (banking), and *Schiedsgerichte* (judging). In 1886, the cooperation of trade firms was expanded by joining with the spinners (mostly located in the south of Germany). Perhaps there could not be a more beautiful example for mutual understanding between trade and industry, for the lasting reciprocal action between the two, as the merger of traders and spinners at the Bremen Cotton Exchange.

Soon the results were noticeable: by the mid 1890s, the first million was reached, by 1905 the second and by 1912, two and a half million bales were shipped through Bremen.

Bremen had become the leading market for cotton on the European continent. Le Havre had fallen behind and Liverpool was just barely ahead. Not only did Germany receive its cotton through Bremen, but also the neighboring countries, Austria-Hungary, Switzerland, Holland, Belgium, and also Russia and Italy were served for most of their needs through Bremen.

This development had a strong influence upon the overall picture of the Bremen economy.

Before the steamship replaced the sailing vessels, most of the ship-owners also owned the freight on their vessels. That was the time of the *Reeders* (merchant ship-owners). They were gradually replaced by large shipping companies, many of which were also stationed in Bremen. Other big lines, some concentrating on passenger traffic, were stationed abroad or in England. While all of Bremen's cotton import had been handled by Bremen ships, now big lines from other countries shared this business. Bremen adjusted to receive cotton by constructing special cranes and larger sheds. The new *Überseehafen* (overseas port) especially strikes the visitor with evidence of a lively cotton trade. The huge new sheds, about 200 meters by 60 meters, are filled cotton bales that had to be stored outside previously. Cranes carrying bales from the ships to the sheds are a normal sight. Everything has been constructed to make the *Löschen* (unloading) better and faster. To make this possible, a well-trained group of workmen had to be developed. The well-functioning operation for unloading into big sheds at the port in Bremen City had been repeated in Bremerhaven. It is especially important for a load of cotton to be moved into sheds since the transfer onto railroad cars takes time. Every bale has to be opened, samples remove, inspected, and judged, and then brought under cover where it might stay some time. Capacity to hold a large amount of cotton bales is a necessary supposition for a functional cotton trade. Therefore, the *Bremer Lagerhaus Gesellschaft* (society to provide storage) has taken extra care to construct adequate storage place. Bremen transportation firms are famous for this branch of the cotton trade.

Bremen is not only an *Eisenbahnhafen* (railroad port), but also takes great pride on its connection with the German Canal system. Its effort to improve both was advantageous for the cotton trade which is a typical railroad commodity. If we mentioned before the lucky combination of import trade and industry, now the same can be said about the Cotton Exchange and railroads.

The cotton tariff has always played a special place among so-called *Seehafen-Ausnahmetarifen* (seaport exceptional tariffs). This shows the advantageous relationship between industry, seaport, and railroad. It is not as important to create an advantage for any of the three branches of trade, but the handling of tariffs can avoid damages for any of the three and also the entire system.

Let me give you a personal example: In 1906, I was asked by the Chamber of Commerce where I worked as a young *Syndikus* (trustee) to attend a meeting with the railroad commission. Present were representatives from the railroad commission in Hannover who were in charge of the cotton tariff then, and also gentlemen from the Cotton Exchange. The theme of the meeting was about lowering the tariffs as a consequence of the construction of the Tauern-rail, connecting the Bavarian Mühlberg and Freilassing. This would have been an advantage for the port of Triest (Italian) and a disadvantage for Bremen. The very able director of the Bremen Cotton Exchange, Geo Plate, made it possible with a very lively speech to convince the gentlemen that lowering the tariff was not necessary. Though this happened more than forty years ago, I still remember this impact of his speech. The railroad people were very impressed and were grateful to the Bremen Chamber of Commerce and the Cotton Exchange for not loosing this source of income. The tariff has not been substantially reduced through the last decades.

The influence of the Bremen cotton trade and the banking system should also be mentioned. Powerful banks from other parts of Germany founded branches in Bremen as for instance the *Deutsche Bank.* Financing was made easy by granting credits—goods on ships and in storage served as collateral.

The Bremen Cotton Exchange had created a powerful instrument in cooperation with spinners, navigation, ports, railroad, traffic, and banks. Ships were granted fast unloading, the commodities were well taken care of, ample stored goods were always available, credit from banks vouched for easy payments, and smooth operation at the Cotton Exchange guaranteed prompt delivery.

My father closes his speech with referrals to both devastating world wars.

Though after WWI Bremen had come back to prewar numbers because of sheer willpower and determination—relatively fast because the ports were not completely demolished—we now, two years after WWII, with more destruction and limitations, will do the same.

For a reference to Bürgermeister Smith, he quotes from the Bible, Letter to the Hebrews, 11:1:

Es ist aber der Glaube eine gewisse Zuversicht des, das man hofft und nicht zweifelt an dem, das man nicht sieht.

But faith is the substance of things hoped for,
the evidence of things not seen.

Faith did not betray Smith. We also will follow the old word of the Bible. Our situation may be compared to that of a ship that is thrown about by the storm:

Zerbrochen ist das Steuer und es reißt
Der Boden unter unsern Füßen auf.

Broken is the steering wheel and beneath us
The ground is torn apart.

We cannot see either the saving coast nor do we behold behind the dark night the light of sunshine. But still we shall cling to our faith that one day a new day will dawn, that our old Bremen will stay alive, and that the Bremen spirit of merchandizing that created the *Bremer Baumwollbörse*, will prevail.

Stanley A. Clem

The American Managers of the Bremen Ports[19]
From notes of Apelt, 1958

In 1945, after the end of the war when there was not much left of the Bremen ports , Bremen was at first under British command. The Americans, however, were interested in funneling their troops through Bremen and were interested in restoring the ports as soon as possible. Bremen became an American "enclave." All the decisions regarding restoration were in the hands of Americans.

When, during the period between the end of May to the beginning of June of 1945, the management of Bremen was again given back to the Senate—at first elected by the military administration—and I was responsible for "Economy and Ports"—the one who had the say about the ports was Colonel Boyle. Actually, the management of the ports was in the hands of the military forces that were assisted by the Weserhafen-Civil Port Authority. Technically, they were advised by Professor Dr. Agatz.

For me, though I was the formal senator of the ports, there was hardly any possibility to participate actively. As for anyone else, it was difficult to even get into the harbor. It took much paperwork to even get a permit to enter the port at all. I had, though, unlimited admission to the almighty Colonel Boyle who had his office at the *Haus des Reiches.* Boyle, usually rather energetic and of harsh military tone of voice, was mostly polite with me. But as to my realm of power, I often had to hear, "Senator, you know you have no control." Therefore, my role was mostly passive at first;

19 Hermann Apelt, Reden und Schriften, page 280

for example, I received all reports about what was going on and what was planned. Otherwise, I was a kind of liaison between the almighty port manager and the Senate and the Bremen offices.

There was mainly the daily complaint of the colonel that not enough workers could be provided. He threatened to hang the Senate if he could not get enough helpers. He even had the manager of the employment office indicted, although that poor man could not help to provide the necessary workers such as bricklayers, carpenters, glaziers—there just were not enough of them.

In spite of the occasional rough manners, Bremen has to thank Colonel Boyle. He was instrumental in the final decision that Bremen was selected to transport the American soldiers, and therefore, both Bremerhaven and Bremen could start with the reconstruction. This decision saved Bremen. And thanks to Boyle's energy this monumental task took place. At first the general cleanup and the repair of the two still-existing warehouses took place. The removal of the mines was done by the British.

Boyle was replaced by Major Harris at the end of 1945. This man was a little more soft-spoken. Instead of "Senator, you have no control," we now heard "Senator, you know we will help you." Major Harris was replaced by Stanley H. Clem.

This man, of German origin from his father's side, was born in the state of Illinois in 1898, and worked as an engineer for the British Navy. He was severely wounded and came to Berlin in 1945. In 1946 he was stationed in Bremen as part of the military government. Here he stayed for five years, until 1951. He never recuperated from his wounds and died in 1958, only sixty years old.

He told me later that the years in Bremen were the happiest of his life. And I must say, that working with this man belongs to my most cherished memoirs, officially as well as humanly. Actually, the original relationship between us was that of the representatives of the victorious and the besieged counties. But in reality, the relationship was one of mutual trust and striving for the common good. Until in 1947 all decisions were again up to the designated senator, Mr. Clem helped our situation rather than blocked it. His great talent for organization and his pleasant, genteel ways made our task easy.

Clem never changed his attitude toward the reconstruction of our ports and considered them "his ports." Wherever he could help us, he did. When we had difficulties, first with getting enough help, then supplying materials—for each ton of iron we had to fight—it was Clem who helped.

He even knew how to enforce his influences at the authoritative places in Frankfurt.

By the end of his time in Bremen, we had become real friends. Aristotle lists three kinds of friendship: because of the pleasure to be together, because of the merit, and because of high esteem. Considering these categories, our friendship began because of merit, not personal, but for the port. This then developed into a relationship that was based on high esteem for each other. This became permanent until Clem, much too early, had to succumbed to the complications of his wounds. I will never forget the weeks I was allowed to spend in his little house in France. I saw him last during a short visit in Bremen. He bore his affliction with outstanding patience. Until the end, his letters expressed his love for the Bremen ports.

All the time he was willing to help and he exercised neighborly love in the truest sense. An example of this is the following: On a cold day, he came home one night without his coat. His astonished wife asked him about this and he told her, a young man had been there who did not have a coat, so he gave him his coat. With this, he did even more that the Holy Martin; that man only cut off a piece from his coat, but Clem gave his whole coat away.

Carl Schurz Gesellschaft[20]

The Carl Schurz Society

Five Speeches (excerpts)

I remember seeing Carl Schurz's memoirs on my father's bookshelf, but I never found the time to read the book. Frankly, I was not too interested—there were many books on bookshelves around the house that were more appealing to me. I had my own set of reading materials and other things to do. Only now I regret that I did not take more advantage of all the stimulating reading material surrounding me when I was young.

My Father was the founder and president of the Bremen branch of the *Carl Schurz Gesellschaft.* As I had mentioned above, I did not know much about Carl Schurz before I picked up *Hermann Apelt, Reden und Schriften* and decided to write my own book about my father's legacy. I even had Schurz's memoirs[21] standing on my own bookshelf (my thoughtful mother had sent it to me), but had never touched it. After having read the five speeches my father gave in honor of this German-American, I became curious about him. I started reading the book about a man who lived from 1829-1906 and made such an impression on my father. I

20 Hermann Apelt, *Reden und Schriften,* pages 330, 332, 334, 335, and 337.

21 Carl Schurz, 1829-1906, *Lebenserinnerungen* (memoirs), 1952, Walter de Gruyter & Co.

could not put the book down. In the end, I was happy that America, my new home, had more appreciation for this fiery German than the German people. He left Germany to find in America what he could not find in Germany. He became a noted politician and worked closely with Abraham Lincoln. Still he never forgot his old home. When I came to the part of the book where Schurz describes his first impression of entering the bay of New York, I was reminded of my father's first impression and also my own feelings while approaching New York. I quote (translated) from page 297:

> "The day of our arrival at the New York port could not have been more beautiful. The bay and the surrounding islands gleamed in sunny splendor. While we, after a four-week voyage across the water desert, beheld this magical show, our hearts trembled with joy. We felt as if we entered, through this gate, a world of happiness and peace."

Founding Celebration, 120th Birthday of Schurz

March 2, 1949

I thank you for coming to our founding celebration of the Bremen branch of the Carl Schurz Society. Today is his 120th birthday. Of all the millions of Germans who went abroad during the last century—be it for political or economical reasons—in order to create a new life in America, there is no name more brilliant than Carl Schurz's. He left his homeland as a political fugitive and rose to highest honors abroad, but he never turned his back on Germany and still stayed attached. Though his wrestling for the good of his old home was never rewarded—in America he was amply rewarded. He worked for the good of his new home and his ideal was a free society.

He wrote his memoirs and there are few such autobiographies that are more worthwhile to read. He wrote in both languages, English and German. The first volume, in German, describes his participation in the tragic revolution of 1848 (tragic for lovers of equality and freedom in Germany) and the second one leads the reader into the struggle between north and south states in America. *(My copy of his memoirs has the second part written in German, so it must have been translated from the English.)* In the center stands the powerful figure of Abraham Lincoln who could not have a more glorious legacy than the one written by a German-born colleague.

After the First World War, the Carl Schurz Society was founded in Berlin with the goal to foster cultural and economical connection between America and Germany. Both nations honor this mediator and patron who demonstrated how one could be a good American and still preserve his love for his homeland. Therefore, it seemed logical to found a branch of this society in Bremen, our tiny republic that had been connected through centuries with the large republic abroad through business and human relationships. I remind you of the fact that already in 1794 Washington had sent one of his first consuls to Bremen, that the Ocean Steam Navigation Company, the forerunner of the *Norddeutsche Lloyd*, chose Bremen for the landing of its vessels. Further I remind you of the keywords: tobacco, petroleum, immigrants, and steamer traffic. And then—there are hardly any families that do not have family connections abroad. Therefore, Bremen had all the reasons to found its own branch of the Carl Schurz Society.

Twenty years ago we celebrated the hundredth birthday of Carl Schurz in the Great Hall of the *Glocke* (a music hall named "The Bell" by Julie Apelt). When I was allowed then to speak to a full audience, I had no idea that a second world war would again tear the connections between our countries.

Now, after this wretched war that brought us so many wounds, we call again for the name of Carl Schurz. The former society had been abandoned in 1933. It is time to pick up the threads again. We in Bremen are willing to mend the tears that this war has caused and, at least, bring back the friendly connections that had existed for 150 years.

We are certain that also abroad the sentiments toward working together find an echo of our endeavors. The connection with the Carl Schurz Society in Philadelphia as well as the presence of the director of military affairs whom I cordially thank for coming here is proving this.

Let us do our work in memory of Carl Schurz.

Greeting the Federal President, Theodor Heuß

February 7, 1952

Mr. Bundespräsident!

In the name of our group of members of the Bremen Carl Schurz Society and their guests, I express my heartfelt welcome here in our Great Hall of the *Rathaus.* We are grateful that you came, in spite of the political unrest.

Special thanks for coming to us in 1952, one hundred years after Carl Schurz who—together with his young wife—set foot on American soil, an event of decisive importance for his own life as well as for the United States of America.

He has served his new homeland with all his power and soul, as citizen and as soldier. Nobody could have striven more truthfully and convinced of the democratic ideal, founded by Washington, Jefferson, and Madison, than he did. Under the guidance of Abraham Lincoln he submitted to collaborate to preserve these accomplishments.

To summarize Schurz's life, the quotation underneath a statue of Carl Schurz says it best:

> "Fearless, independent liberal reformer, Schurz fled Germany after the abortive revolution of democrats against autocracy.
>
> In 1852, he arrived in America accompanied by his bride. His versatility lifted him quickly out of obscurity.
>
> His career in his new homeland made him a diplomat, orator, soldier, editor, senator, cabinet officer, biographer of Lincoln.

> Attained highest offices open to a citizen of foreign birth. Seeker of justice for the Negro [sic] and Indian [sic]. Founder of civil reform, he was the nation's most distinguished immigrant of the nineteenth century."

As closely as the new home had gripped his soul and unchanged loyalty, he never forgot his old German home. He was always interested in the fate of Germany. In 1866, he wrote to his brother, "I have to confess that I almost think more about Germany than of Germany."

Even today, during our sorrowful and complicated time, he might have said the same. And I am sure that thoughts about the Marshall Plan and peace negotiations would have found a zealous and truthful helper in him.

So he may serve both, Germans and Americans, as a common model. What could connect us more than common models?

One Hundredth Anniversary of Carl Schurz's Entering America

October 1952

On September 17, 1852, Carl Schurz entered the United States together with his young bride to build a new life on American soil. September 17 is also the date when, 55 years earlier, the Federal Convention in Philadelphia, city of brotherly love, had ended their work and the constitution of the new nation was signed. The American constitution could be compared to the *Magna Carta* for the English constitution. Both were sown from similar seeds and are still workable, unlike so many other constitutions that did not last. The admirable deed could only be accomplished by the unity of spirit of the fathers of these constitutions. Freedom and Human Rights were the foundation of both. The same spirit moved the young rebel Carl Schurz to fight in 1848 which, after utter failure, led him to choose America as his new home.

Maybe it is chance that the date of his entering America and signing the United States' constitution fell on the same date, maybe premonition. Carl Schurz earned in the new country what the old one had denied him, freedom of thought and security. Both belong together.

It was his goal from the beginning to keep the flame, lit by the young United States, going and keeping it clear of debris. He would be the guardian of that flame.

Carl Schurz has done much for his new homeland. He helped President Abraham Lincoln and later President Hayes, both of the same spirit, to establish their ideals.

Also for his old homeland he did not live in vain. While he—a common model for his old as well as his new co-patriots—leads both of us, Americans and Germans, together in his name, will he not also influence us both beyond his grave?

Therefore, his memory should be blessed.

Speech to Remember the Death of Carl Schurz

May 13, 1956

Fifty years ago, Carl Schurz said his last words, "It is so easy to die." This reminds us of the words of Lord Byron in one of his poems, "Old man, it's not so difficult to die."

This sounds similar, but it is quite different. Byron expresses bitter disappointment and dissatisfaction, Schurz in contrast looks at death in a positive way. He accomplished his goals. Byron was the great romantic of the *Weltschmerz,* Schurz the idealist of action.

Schurz was a doer. Without regard to his own future, he fought for his ideals. He did not succeed in the old country, so he looked forward to a new home. Here he met Lincoln and found that this great man had similar ideals. When in 1860 the American people chose Lincoln to be their president, Schurz could say about himself, "I did my part." Indeed—his numerous fiery election speeches and writings did their part in the victory—maybe the most important outcome of an election in the history of the United States. After Lincoln's death, he also fought for the Civil Service Reform and could say the same. He did his part and therefore he could say, "It is so easy to die."

Therefore, he is our model in life and death, and also a symbol for all the common good that connects both nations, the American and the German.

Speech at the Ten-Year Celebration of the Carl Schurz Society

November 24, 1958

This winter is the tenth anniversary since our Bremen branch has been founded. Ten years are not a long time span, especially in our fast-moving time. However, not long ago the United States was fighting us as enemies and they were the victors, we the besieged. In every war, there are the winners and the losers. This is old history. But the relationship between the two does not have to be inhumane.

An old wish of mine has been fulfilled recently. In Madrid I was allowed to see the original painting by Velasques, *Las Lanzas* or "The Surrender of Breda." It could not have been expressed more nobly and beautifully how the conqueror can still be human and feel for the defeated as the artist shows in the deportment of the victorious Spanish general Spinola and the defeated Commandant Justin von Nassau. The besieged knows he has lost, but still retains his dignity.

Looking at this outstanding painting brought back what it meant that America, the victor, is reaching out her helping hand to us, the besieged.

This friendly gathering in honor of our mutual patron, Carl Schurz, is confirmation and expression of this attitude of the winner.

As I mentioned above, I was motivated to read Carl Schurz's memoirs. I own a copyrighted edition from the year 1952 (the year I set foot on American soil for the rest of my life) and it has been published by Walter de Gruyter & Co., Berlin. The second part of my copy must have been translated from English to German because the entire volume is German. It also must have been slightly abridged. Since I am a German teacher and have been asked frequently if I learned to think in English since coming to America, I would like to quote Carl Schurz here (page 303):

> *"Since I have become known as speaker and writer in the English as well as in the German language, I have been asked frequently whether I, while speaking or writing, think in English or German, and if I am constantly translating from one language into the other. My answer was that, while speaking or writing in English, I also think in English and that, while speaking or writing in German, I also think in that language. And if I am thinking without expressing in words or letters, I don't know in what language this takes place."*

My answer would be the same as his.

Deutsche Gesellschaft zur Rettung Schiffsbüchiger

German Society to Rescue Shipwrecked People[22]

Speech Given at the Rotary Club

May 1936

This is the last speech selected by Dr. Spitta and my mother that took place before the war ended in 1945. During the time from 1933 to 1945 my father was working as an attorney and I believe it was hard for him to make a living this way. Though now he could speak freely about his daily chores, he still had to be very careful not to say any uncomplimentary things about our leader since, as an ex-senator, he was closely scrutinized by the Nazis. So at our dinner table we listened to the stories about how he was harassed by unhappy wives, marching right into his office, demanding justice against brutal husbands. He had to listen to these people because, among other branches of the law, he also dealt with family court issues. Instead of a set salary for senators, his income now became sporadic. Still he had time to dedicate energy to his hobbies, the *Kunstverein* (Art Association), the *Goethegesellschaft* (Goethe Society) , the Rotary Club, and others. Therefore, when asked by the Rotary Club to speak about his pet project, the *Deutsche Gesellschaft zur Rettung*

22 Hermann Apelt, Reden und Schriften, Deutsche Gesellschaft zur Rettung Schiffbrüchiger, Page 387

Schiffbrüchiger (German Society to Recue Shipwrecked People), he was more than happy to do so.

Honored members of Rotary.

From early on rescue shipwrecked people occupied the imagination of mankind and poets. Homer's divine sufferer Odysseus throws the lifesaving veil to Leucothea (Greek sea goddess). In Shakespeare's tragic-comic *The Tempest*, it is the spirit Ariel who saves the drowning people. Everyone enjoys hearing about these wonderful rescues. But only lately something has been done about the saving of them. At first there were a few local groups in England at the end of the 18th century. In the beginning of the 19th century, the Prussian state started with a few rescue stations on the Baltic Sea. Not until 1824 were larger organizations established. In this year the large English society, as well as the two Dutch societies, were founded for recuing shipwrecked people. It took forty more years for Germany to follow. In 1860, the Hanover brig *Alliance* went down with the entire crew. Influenced by this disaster, two citizens of the Bremen port city Vegesack turned to "the entire German Nation" for not having observed, as other nations had done, the "first duty of humanity." This wake-up call initiated first the foundation of some local societies until, in 1865, the *Deutsche Gesellschaft zur Rettung Schiffbrüchiger* was founded in Bremen. It combined all the other local organizations. This led to unification in the area of rescuing shipwrecked people and thus overcame the German menace of fragmentation by borders and parties even before 1870 and 1933. As in England and in Holland, the entire rescue system lies in the hands of volunteers. Sacrificing their own lives to save others, more than one thousand courageous men make this possible, and to a lesser degree all of those who give their small contribution in order to run the necessary equipment and to maintain the stations.

According to the same principles the French society was founded in 1865 and others in other European countries with the exception of Denmark and Sweden where already the state had developed rescue stations.

The high value of these rescue activities is expressed in the fact that the highest power of the countries are the protectors of the societies—in England the Kings since George IV, in France the presidents of the Republic. In Germany Wilhilm I, King of Prussia, was the patron and kept the protectorate when he became emperor. After his death, his grandson took over. Today the protector is the leader and vice-president Adolf Hitler …

I find remarks about Hitler very seldom in my father's speeches and writings! In Germany at that time, 1936, one had to be extremely careful to be respectful of the Nazis. The rest of this speech consists of statistics about the society and the devastating result of World War I. Membership had been drastically reduced and my father urged more interest in bringing back the society to its pre-war excellence. What World War II did to the Society, I do not know, but it must have been disastrous since, along with the Bremen fleet, the rescuers must have been destroyed too. I still remember the little replica of a rescue vessel hanging in the hallway of our restored house in Bremen. Visitors contributed money through a slit. Being the leader of the Society to Rescue Shipwrecked People was one more voluntary chore my father took upon himself in his busy life. I learned from the Internet that the organization is now in good shape and still depends on volunteers for sustenance.

Seefahrtsschulen[23]

School for Navigation

My father was very interested in having good schools to produce top navigators. In their book, *Hermann Apelt, Reden und Schriften,* Dr. Spitta and my mother selected four speeches, held between 1952 and 1955:

1. *Seefahrtschule, Bremerhaven* (opening of the school after destruction in WWII), 1952
2. 75 Year Celebration of the *Seefahrtschule* Bremerhaven, 1954
3. Foundation of the New Building for the *Seefahrtschule* Bremen , 1955
4. Farewell to the Navigation Students, 1955

The last speech was held just before his official retirement from the Senate. The navigation school in Bremerhaven had been housed in a temporary location and from now on students would be trained in the new building in Bremen. I chose the first and the last of these speeches to share:

23 Hermann Apelt, Reden und Schriften, page 270

Seefahrtschule, Bremerhaven

March 31, 1952

Honored Friends,

When German navigation and German seamanship have earned a good reputation in the world, German schools to teach these subjects may rightfully take some credit for this.

The origin of navigation education is about two hundred years old, while navigation has been with us since the beginning of mankind. If we follow the Bible, the beginning of the history of man started with a ship: *Noah's Ark*.

Since ancient times, the art of steering a ship has always been highly esteemed. The old stories about the voyages of the Argonauts and the misguided searches of Aeneas have handed down to us names and fates of helmsmen: here Tiphys, there Palinurus.

Scanning the pages of Plato's dialogues, we find again and again remarks about the art of leading a ship. This is also used as a metaphor for leading a state. It is written in the *Republic* "The helmsman has to take care of the time of year and day, of sky and stars, of air conditions and everything having to do with his field if he truly wants to be a leader of the ship."

In a beautiful way Plato compares the leaders of state and ship: "Both have to guard the security of their subjects by using the art of decisiveness gleaned from their own feel for responsibility rather than following written instruction and therefore bring everyone home safely."

In Plato's time, there were no instructions to guide ships with the help of science, no knowledge of arithmetic, measurements, and weights—the art of steering a ship was based on practice and experience. Indeed, it was considered a trade. And, as with other trades, it was carried over to new generations by apprenticing. Of course, the ships were made of wood and they had sails. In medieval times, when the magnetic needle became known, the compass was invented.

The real progress came when the great explorers—Columbus, Vasco, Magellan—cruised the world, when European navigation changed from coastal to overseas voyages, when progress was also made in the exact sciences, and as astronomy, and nautical science became necessary for navigation.

The fact that Germany did not partake in these new discoveries has political reasons. Germany, as well as Italy, were splintered countries at that time and did not stand behind their large seaports. Therefore, other more centralized countries rose in the race for discovering the world: Spain and Portugal. However, Germany did contribute to promote scientific navigation: Peurbach and Regiomontanus in Nürnberg. Martin Behaim tied the connection between the astronomy of the Germans with the nautical skills of the Spaniards and Portuguese.

Then came the period of the great German reformers: Copernicus for astrology, and Martin Luther for religion. They were almost contemporaries, Copernicus lived from 1473 to 1543 and Luther from 1483 to 1546. All of these developments led to an improvement in nautical science and it became necessary to educate the future navigators in both, theory and practice. Therefore, it became necessary to have navigation schools.

Not only because of progress in nautical knowledge, but also the building of ships had progressed, these schools became necessary. The wooden sailing vessels were replaced by motorized iron vessels. The invention of the steam engine created a whole new era of navigation.

If one could call the development a marriage of science and practice, so no one could call it a marriage of technique and practice. Therefore, both navigation schools as well as nautical engineering schools became a necessity. The first German navigation schools were founded in the middle of the 18th century. In Bremen, this happened in the year 1789. That was before the founding of Bremerhaven in 1827. The idea to build a navigation school in Bremerhaven was backed by the interest of the German Reich, and in 1878, the building was finished and the first class held. One year later the first class of a new engineering school started. In 1929, the 50-year-old school was celebrated with a party and a report, *50 Jahre Seefahrtschule Wesermünde/Gestemünde.* I used this report several times.

In September of 1944, the school building was partly destroyed. But the lessons continued until January 1945. After the occupation, first by the English, then by the Americans, the continuation of the schooling was not permitted at first. But then, thanks to friendly negotiations with the Americans, permission was given to start instruction again, and by this time the Wesermünde/Gestemünde area had changed its name to Bremerhaven.

While in Bremen City, the navigation school had been completely leveled, so that instruction had to be given elsewhere, in Bremerhaven part of the building was still standing. It was possible to reconstruct the building so that now it can also serve the students for navigation engineering.

Honored friends, it is an important, enjoyable step that we took toward completing this reconstruction project.

I know that not all wishes have been fulfilled. We are still not offering all the courses we had before the war. Please, be patient. The reconstruction of our fleet is still in the early stages and we are still not sure yet how many officers we will need in the near future. Also I don't have to mention that we have to be careful with our state expenses. Let us be grateful that our building has been repaired in what I believe is an enjoyable manner. Everything beyond that is up to the future.

Therefore, I put the key to the new navigation school building into your hands, Herr Oberseefahrtsschuldirector Berger. *(This long word means Super Director of the Navigation School.)* May the renovated school be the worthy continuation of the more than 70-year tradition. Also, may these words be true:

Und neues Leben blüht aus den Ruinen.

And new life may blossom from the ruins.

Verabschiedung der Seefahrtschüler

Farewell to the Navigation Students

Bremen, December 16, 1955

Gentlemen,

You are at the beginning of your career. My own career—my official one—is ending soon. *(My father retired officially on December 30, 1955.)* I am very grateful to be permitted to speak to you and hand out your well-earned diplomas as one of my last acts of service.

Times are changing. It has not been long since young pilots, helmsmen, and captains were ready to serve, but the ships were missing. Now we have—and we are grateful for that—a German trade fleet again, which grows continually. But now our demands seem to be changing. Now we have the ships, but are missing the men who are able to serve as officers and captains on these ships. Therefore, I welcome you with double joy: first, I do not have to worry anymore about the problem of what to do with all the young men who are ready to serve our country as navigators, and second, now we have all of you ready to fill our demands. Every one of you is welcome; everyone is filling our needs. We need all of you to supply the necessary demands a ship's crew requires. Every one of you can leave this school to use what you have learned here in practice and continue your education by serving on one of our ships. Gentlemen, the profession you have chosen is surely a beautiful one. It stimulates the imagination, but it is also a difficult job, demanding full responsibility. Just think of the weather over the last two weeks with heavy storms and complicated fog conditions that demonstrate to us what important decisions helmsmen and officers of a ship have to make.

But it is not only <u>this</u> responsibility, caring for the ship loaded with people and wares; the crew and their leaders have another responsibility. As Germans, as officers of German ships, they are also representatives of Germany abroad. In every foreign port where German trade vessels land, their crew and officers have to demonstrate through their deportment what others have in their mind about German navigators. The opinion of the world about Germans, their character, their values and what they do not value, is influenced considerably by the way German navigators behave and act in foreign ports.

Gentlemen, I am certain that you are ready and capable to execute both of these responsibilities. And with all my heart I wish you good luck in your further endeavors.

Fine Arts[24]
Kunsthalle in Bremen

Art Museum

Jahrhundertfeier des Kunstvereins

Besides my father's love for poetry and music, he was motivated by my mother to develop an attachment to other arts to the extent that he devoted much time and energy to promote the situation of our *Kunsthalle* (Art Museum) and Fine Arts in general. During the war, he helped to save valuable pictures. I chose to translate two speeches from the time after WWI during the inflation.

24 Kunsthalle, Hermann Apelt, Reden und Schriften, page 297

Two Speeches at the 100-Year Celebration

November 4, 1923

At the Event in the Art Museum

Sad as our times are, and as seldom as we invite people to our events and celebration, we believe yet that it is not only our right but also our duty to celebrate the hundred-year birthday of our art society.

When in 1823 our ancestors founded the art society, our fatherland had just recuperated from a deep depression, but though there was much to wish for, at least our country was free; the enemy had fled.

Today, one hundred years later, the enemy is still inside our country and we have no weapons to defend ourselves.

Blindlings von einer Stunde zur andern,
Wie Wasser von Klippe zu Klippe geworfen,
Jahrlang ins Ungewisse hinab.

Blindfolded thrown from hour to hour
From cliff to cliff like water
Year after year into the unknown.

Even though the political and economical Germany may be given to the discretion and power of traitorous enemies, it is our own responsibility to see that they cannot break the spiritual Germany. In spite of all lamentable destruction of the spirit as well, the common possession of what is left is our last and strongest chain that holds all Germans together. The German people will not be ruined if they manage to keep their spiritual heritage—not as dead, but as daily renewed possession; not as buried, but as growing substance, not in luxurious pillows, but on raw ground, always new, not processed, but processing. Only from living spirit can Germany be born again. A hundred years is a long time span, measured with human experiences. But a hundred years are nothing when compared to eternity. Let us be happy looking back onto hundred years of working together to uphold Fine Arts. Let us be joyous that in the reflection of German art, in the works of our masters, a dawning, an inkling of eternity, captured by our masters, ray by ray, has been kept by our perishable eyes.

Let us take what has been expressed by these works of art as a guarantee for the everlasting value of our nation, which—and that be our belief and our credo— in spite of all disguising and disfiguring smoke and fog of the present, will remain with us forever.

At Dinner in the Essighaus

Restaurant in Bremen

Honored Friends!

This house, where we are together now, has the year 1618 inscribed over the entrance. Up to that point these kinds of houses were built. Then the 30-Year War came and with it never ending misery. But the old patrician building outlasted the war and many other events. Be it our symbol for being hopeful for the future.

If we decided to invite our friends in spite of difficult times, it will be in this spirit. I greet all of our friends: artists, artisans, and art critics. *(This is a pun. My father used the words: Künstler, Können, und Kenner. These words mean: those who have the gift to create, those who are able to produce artistic things, and those who understand art and can debate and criticize it. I would add another "K" word: Käufer. Those are the buyers. My father thinks of that also.)*

We are happy that all three of these areas have sent representatives. One more important factor for the world of art is the business side; we need to foster trade. In old times there were the *Mäcens* (rich people who helped starving talented artists), but nowadays, in our democratic times, the task falls to you. The museum, where art is exhibited, should not be a mausoleum but rather a blooming garden, brimming with life.

Therefore, we are grateful to our gardeners. *(Here he reminds us of the past president of the art museum, Gustav Pauli, now working in Hamburg, and Emil Waldmann, who was still alive in 1923, and others that made it possible to have such a wonderful institution to promote art.)*

May the *Kunstverein* be permitted so that all of them, *Künstler, Können, Kenner,* and *Gönner (new pun, meaning promoters, guardians, collectors)* will continue to work together; only then will it continue to flourish.

In the beginning, there was the Bremen *Kunstverein* (Art Association). The names Klugkist (the founder), Gustav Pauli, Emil Waldmann, Günther Busch and Rudolf Alexander Schröder are all closely related to the *Kunstverein* and its building, the *Kunsthalle.* My father was active as its manager for many years, but had to step down after the change of power to have a Nazi, Schulrat Castens, take over. Under the Nazi regime, the direction of goals for the *Kunstverein* was drastically changed.

Three Speeches to Honor Bremen Citizens

Gravesite Speech for Mathilde Becker[25]

1926

My father was frequently asked to hold eulogies of beloved Bremen citizens. I selected one of those speeches, the one to honor Mathilde Becker, the mother of Paula Moderson Becker, the daring modern artist who died much too young at the age of 31. She was the wife of the painter Otto Moderson. I was distantly related to her twice: through the marriage of my mother's sister Lotte to Paula's brother Henry and also through the marriage of my sister Dorothee to Wulf Rohland, son of Emilie, Paula's older sister. Mathilde Becker was my godmother. She was like a real grandmother to us children and we had spent many happy hours playing in her comfortable house on the Schwachhauser Heerstraße and in her beautiful garden.

Dear fellow mourners,

You went, whether we believe it or not; we have to believe that you left us.

Not long ago the solemn friend stepped close to you and led you to that dark border that lies between life and death—but once more, your strong will to live conquered the almighty. Now we believed we had you back for good, you indestructible one. But you knew better, you cherished every day as an extra gift and lived your last days to the fullest. And then he came, quickly and peacefully, without fight or bitterness, to detach the thread.

25 Hermann Apelt, Reden und Schriften, Page 327

Now we have pain and thanks in equal measure. Every word that repeats the painful loss has to become a word of thanks that you were granted a full life and that we could share this life with you. Every thought trying to understand how such fullness of life can leave us, wants to remind us: You belonged to us, and that treasure nobody can take away—you will remain ours, never to be lost. Though we do not see you anymore, your memory lives on, forever in those who knew you, you perfect one.

The cornucopia of life and love; it flowed from you and returned to you. You opened your great, warm heart to the entire world.

For you it was:

Natur ein Buch lebendig,
Unverstanden, doch nicht unverständlich,
Denn du hattest viel und groß Begehr,
Was wohl in der Welt für Freude wär',
Allen Sonnenschein und alle Bäume,
Alles Meergestad und alle Träume,
In Dein Herz zu sammeln miteinander.

Nature a living book,
Not understood, but understandable,
For you had great desire and yearning,
To know what all the world has to offer,
All the sunshine and all the trees,
All the beaches and all the dreams,
To gather in your heart together.

Speech for Clara Rilke-Westhoff[26]

70th Birthday Party

Worpswede and Fischerhude are art colonies closely situated to Bremen. Here the sculptress Clara Rilke-Westhoff, a good friend of the paintress Paula Moderson Becker and wife of renown poet Rainer Maria Rilke, lived and worked. She studied her art under famous sculptors in Paris, one of them being Auguste Rodin . It has been told that Rilke was a good friend of both artists; and for a long time he was not sure whom he liked better, Clara or Paula.

Honored Frau Rilke-Westhoff!

By taking the courage to be the speaker today I want to express my regret that another one who would be more apt to be in my place is forced to stay away because of illness. I am sure he dwells among us with his thoughts *(Rainer Maria Rilke, Carla's husband).* Since I am not the ordained speaker here, at least I can be the representative of several others.

I bring to you the heartfelt greetings of the Senate, the *Kunstverein,* and many friends, present and absent, who want to partake in this birthday celebration. We greet you proudly as a child from our town. Though Worpswede and Fischerhude are not parts of Bremen politically, we still consider both places as belonging to the Bremer spiritual realm.

If one says that Worpswede and Fischerhude lie on the border of the political borders of Bremen, one could rightly say also that Bremen is situated on the borders of the art world of Worpswede and Fischerhude.

26 Hermann Apelt, Reden und Schriften, page 316

Honored Lady! You are completing the seventieth year today and have reached a biblical age. Though age is no accomplishment by itself, but a gift of God; however, aging gracefully and keeping young in spirit is. The word of Seneca of old comes to mind:

Longa est Vita, si plena est—Actu illam metiamur non tempore.

Life is long when it has been fulfilled. Let us measure
it according to content, not number of years.

You, honored Septuagenarian, have not only received the number of years but also the fullness of life. It is enough to mention Leipzig, Paris, Rome and Worpswede.

If the present times are dismal and oppressing, two things no one can take away from you: memory and the ability to create.

I quote Goethe:

Denn es ist ein zweites Glück,
Eines Glück's Erinnerung.

For it is second happiness
To remember happiness.

In summary, thank you for all your gifts to us as an artist and as a person. We hope that you and your work will be with us forever more.

Speech to Honor Rudolf Alexander Schröder

On His 70th Birthday[27]

In the Old Hall of the *Rathaus*

1948

Since this Bremer poet and lover of the arts had been elected to be the director of the Bremen Art Society after WWII (he accepted the honor, but gave the job to Dr. Günther Busch) and had received the role of *Ehrenvorsitzer* (Honorable Director) in 1957, I will at least mention this rather long speech. Schröder was also nominated *Ehrenbürger* of Bremen (honorable member of our city). He was a prolific writer and poet, loved the arts and was highly regarded by everyone. I happened to know him quite well since I spent three months with him in Bergen, a small town in the Alps where he and many other Bremen citizens had gone to avoid the constant bombing in Bremen. When I, weak and exhausted from scarlet fever and just released from the hospital in Traunstein that morning, came to his doorstep, he and his sister Dora with whom he lived, embraced me and took me in to recuperate. Nobody had enough to eat in May of 1945, so it was a gift from heaven for me to be accepted by them. It was a very orderly household and Dora took good care of both of us. As soon as I was feeling better, I helped them as much as I could. My parents were very relieved to hear that I was with the Schröders, their good friends.

---

27 Hemann Apelt, Reden und Schriften, page 439

This address in his honor is mostly about Schröder's poetry and I find it difficult to even summarize this speech. It must have taken several hours to deliver it. It has many quotations in it, several about Bremen's beautiful gardens. However, my father was very dedicated to him. I shall translate just one paragraph:

> Among all of the poems, the one about Bremen is the most impressive, created during 1931, the year of the height of the depression when his hometown was suffering serious deprivation. The deep emotional upset of the poet's soul seems to influence the rhythm of the poem directly. The dactyl in the second foot gives the verse some peculiar feel of ascending and pressing, as then the masculine rhyme of every third and sixth line has the tone abate and therefore bestows the ending a special vigor.

And now, you probably want to know this verse:

Herrin, heilige, die wir meinen,
Weil du unsere, wir die Deinen,
Da Du friedetest Strom und Strand,
Will im Herde die Glut erkranken,
Weil die Scheiter in Asche versanken,
Hier sind andere! Nimm den Brand!

Mistress, holy one, whom we mean,
Because you are ours, we are yours,
While you conquered river and beach,
The fire in the stove went out,
Because the embers drowned in the ash,
Here are others! Take the torch!

> The poet does not speak for himself. From the feeling for the community, out of feeling deep sorrow for the future of the beloved city, he becomes the spokesperson for all—he gives the pledge of loyalty for all.

My Father, the Goethe Admirer

My father loved Goethe and we had several sets of his complete works in our house. Goethe worked all his life on his *Faust* and created a masterpiece. My father loved to speak about controversies and certainly found many of those in literature, even in works of his beloved Goethe. Therefore, I selected Father's speech about the first verses from the prologue to *Faust*, followed by two treatments of *Iphigenia* and another one about Goethe's *Theory of Colors.*

Speech on the First Verses from the Prologue to Goethe's Faust[28]

Goethe's position to the world systems of
Ptolemy, Copernicus, Pythagoras, etc.
At the Rotary Club
December 13, 1950

The first verses in Goethe's *Faust,* the songs of the archangels Raphael and Gabriel in the Prologue in Heaven, are:

Raphael	Translation by Bayard Taylor[29]
Die Sonne tönt, nach alter Weise,	The sun-orb sings, in emulation
In Brudersphären Wettgesang,	Mid brothers-spheres, his ancient round;
Und ihre vorgeschrieb'ne Reise	His path predestined through creation
Vollendet sie mit Donnergang.	He ends with step(s) of thunder-sound
Ihr Anblick gibt den Engeln Stärke,	The angels from the vision splendid
Wenn keiner sie ergründen mag;	Draw power, whose measure none can say;
Die unbegreiflich hohen Werke	The lofty works, not comprehended,
Sind herrlich wie am ersten Tag.	Are bright as on the earliest day.

28 Hermann Apelt, Reden und Schriften, page 361

29 Johann Wolfgang von Goethe, *Faust, Part One* The Bayard Taylor translation, revised and edited by Stuart Atkins, Collier Books, New York, New York, Collier-Macmillan LTD, London. Fourth Printing 1973.

Gabriel

Und schnell und unbegreiflich schnelle	And swift, and swift beyond conceiving
Dreht sich unher der Erde Pracht;	The splendor of the earth goes round,
Es wechselt Paradieseshelle	Day's Eden-brightness still relieving
Mit tiefer, schauervoller Nacht;	The awful Night's intense profound;
Es schäumt das Meer in breiten Flüssen	The ocean-tides in foam are breaking
Am tiefen Grund der Felsen auf,	Against the rocks' deep bases hurled
Und Fels und Meer wird fortgerissen	And both, the spherical race partaking,
In ewig schnellem Sphärenlauf.	Eternal, swift, are onward whirled.

Seldom have German poets achieved to glean such fullness of sound from our harsh German language. The beauty of these verses has been recognized universally. The English poet Shelley, who tried a translation, called them "this astonishing chorus" and thinks it impossible to recreate the melody of these verses in another language.

But no fruit is so beautiful that it could not fall prey to wasps. And the German schoolmaster could never hide. Even during at Goethe's life, some critics found—while not doubting the beauty of the language—that the first and the second verse demonstrated a contrast in the way the astronomers explained the world.

The *first* verse seems to follow the system that Ptolemy had summarized regarding antique findings and as the later antiquity and middle age saw the world: in the middle the immobile earth and sun, moon, and stars circling around it. The *second* verse seems to follow the picture as Copernicus formed it: in the center the sun, the earth moving around him, at the same time turning around its own axis.

So, one time it is Ptolomy and the other time Copernicus. Is that not for some schoolmasters rightly disturbing, even an insulting contradiction!

But are Ptolemy and Copernicus the only architects of world systems? Are there not any other possibilities than those two? Are there not between, before, or after others who could tolerate both, the poet and the schoolmaster? I should also mention that Copernicus, even though he allows the sun to be the center of the universe, he, the sun, does not stand still but turns around his own axis. As Schiller says so beautifully:

Da, wo jetzt, wie unsere Weisen sagen,
Seelenlos ein Feuerball sich dreht.

There, where now, as our savants say,
A soulless fireball is turning.

Neither will I elaborate about the fact that according to contemporary theory the sun is the center of *our* planetary system, but races (with all the planets) top speed on an unknown path toward an unknown goal.

Neither one would be enough to vindicate Goethe. The turning about itself is hardly a path and the movement of the entire system is so far beyond our understanding that it hardly helps to interpret Goethe's poetic work of art.

In the last two lines of the verse of Archangel Gabriel the concept *Sphärenlauf,* translated by Bayard Taylor as "spherical race," leads us to the school that taught about harmony of the heavens, the Pythagoreans.

Their picture of the world is kept with us through Philolaus who lived around the same time of Socrates. (ca 354 B.C.) How did he see the relationship of movement between Earth to sun, moon, and stars? This is what he thought: he had the sun circle, not the earth, but together with the earth a central fire or "hearth of Vesta," positioned in the center of his system. Around this fire circled on the plain of the zodiac (the ecliptic) the five major planets, Venus, Mercury, Mars, Jupiter, and Saturn, also the sun and the moon, each in his own sphere. The outermost sphere is the sky with the fixed stars. The earth also circles the central fire, but on a different plain, the equator. The two planes are angled to each other. This theory would agree with scientific observations, but now he adds a mythical hypothesis: he invents another heavenly body, the so-called *Gegenerde* (anti-earth) that circles between Earth and Central Fire. *(Actually Philolaus believed in the harmony of numbers and needed one more heavenly body for his system of the world to make it ten. But my father did not want to go this far into the Pythagorean system.)*

Here we have neither Ptolemy nor Copernicus, but we have both, Sun and Earth circling. Day and night, as well as the seasons, are regulated by the different speeds. Earth completes its circle in 24 hours, the moon in a month, the sun and the inner planets in a year, Mars in two years, Jupiter in twelve years, Saturn in 30 years, and the fixed stars in an infinite number of years.

Simultaneously this system fits in with the basics of Pythagorean's teaching of harmony of the cosmos and spherical harmony. Even light and sound are included in this theory. But still, all of this is not quite satisfactory. Though the sun is completing its destined journey, though *Fels und Meer* (ocean tides and rocks) are hurled away by Earth's spherical race, but how about the turning around its own axis? It seems that this is missing in Philolaus' theory.

My father elaborates this quite in depth, even cites his own grandfather, Ernst Friedrich Apelt[30], who knew about Philolaus through a thesis by August Böck of 1819 which he used and supplemented in his own works about *Die Epochen der Geschichte der Menschheit* (Epochs of the History of Man). Goethe most likely did not know about Philolaus.

Anyway, Goethe might not have known all of these details; neither would he have been bothered by the critics. He might have smiled and explained that it is the right of an artist, be it in the field of painting, writing, or science, to look beyond nature and allow possible inconsistencies.

In a dialogue with Eckermann, his good friend, he points out several examples of this and closes with this statement: "At all times we should not criticize an artist with painstaking little controversies. We should take and enjoy what has been created with a free and bold spirit."

And so, my father concludes his speech:

I think Goethe could use this *dichterische Freiheit* (poet's right) to defend his own verses. If he was inclined to describe the racing sun of

30 Ernst Friedrich Apelt, 1812-1859, German philosopher and factory owner. He wrote several books. *Die Epochen der Geschichte der Menschheit,* Eine historisch-philosophische Skizze, Jena, 1851, 2 Bände; *Johann Kepler's astronomische Weltansicht,* Leipzig, 1849; *Die Reformation der Sternkunde,* Jena, 1852; *Die Theory der Induktion,* Leipzig, 1854; *Metaphysik,* Leipzig, 1857; *Religionsphilosophie,* Leipzig, 1860.

Ptolemy in his first verse, but the turning earth of Copernicus in his second verse, so he could not be touched by voices of critics and offended by controversy of logical thinking. His verse remains:

"Herrlich wie am ersten Tag."

Splendid as on the first day.

Speech on Goethe's Iphigenia[31]

At the Rotary Club

March 22, 1935

This was the time in my father's life when he was not working in the Senate. This was the time of Hitler's rule and a Nazi Senate. The ex-senators had to return to their old jobs to make a living. My father worked as an attorney again. He had more leisure during this time and was frequently asked by various organizations to speak.

Dear Fellow Rotarians.

Today is the day of Goethe's death.

It might be appropriate—while according to date, though not contemporary—to speak about Goethe's *Iphigenia.*

Iphigenia is the purest expression, the noblest poetic form of the ideal of our classic era, of the ideal of humanity—told by Herder, formed by Goethe, and lived by Humboldt. Also by the idealistic masculine power of Schiller and, thought more strictly, the teaching of duty by Kant and Fichte.

This spiritual-moral creation—united in its threefold meaning as the German idealisms in the right understanding—was, until now, the last one of European importance.

As far as it, overlaid by other thoughts, has stayed alive, should not be examined. In any case nothing of same value has been substituted for it.

Today we are anticipating a time that shakes everything, that seriously wants to change values, doing this with solemn ambition, also—or better

31 Hermann Apelt, Reden und Schriften, page 343. Though the spelling is *Iphigenie* in German, I chose to use the English spelling of "Iphigenia" throughout this document.

primarily—in order to renew the moral thought structure. The ancient ideas are paling—behold, everything has to become new!

To know that the moral perspectives are also changing does not need today's experience. Every speck of knowledge about the development of mankind proves it. Nevertheless—as certain as every era has its own moral pathos, as much as it might differ in emphasis, clothing, outer appearance—from the Greek dramatists and Plato to the Gospels and from there to the teachings of humanity of our classics there exists a common overall truth and immortality. It may have new forms, it may retreat behind necessities brought on by outer conditions that overlap it, but it will never need to contradict it. As difference and unity go hand in hand, or better, the sameness may appear different, will be clarified through the various judgments that Goethe's *Iphigenia* has experienced. Some critics see the drama as genuine "Greekdom," others merely as Greek appearance. Even if Schlegel called Goethe's drama an "Echo of Greek singing" and if otherwise the British writer Lewis said, "We can't measure Goethe's *Iphigenia* with Greek rulers any longer; that play is German,"—this may not be important to us. But Schiller's judgment is more significant. One time in the treatise of 1787 he indicates, "One cannot read this piece without being touched by a certain breath of antiquity, here one finds the overwhelming tranquility that makes every antique work so unattainable." Another time, in a letter to Körner in 1803, he calls *Iphigenia* so amazingly modern and non-Greek that one cannot understand how it was possible to ever compare the play with a Greek drama.

Both opinions are correct and incorrect at the same time, each one gives us part of the truth. And maybe it was the happiest formula—I believe it comes down from Victor Hehn—that Goethe's *Iphigenia* presents the true marriage of Faust and Helena. Nobody can proclaim to be just "living in different times." Everyone, even the greatest, is firstly a child of *his* time, but according to his greatness, one will be more, the other less, independent of his contemporary era.

Shakespeare's Romans certainly weren't genuine Romans but pure Elizabethans. But, at the same time, they were more than that—and with this *more* they had their share of Roman greatness.

Likewise, we will not meet genuine Romans in Goethe's *Iphigenia* but real Germans of the 18th century in Greek clothing. But they also are *more* than that—and with this *more* they have their share of the Greek spirit or even better: they are conjointly members of a higher empire of that Germans and Greeks have equal shares; in that the best of Germany meets the best of Greece.

Schiller founded his later judgment, rebuking the "Greekdom" of Goethe's drama, firstly with the words, "She is completely moral." Well, this might be so—but even if the Greek tragedy was not exactly "only moral," at least it was "also moral." Point in case, it strove to answer moral questions. That it also strove to gain pure humanity makes it partly so immortally valuable—and in this striving it meets here with Herder and Goethe. This becomes especially clear when one is familiar with the development of the saga about *Iphigenia* and the treatment of it here by the Greeks and there by Goethe.

Racine begins the preface to his *Iphigenia* with the words: *"A rien il n'y de plus celebre dans les poetes que le sacrifice d'Iphigenie."* (Nothing is more renowned among poets than the sacrifice of Iphigenia.)

Indeed—few materials have had such importance in the European dramatic literature as the sacrifice of Iphigenia. All of the great Greek tragedians have used the material, though the plays by Aeschylus and Sophocles have been lost and only the two plays by Euripides remain. For both, the classic French as well as the German stage the treatment of the material, there by Racine, here by Goethe, signify a zenith. How much Goethe was involved in the concept of Iphigenia, is apparent in the fact that he was planning to write another play, *Iphigenia in Delphi.* Schiller expressed his interest in the material by translating *Iphigenia in Aulis* by Euripides. Finally it should not be forgotten the influence on the modern opera by Gluck's two treatments of *Iphigenia.*

The subject of the saga of *Iphigenia* is the sacrifice of man and especially of one's own child. For the people of Athens at the time of the tragedians, the time of human sacrifice was over—but its decline remains a typical example for the transition from more coarse to more human manner, a symbol for the division between barbarism and morality.

Almost all nations have at some point in history been involved with human sacrifice (the most poignant form of which is the sacrifice of one's own child), but no place has this struggle happened so obviously as in Greece and with the Jews. Often and rightfully so has this been mentioned in research of the Old Testament and the Greek sagas. There are parallels from mythical times: there Abraham and Isaac, here Agamemnon and Iphigenia. In both cases the gods are satisfied with the obedience and substitute an animal at the decisive moment. ...

The material about Iphigenia has three parts:

1. Iphigenia's sacrifice or *Iphigenia in Aulis.*
2. Iphigenia's liberation or *Iphigenia in Tauris.*
3. Iphigenia's return home or *Iphigenia in Delphi.*

The subject of the first part is the sacrifice of the child, the second is about human sacrifice in general, in the third the human sacrifice is just background and the reason to commit revenge. Because no play from the third part remains today—even Goethe's *Iphigenia in Delphi* is just a plan—we may just concentrate on the two others. We have both in the treatment by Euripides, then the first by Racine and the second by Goethe. Therefore, we have the possibility to compare the plays in ancient and modern versions. Racine did the comparison by himself; Schiller did it for Goethe as did later some others. The point is to demonstrate that the striving for humanity was not invented by Goethe, but that at least a direction toward this striving already existed with the Greeks.

Homer does not know anything about Iphigenia's sacrifice. According to him King Agamemnon offers his daughter to the angry Achilles for marriage. Odysseus is the go-between. According to Homer there are three daughters besides the baby Orestes and Agamemnon feels obliged to soothe Achilles' ruffled feelings so the Greeks can besiege the Trojans. According to Herodot the idea of human sacrifice was started by the Barbarians in Tauris and somehow the figure of the goddess was entwined with that of the virgin daughter of Agamemnon.

Since now a lengthy contemplation about the origin of the saga about Iphigenia follows, I leave portions of the speech out and just give the essence of it. It shows that my father had actually read and studied many ancient and modern authors and was trying to prove that there was a trend to humanize cruel barbarian rituals.

The summary of the drama of Aulis is this: The Trojan prince, Paris, has robbed the Greek ruler Menelaos' beautiful wife, Helena, and the Greeks are revenging this robbery by attacking Troy. On the way, the Greeks' fleet is stuck by the absence of wind and the goddess Diana (also called Artemis, responsible for birth) demands the sacrifice of the king's eldest daughter. This, in Goethe's play, is told to the Taurian king Thaos by Iphigenia herself. She was not really killed but taken away by the goddess, replaced by a female deer, and carried from Aulis to Tauria to become Diana's priestess there. The essence of the old Greeks' tales is that the father really killed his own daughter for political purposes. There are citations from Ovid, Aischilos, Sophokles, and indications of Pindar, Lucrez, Virgil, and Horaz, even of Fredrick the Great (in French) quoting Racine, to prove the point that the sacrifice really took place, but that somehow even the ancient poets had to find a more human ending.

In 1935, my father was then almost at the age of retirement, but still fully occupied by his profession and found the time and leisure to read texts in their original language and even do the most difficult of all composing: comparison and finding agreements and contrast in his studies. I remember him coming home, having the midday meal with us and then lying down on the sofa, book in hand, glasses on his nose, but soon fast asleep for a few minutes, getting up refreshed and leaving again for work until 8:00 in the evening. How could he do all this in one day? Now back to Iphigenia in Goethe's play (I shall continue this long speech a little)...

Now to Iphigenia in Tauris. Here we find essentially in the plays of Euripides, Racine, and Goethe that now Iphigenia is priestess in barbarian Tauris, serving a king who believes that the goddess needs human blood, and who hates the Greeks and will kill any Greeks that shipwreck on their shores, but is amazed by her apparent humanity. Orest, who was a mere baby in Aulis, is now a man followed by furies for the murder of his own mother, and has no idea that his sister is still alive and no less the priestess who will conduct his sacrifice. He is promised by the oracle of Apollo that he will be redeemed if he brings Diana's statue home to Greece. Therefore, to the crime of murdering one's child, the crime of slaughtering one's relative is added. Other versions, again cited from ancient writers, suggest the killing of the host on Taurus, which introduces the sacred cow of the Greeks: the breach of right of visitors to be treated humanely. Finally, using the theatrical medium of "*deos ex machina*" (either a mechanical device or, as in this case, an un-introduced person or god that is used to advance the plot of a play), the goddess Athena appears and demands a change in the traditional way of human sacrifice: instead of *killing* the person, it will only be indicated by making a small incision at the neck. Then everyone is satisfied: the goddess has a little blood, the man or woman is still alive. This leads to the final comparison between Euripides and Goethe:

1. Euripides lets his Iphigenia lie to Thoas and succeed in getting away with her brother alive and the statue of Diana. Goethe has his Iphigenia listen to Pylades' invention of lies, but she can't follow through and speaks the truth.
2. Euripides has Thoas give in to the fact that he loses his priestess as well as the statue. Goethe's beautiful ending has the statue stay in Taurus.
3. In Euripides' drama, Thoas' intentions of bloody revenge are only checked by the appearance of Athena. In Goethe's play, the declaration of truth changes Thoas' mind.
4. In Euripides' version, the reversal of human sacrifice is triggered by divine order. Goethe has Iphigenia do this through her purity.
5. Euripides has the successful flight and healing of Orest occur as a consequence of the oracle in Delphia. Goethe has both occur as consequence of Iphigenia's pure human character.

However, even if Goethe went farther in his way to show human perfection, we also find the same tendency in Euripides. There is a difference, but the difference is not a contrast. The tendency is the same—toward pure humanity. The greatest variance in Goethe is that he denies the lying and stresses telling the truth. There is a parallel to the story of Philoctet in Sophokles' drama where Neoptolemos first lies and then tells the truth. Odysseus, the king of lies, is rebuked by a changed Neoptolemos.

So, reverence to human life—*you shall not kill*—truth as a fundamental part of human morality—*you shall not bear false witness against thy neighbor*—has been taught by the Greek tragedians there and by Goethe here—each one in their own language in their own time.

However, this very last step: to tell the truth by one's own conviction is only found in Goethe's play. Sophocles still needs to insert the appearance of Athena to accomplish what Iphigenia does by herself, to conquer the wrath of Thoas and to heal her brother's madness.

This *(and I quote my father as he ends his speech)* is the meaning of the following verse that Goethe wrote in a copy of the *Iphiginia* in the possession of the actor Krüger in 1827, I *(my father)* own the original copy of this verse which gave me the idea to make this speech.

Was der Dichter diesem Bande
Glaubend, hoffend anvertraut,
Werd' im Kreise deutscher Lande
Durch des Künstlers Wirken laut.
So im Handeln wie im Sprechen
Liebevoll verkünd' es weit:
Alle menschlichen Gebrechen
Sühnet reine Menschlichkeit.

What the poet is dedicating
In this volume believing hopefully,
Will within German lands
Be expressed loudly through the artist.
Therefore through deed as well as speaking
Be the message spread lovingly:
Every human inadequacy
Will be redeemed by pure humanity.

I find it interesting to compare two writings about the same subjects (one a speech, the other an essay) about the same subject, created 25 years apart—the speech in 1935, the essay in 1960. Both were written during a time when Father was not occupied by all the time-consuming work in the Senate.

Zwischen Euripides und Goethe[32]

Between Euripides and Goethe

Essay in the *Jahrbuch der Goethe-Gesellschaft*

1960

My father was always interested in Greek mythology and the ancient tragedians. More than my older sisters, I benefited from this interest. My father and I took frequent walks together and he loved to narrate many Greek stories and found me to be an attentive listener. For Christmas and my birthday, I received books telling these stories. In fact, my background in Greek mythology was sufficient to teach a course about this subject while substituting long-term at one of the Hayward high schools in California. However, while I was satisfied just knowing the main plots of the stories, my father was probing deeper into the various versions and tendencies of the ancient writers who had created them, as well as the modern playwrights and composers of operas dealing with Greek material. Since he knew Greek, Latin, and French, besides German and English, he had been able to read everything in its original form. Having relied heavily on Racine as one step between Goethe and Euripides in his speech in 1935, when he had been replaced from his demanding job as senator for the ports, navigation, and traffic by a Nazi and had "only" his clients from his attorney office

32 Goethe, neue Folge des Jahrbuchs der Goethe-Gesellschaft, herausgegeben von Andreas B. Wachsmuth, Sonderdruck, im Buchhandel einzeln nicht käuflich. 22ster Band, Hermann Böhlaus Nachf. /Weimar 1960.

to take care of, he was retired now in 1960 and only worked part-time. In his last year of life, he went back to the story of Iphigenia and now added another step of his comparison between Goethe and Euripides: the opera by Christoph Willibalt Gluck (1714-1787). Maybe the performance of this opera in the Bremen Theater had triggered this second research. This time he did not speak be wrote an essay for the Goethe Society in Weimar. This essay was printed and published two years after my father's death.

Years ago, I occupied myself with a comparison of the two dramas about Iphigenia on Taurus, treated by (ancient) Euripides (480-406 B.C.) and (modern) Goethe (1749-1832 A.D.). I intend to show that Goethe's striving to demonstrate humanity is not meant to be a contrast to Euripides, but rather that both great playwrights are moving closer to a common goal step by step. My motivation was the beautiful dedication that Goethe wrote in the *Iphigenia* book of the actor Krüger on March 31, 1827. The last two lines are as follows:

Alle menschlichen Gebrechen
Sühnet reine Menschlichkeit.

All human deficiencies
Are redeemed by pure humanity.

When I held the speech on Goethe's death date back in 1935, someone from the audience mentioned to me that it had been Gluck's opera that had motivated Goethe to work with the material. Only now (after retirement), I found the time to examine this question and study this problem: Did Goethe merely noticed Gluck's libretto or did this opera really inspire him to write his drama?

The first performance of Gluck's French version of *Iphigenia* took place on May 18, 1779 in Paris. At this time, Goethe had just finished the first prose version of his *Iphigenia*. This excludes the theory that Goethe was motivated to start working on the material. However, Goethe had seen a performance of Gluck's *Iphigenia in Aulis* (in 1774). So he probably knew about the other opera and it is possible that the composer and the playwright were working at the same time on the same material.

Goethe was familiar with Gluck and even wrote the text to a cantata for a niece of Gluck. But did Goethe really *need* any more motivation to treat the *Iphigenia* material? He had been familiar with Jean Racine from his youth on, and often spoke to Herder and Winkelmann about the Greeks. Neither was Gluck the first opera composer who was interested in Greek writings. Already in 1759 the Italian Traetta had composed an *Iphigenia in Tauride.* Gluck's libretto derives from the French poet Guillard (1752-1814) who got his ideas from the playwright Guimond de la Touche (1723-1780) who wrote his *Iphigenia*. This play is more or less derived from Euripides' version, but also shows essential differences.

Now follows a minute description of Guillard's play that has more characters then the one of Euripides as well as Goethe's. Iphigenia has two friends, Ismene and Eumene, who assist her in trying to help the two captured Greeks. Thoas' assistant is not Arcas (Goethe), but Arbas, the name only differing by one consonant. My father quotes several lines in French, demonstrating that he studied Guillard's work in that language.

The result of my father's research of comparison between Guimond and Euripides is, in a nutshell:

1) Guimond emphasises Iphigenia's aversion to the custom of sacrifice more. In Goethe's version, the Barbars have desisted from sacrifice altogether.
2) While in Euripides' play the attack of Orest's madness is just told, Guimond has it acted out on stage, as has Goethe.
3) Just as in Guimond's play ghosts of mother and Aegisthos appear and Orestes also thinks that his friend Pylades is a shadow, Goethe also has the three appear as shadows, but in an amicable relationship.
4) In all plays, Iphigenia exudes a soothing influence on Orestes. Here Guimond touches a motive that for Goethe becomes the main motive to work with the material of the Iphigenia saga.

5) Guimond is following Euripides in having Iphigenia write a letter to one of her family members in Argos (to brother Orestes in Euripides', to sister Electra in Guimond's play). Goethe does not use the letter motive since the acknowledgment of brother and sister happens independently.
6) No "*deus ex machina*" in Goethe. Instead he finds the truly humanistic solution, while Guimond—in contrast to Euripides—has the men plot to kill Thoas. Euripides denies this because it interferes with the Greeks highly respected law of honoring one's host.
7) It seems more than pure chance that the names for the king's assistance, here Arcas, there Arbas—though the two characters are rather different—sound so similar. And there is a third similar name in Racine's Iphigénia: Arcas: he is King Agamemnon's loyal servant in Aulis who fetches Chlytemnestra and Iphigenia from their home in Argos.

My father definitely took his research to Weimar and asked at the Goethe-Gesellschaft as well as at the library for a copy of Guimond's text. The playwright died in 1750 when Goethe was one year old. His play had been printed and staged shortly before his death, but none of the above mentioned literary places had copies available. According to my father this Guillard was not a very famous writer or else his works would have been easily available in Weimar, the seat of German literary culture.

Racine might have influenced Goethe with his fragment of *Iphigénie en Tauride.* Goethe might have known this unfinished play. These are some points of contrast between Goethe, Racine, and Euripides:

1) In Racine's play Thoas has a son, in Euripides' drama there is no son, and in Goethe's version Thoas had a son but he was slain in the war.

2) Racine has the son of Thoas love Iphigenia passionately, no love motive in Euripides, and Goethe lets Thoas woo for Iphigenia's hand.
3) Racine keeps Thoas ignorant of Iphigenia's royal descent. The same is true for Goethe's play. It is typical in Racine's play that King Thoas is against a marriage between his son and his priestess because of the difference in background.
4) Even more pronounced is Iphigenia's aversion to sacrifice humans for the goddess.

No one will know if Goethe has been influenced by Racine or Guillard. This might be regrettable from both literary and philosophical point of view. It is always worth the effort to follow the reappearance of poetic material through the course of time. It would not be without enticement to see which of the two following possibilities concerning the relationship between Goethe and Racine, as well as Goethe and Guimond would be true: whether two not too distant in time (about 100 years between Goethe and Racine, about one human generation between Goethe and Guimond) would treat the same material and come to the same conclusion, or if one had altered the motives and had influenced the other.

However, to judge the aesthetic value of Goethe's drama—be it that he had been influenced by Racine or by Guimond—it does not infringe on Goethe's legacy one way or the other. The lesson of humanity in Guimond's work sounds a little preachy. Only in Goethe's *Iphigenia,* humanity and its redeeming, healthy, and compromising power found its living manifestation.

Only when also the character of King Thoas is included into the circle of humanity, there could be a solution without "*deus ex machina*" and without the idea of murdering the host. Only through the beautiful thought that Apollo had not meant the picture of his sister to be brought to Argos, but of Orest's sister, Iphigenia, an all consoling solution could be found.

As both, Orestes and Iphigenia, detest lies and untruths and therefore prove to be of one family, as this noble characteristic leads to recognition of the siblings—between us shall be truth, says Orestes—and as then the same feeling in Iphigenia's breast leads her to be truthful to Thoas also and he is overwhelmed by Iphigenia's purity and morality; that is completely Goethe and neither Euripides nor Racine nor Guimond. And maybe it is not an exaggeration to say that just the song of the Parzen in its beauty and grandness overshadows the entire drama of Guimond.

Afterword

When Goethe, in his letter to Schiller on January 19, 1802, calls his Iphigenia "bedeviled human," one could detect a recant or at least a limitation to his declaration for humanity. But even so, there is no more beautiful recant of a recant than the verses that, as already mentioned, the elderly Goethe dedicated to the actor Krüger. Also the words that Goethe wrote at the same time to Zelter sounded a little resigned—"Why should I remember those days when I felt, thought, and wrote all of that"—cannot minimize the weight of those verses.

Just as Gluck and Goethe worked on the same material in the year 1779, unaware of one another, and just as only a few weeks apart both Taurish *Iphigenias*, drama and opera, experienced their first staging, the drama in Ettersburg, the opera in Paris, so it came to pass half a century later that both works followed each other with only a distance of one year on the stage in Weimar. Both performances were made immortal by Goethe's words. On June 12, 1826 Goethe wrote to the singer Frau Milder:

Das unschuldvolle, fromme Spiel,
Das edlen Beifall sich errungen,
Erreichte doch eine höhres Ziel
Von Gluck betont, von dir gesungen.

The innocent, pious play,
That earned honorable applause,
Achieved an even higher goal
From Gluck composed, sung by you.

On March 31, 1827, he wrote to the actor Krüger, who had played Orestes, the verses that have already been mentioned above.

Goethe's Color Theory[33]

Speech held in the second half of WWII

Goethe lived 1749-1832

In his treatise about the *Farbenlehre* (Theory of Colors), Goethe's view contradicts that of Isaac Newton. While Newton uses mathematic formulas to develop his theory that light consists of seven different components, each, as we know now, of different wavelength, Goethe states that light cannot be divided. If impurities get into light, colors develop. Goethe was adamant about this and tried to prove Newton's wrong. This became a regular fight because Newton seemed untouchable in his realm as a physics specialist and mathematician. I loved physics in high school and learned, of course, Newton's way of explaining colors, but was also impressed with Goethe's idea of the *Urphänomen* and indivisibility of white light. How can something white contain seven colors? We could see the rainbow, but how does one explain those seven colors? Anyway, my father and I studied Goethe's book together and I did not become much wiser. Neither did I understand the wave theory. But I agree with Goethe that light is beautiful and should not be touched or dissected. Now I shall let my father speak…

33 Hermann Apelt, Reden und Schriften, Page 353. Excerpt of a speech titled *Goethe als Forscher und Denker*

The battlefield narrowed when Goethe had constructed his own Theory of Colors and defended it against Newton's Optic.[34] *(Newton died before Goethe was born.)*

It is possible that the battle in its concrete form, according to the formulation of the debate, may be based upon a misunderstanding. Could it be that Goethe did Newton injustice? Could it be that there is some common ground that rectifies both theories? But for us this is not essential, though for Goethe it was very important to believe in the unity of light and to disregard the divisibility of light into seven colors as Newton teaches. For us this fight has symbolic importance; Goethe's reason has a deeper root than the controversial issue. Newton, master of the natural sciences, condenses everything into a mathematical formula—his idea is objective—and Goethe, the teacher of the *Urphänomen* (archetype, an original model), has an idea that everything that we behold with our senses can be explained with one form—his idea is subjective. Those two ideas are representing opposite standpoints. But besides this controversy Goethe's *Farbenlehre* (Theory of Colors)—by the way his longest piece of writing—is a book of immense wealth of material and written in beautiful language, as probably few scientific works.

Goethe felt that the domineering and demanding claims of the mathematical sciences attacked the nucleus of his thinking. Especially he felt personally attacked if the issue was "light." To him—the man of visual sensitivity to whom the sense of sight was the most perfected—the eye was comparable to the sun, and to him it was a crime that the mathematicians also dissected the light and subdued the colors to calculation. Especially in the realm of light, he believed strongest in the *Urphänomen,* and used it to contradict the hated idea of cutting up the light. This is the only explanation why Goethe became a grim and inconsolable controversialist and even went so far to attack his great dead opponent and to suspect him of fraud. His fight against the deceased was not about a scientific theory; it was a battle of upholding his inner core and at the same time to uphold truth for the coming generation, even for mankind. If he was understood or not, he still aided the sciences to build the dam that the German idealism, classicism, and romanticism was erecting against Western dissolving influences, as the teaching of mechanics and the French revolution. (My father compares these influences with a flood.) This flood was halted, but not for long. Then it destroyed the dam and broke with all force

34 Sir Isaac Newton, 1642-1727. Johann Wolfgang von Goethe, 1749-1832.

into the 19th century. In the future, will this flood turn around? Or maybe we stand already in the backwater?

So much for the reference to Goethe's Theory of Colors. The title of the speech is *Goethe als Forscher und Denker* (Goethe as Scientist and Thinker). The entire speech is about Goethe's wish to make us all understand the dangers of analytical and abstract thinking. Synthesis is his way and this includes to stay in the realm of our senses and not to touch things we cannot understand because of the way we are created. I quote another paragraph in this speech and attempt to translate it (from page 356):

> *Goethe erklärte es für das schönste Glück des denkenden Menschen, das Erforschliche erforscht zu haben und das Unerforschliche ruhig zu verehren. An dieses, das Unerforschliche, wollte er nicht rühren lassen. Daß die mechanische Betrachtungsweise ein ihrer Sphäre entzogenes Unerforschliches nicht anerkennen wollte, schien ihm unfromm und Vermessenheit.*
>
> Goethe declared that for the thinking human being the greatest happiness is to have researched the discoverable and to quietly admire the things we cannot grasp. He did not allow touching things beyond our knowledge. To him it seemed disrespectful and anti-religious of the mechanical way to research things that could not be researched with our senses.

Schillers Dramas[35]

Schiller lived 1759-1805

Speech to Celebrate His 200th Birthday

Given in 1959

Schiller's and Goethe's poems and dramas were the nucleus of German literature taught to us in our German classes. I can still recite passages from Goethe's *Torquato Tasso* and Schiller's *Wilhelm Tell.* My father not only knew all those dramas almost by heart and had seen each one at least once on stage, he also compared them and found their common denominator. While Goethe's talents and interests were multi-faceted, Schiller's were concentrated on literary works. His dramas are especially beautiful and expressive. I do miss this part of my earlier life more than anything else. Here in America, German drama is not performed, mostly I think, because there are not many, if any, good translations. How does one translate something so perfect anyway? So I let my father explain the most famous of Schiller's dramas.

The great theme, the keyword of Schiller's thoughts and writings, is "freedom." His good friend Goethe says, "All the works of Schiller are saturated with the idea of freedom."

As the light breaks up into many colors with the prism, so does the light ray of freedom of thought, of thinking and life, of mankind

35 Hermann Apelt, Reden und Schriften, page 395

breaking up into various ways: from the physical freedom via the political independence to the inner and outer political freedom, to the outer and inner spiritual freedom, and finally to the moral freedom of responsible action. All these fractions mirror the thought of freedom in Schiller's thinking and poetry.

The title page of his drama *Die Räuber* (The Robbers) displays an agitated lion, surrounded by the words *in tyrannos.* This preface to his first work would have also been a fitting preface to his last work, *Wilhelm Tell.* There the misled fight of one person against despotism and injustice, here the fight of a whole nation for freedom and rights.

In *Fiesco* it is the battle for political freedom.

Kabale und Liebe is a courageous indictment against the absolutism.

Maria Stuart's futile fight for physical freedom eventually leads to inner freedom.

Johanna dies to gain the freedom for her fatherland (France) against the English conqueror. She also wins back the threatened inner freedom of her soul. However, in no other drama of Schiller is the thought of freedom expressed more forcefully and ravishing than in *Don Carlos.* The Netherlands is the background for the drama. In a peculiar way the relationships of love and friendship are woven together with the battle against force that stifles him and the interceding of Posa in favor of the Netherlands and freedom at all, culminating in the famous words: *Give me freedom of thought!* (Allow me to think what I want!) And as the *Räuber Moor* is giving himself over to the judge, so does Posa take his own life in order to save his friend and also freedom.

It was Schiller's very own experiences that led to the creation of his powerful dramas. He had to suffer spiritual oppression bitterly. The fate of Schubart[36] had shown him what was waiting for him if he would allow his spirit to run freely. Only the flight from Württemberg could save him. But he had to pay dearly for his freedom. "*Die Räuber,*" as he writes later, "cost me my family and my homeland." And even if he gained physical freedom through the escape, he now had to endure tough economic difficulties. He writes to the Danish poet Baggesen in 1791:

36 The poet Christian Friedrich Daniel Schubart was held in the prison *Hohen Asperg* in Württemberg from 1777 to 1787 without interrogation, indictment, or sentence. Schiller was able to flee to the *Kurpfalz.*

"Von der Wiege meines Geistes an bis jetzt, da ich dieses schreibe, habe ich mit dem Schicksal gekämpft, und seitdem ich die Freiheit des Geistes *zu schätzen weiß, war ich verurteilt, sie zu entbehren."*

"From the cradle of my spirit until now, while I am writing this, I had to fight with my fate. Since the time I appreciate the *freedom of the spirit*, I was condemned to do without it."

Needless to say, for Schiller *freedom* never meant *licentiousness.* Above all stands *moral freedom.* Here he becomes close to Kant. So it says in a letter to the Duke of Augustenburg on July 13, 1793:

> *"Nur seine Fähigkeit, als sittliches Wesen zu handeln, gibt dem Menschen Anspruch auf Freiheit; ein Gemüt aber, das nur sinnlicher Bestimmungen fähig ist, ist der Freiheit so wenig* wert *als* empfänglich."
>
> "Only the ability to act as a moral person gives one the right to freedom, but a human being that only acts from sensual stimuli is neither *worthy* of freedom *nor receptive."*

Schiller's *aesthetic* world is also governed by the idea of freedom. He calls Fine Arts *"Daughter of Freedom"* and *"Free Sons of the Freest Mother."*

"Freedom in Appearance" was his formula for the concept of *Beauty.* And his theory of the *Tragic* was based on the concept of the *Independence of the Laws of Nature.*

As Goethe with his *Götz von Berlichingen* and his *Leiden des jungen Werthers,* so also Schiller had extraordinary success with his *Die Räuber.* He became famous at the age of twenty-three. However, *Fiesco* and *Kabale und Liebe* could not reach the success of *Die Räuber.* But with *Don Carlos* Schiller won, on a higher level, the applause and hearts of a large audience. And when he, several years later—he dedicated this pause mostly to history and philosophy—returned to drama and stage; there was no doubt that he—even if Kotzebue and Iffland knew how to please the masses—was the master of German tragedy.

In the remaining short time span, when he wrote no less than four dramas, his renown was steadily rising. This even continued half a century after his early death. No other German poet had been given this measure of veneration and love by the people as Schiller.

The curve of his glory reached its zenith in the middle of the 19th century. The commemoration of his 100th birthday anniversary was celebrated with an incomparable feast, shared with the entire nation. How high the excitement in Bremen rose can be read in old reports. The citizens expressed their elated feelings with a parade of torch bearers on the market place. It might have been the only time that a German writer has been glorified in this way by his nation. Schiller's influence reached far beyond Germany's borders. How deep an impression he made on Puschkin and Dostojevski *(the English version)* is well known. I will never forget when my great-grandmother, who was Swedish, told us children about the Schiller festivities in Upsala that she had attended in 1859.

Schiller had the gift of expressing the noblest feelings of the people with the flow of his thoughts and the power of his words. How his message of the *ideals of freedom* must have echoed in the time of utmost oppression by Napoleon whose figure had darkened the horizon already at Schiller's time!

Just before I came to this country, I had the chance to see an excellent performance of *Don Carlos* that I preserved in my memory all my life. This play, as well as *Torquato Tasso* by Goethe and *Der Prinz von Homburg* by Kleist, gave me the understanding of the struggle of young, talented human beings to be heard by the world, only to be subdued and crushed by the harsh and overruling powers above them.

As we all know, Schiller died of consumption, a poor man, only 46 years old. However, he died a free man.

My father points out that not everything was a bed of roses for Schiller. How critics and other negative voices diminished his reputation; how it became almost a wise thing to say derogative things about Schiller. But those times have changed and in his day (in 1959), Schiller was judged again more justly. Looking back, my father says:

… more of Schiller's spirit (freedom) and less of Nietzsche's spirit (superman) would have been healthier for our nation. I dare to say that

Schiller-nearness means spiritual-moral ascent; Schiller-distance means spiritual-moral descent ...

In the prolog to *Wallenstein's Lager*, it says:

Wer dem Besten seiner Zeit genug
Getan, der hat gelebt für alle Zeiten.

He who has worked for the best of his time
Has lived for all times.

My father ends his speech with Goethe's epilogue to Schiller's *Glocke*:

Denn er war unser! Mag das stolze Wort
Den lauten Schmerz gewaltig übertönen!
Er mochte sich bei uns, im sicheren Port,
Nach wildem Sturm, zum Dauernden gewöhnen.
Indessen schritt sein Geist gewaltig fort
Ins Ewige des Wahren, Guten, Schönen,
Und hinter ihm, in wesenlosem Scheine
Lag, was uns alle bändigt, das Gemeine.

For he was ours! May the proud word
Powerfully overrule the loud pain!
He would be here with us, in our secure port,
After a raging storm, getting used to constancy.
Meanwhile his spirit progressed immensely
Into eternity of truth, purity, and beauty
And what's left behind him without essence,
Was, what restrains all of us, the vulgar.

Alcestis[37]

Essay from the Weser-Zeitung, March 1914

Another debate about a controversy, this time a performance of the ancient play *Alcestis* (in a modern version) which was performed in our local Theater. Since I am always interested in Greek Mythology, I selected this essay, written just before my father enlisted as soldier.

Dilettantes are planning to present a performance of *Alcestis* by Euripedes at our *Stadttheater* (Bremen's theater). This will be the translation or more correct, the condensed copy of Euripides' written by Hugo von Hofmannsthal. Apparently this is a double risk: on one hand the difficulty of acting the play, on the other hand the antiquity of the material and moreover the unaccustomed world of feelings and thoughts. But perhaps this dilettante try is justified by choosing a play that is not frequently shown on our stages.

The literary circles in Germany were well acquainted with the story of Admetus and Alcestis at the time of the classics. Wieland has treated the saga dramatically, then Herder. Goethe has written a humorous farce about it, *Gods, Heroes, and Wieland.* Gluck has used it for one of his operas. Today the material is not popular anymore. Wieland's and Herder's pieces are forgotten; Goethe's satire has kept its vigor still, but naturally people see it more as a literary-historical piece. Gluck's Alcestis does not belong to those performances that are favored by repertoires of theaters and opera houses. And Hofmannsthal's copy has not stirred up much interest so far. Therefore, I would like to give a short introduction to the play.

37 Hermann Apelt, Reden und Schriften, page 367, *Artikel über die Alkestis.* Though the spelling is *Alkestis* in German, I chose to use the English spelling of "Alcestis" throughout this document.

The Greek saga of old tells us Apollo had slain the Cyclops, the servants of Zeus. For punishment, Zeus expelled him for a while from Olympus and forced him to serve a mortal. Apollo found friendly reception in Pherae, at the home of Prince Admetus. Here he served by caring for the cattle with other shepherds; here he sat with the slaves at table, he a slave himself. But friendship between him and his hospitable host kept them amicably together. The peaceful presence of the god was felt by people as well as by animals—his zither playing even tamed the beasts of prey, so that wolf and fox joined the herd peacefully. After a while, the god was forgiven and returned to Olympus; and Admetus had become king after his old father had retired. He married the beautiful young Alcemis who gave him two lovely children and lived a happy and blessed life at her side. Then Apollo heard that the Moirai (goddesses of fate) had decided that Admetus should die. He felt pity and gratefulness to the man who had taken him, the exiled god, into his home and had treated him well. He persuaded the strict Moirai to let him live, provided he could find someone who was willing to die in his stead. Happily he made haste to go to the house of his old host. Meanwhile Admetus had asked all of his family and friends if someone would be willing to die in his stead but no one would, not even his old parents. But then Alcestis, the queen, had decided to give her life for that of her husband. And therefore she had died.

This preface we hear in the prologue of our play from Apollo who is leaving the house of Admetus, fleeing from the unclean odor of death when he met Thatanos, the god of death who was sure of his prey. The content of the actual play consists of the farewell, the death, and the funeral of Alcestis and the appearance of Heracles who retrieves the already buried woman from the grave and leads her back to her husband. As in the saga of Orpheus and Eurydice, so it is here: the wife, who has already died, is supposed to return to her husband. But here we have a double motive: the dead wife, brought back to life by Heracles wrestling with Tathanos, had already thrown in her lot to die for the life of her husband by her own free will. Though we are willing to feel for the wife for whom her own death is less horrible than the idea to live without her husband, we feel a *strong dislike* for the husband who asks his family to die for him and agrees to see his wife die in his stead. Had he asked his wife too? In the play by Euripides, it seems like it. According to Hofmannsthal's version he did not. Since the wife had declared by her own will that she was willing to die, one could say that it was not his own choice, but fate. However, would he have, if the question had been put before him, rejected her sacrifice? And even if this had been so, there still remains that by asking the others his life-craving request he did trigger the fateful event.

Our German saga also knows of a similar example: the tale of the poor Henry (*Der arme Heinrich* by Hartmann von Aue, written in the 1190s). But this is for us only acceptable because here the knight is changing his mind at the eleventh hour and rejects the sacrifice. Wieland felt, when he copied the material according to Euripides that he was justified to do better than the poet and to change the plot: by turning it into an amicable race between the two spouses, of whom each one was willing to die for the other. Goethe punished Wieland in his farce for that sharply. Whether or not our own feeling weigh more for Wieland's or Euripides's interpretation, from the point of view of the Greek poet, Goethe's opinion was justified. For Euripides the acceptance of the sacrifice was something natural and that it could throw a shadow upon the king's character did not enter his mind. He allows Admetus to fight with the gods about demanding this sacrifice and also his old father about refusing to give his life for his son's, but never accused himself for asking others to die for him. Therefore it is not Admetus' conflict in regards to his wife that is the main contents of the play; such a conflict does not exist for Euripides. The fate of Alcestis has been decided before the play begins; only the farewell is shown. The dramatic conflict into which Euripides puts his hero is quite a different one: it is between the concentration of his own suffering and his duty to be hospitable. Not death of a spouse nor the sacrifice of death are the actual themes of the play, but the royal mind of the man who conquers his personal sufferings in order to be a genuine host and king. Therefore, he hides before Heracles, who enters during the preparations for the burial, that Alcestis has died. He is afraid to send the guest away from his threshold. Only from the mouth of an old servant the guest hears that the person whose funeral is going on is not a stranger as Admetus has told him, but the mistress of the house. In order to redeem this evidence of pure, royal hospitality, the semi-god goes and fights with Tanthalos, the god of death. He wins and Alcestis is alive again and returns into her husband's arms.

Though we have difficulties agreeing with the foregone conclusion granted the king's naïve crave for life, just as well we find it hard to understand the overwrought esteem for hospitality. However, different times have different standards and hospitality was very important to the Greeks. Whoever wants to enjoy the beauty and greatness of classical poetry must also live with the suppositions it is founded upon. The holiness of the rights of one's guests is the center of the play. Admetus, the host, is the protagonist of the drama, Admetus, who exercises maximum hospitality to god and semi-god, and he receives in return maximum thanks.

Hofmannsthal did not shy away from following Euripides in the course of the plot. He did not change the play as Wieland had done. But still, he could not take the entire work by Euripides. Though he did not touch the material, he still used softer outlines. The powerful trimesters have been replaced by flexible five-footed iambs; many a harshness and acerbity have been mellowed. The strict rhythm of the Euripideaen choir of the old men has been partly dissolved into correspondence of the people, and partly compensated by funeral hymns of the women and maidens in soft, insinuating rhymes.

Would anyone therefore judge Hofmannsthal? Though he would not say with Wieland, "My audience, Euripides, is not the same as yours," still he must not insist rightfully that he is different from the old Greek. No writer can dispose of himself unless he wants to quit being a writer. Any translation of another poet's work will result in something new. Also in Schiller's translation of the *Aeneid,* Old Virgil would have recognized the congenial writer but hardly his own self. And who would quarrel with us about Schiller being closer to us than Virgil? And Hofmannsthal closer than Euripides?

While translating this speech I had to return to the original German story several times. I have never seen *Alcestis* on the stage, and I would love to have known my father's reaction to the actual play back then, in 1914. At least he saw the play well dramatized!

Speech About Kant[38]

For His 150th Birthday Celebration
At the Philosophical Society in Bremen
July 1954

In this speech, my father defends the importance of Kant's work for all philosophers. At the time that my father gave this speech in 1954, Königsberg was located in behind the Iron Curtain in East Prussia. It currently part of Russia.

Honored Friends!

In these days, our thoughts go again and again to Königsberg, the city where Immanuel Kant was born, where he taught and worked and died 150 years ago. There this celebration should have taken place. However, it adds to all the painful experiences we had to suffer that Kant's city is not German anymore. Kant's mortal remains are resting beneath the shambles of his grave and those of the sacred old cathedral.

But the memorial that he has set himself belongs to a different realm which no enemy bombs can destroy. Although decades later some say that Kant is out of fashion and doesn't count anymore. This could be so and nobody will state that everything Kant has said is unequivocally correct and uncontested. Neither with the contemporary nor the succeeding philosophers has he found unlimited agreement. How could it be different, considering the revolutionary thoughts such as those of Copernicus?

Those who consider themselves his loyal students have very different points of view. The meta-critics, however, trying to remedy his teachings, wound up with entirely different systems, even contrary ideas. And the opponents expressed their bitter refusal.

---

38 Hermann Apelt, Reden und Schriften, Page 393

Philosophy will never speak with finality. If she would try she would dig her own grave and crystallize to the immovable dogma from which Kant had set her free.

It says in the *Prolegomena,* "It is not feasible that mankind will ever cease to search beyond reason (metaphysics) just as it not feasible to give up breathing."

May it be much or little that we can gain permanently from his thoughts—and I think there is very much to use as basis for our thinking and support for our willpower still today—be that as it may, Kant still remains the greatest contributor to German philosophy. Nobody who wants to be taken seriously can omit him.

Especially those who fight him the most or try to abnegate him most arrogantly by trying hard to contradict the already declared dead philosopher, demonstrate thus how forceful his legacy is. Everybody has to confront him, either positively or negatively. He will never be forgotten. Even if we deny everything he said, his critical thinking shows us new ways. His questions and answers cannot be ignored, regardless if we agree or not.

Even if one does not accept any of his formulas, it remains that his critical thinking shows us new ways, that his questions demand new answers, no matter whether his own solutions are accepted or not; the spirit of his writings remains and can never get lost as well as the sentiment expressed in the teachings about freedom, about invulnerability, and about the goal of global peace between nations, created through negotiation rather than wars. And it was East Prussia, Kant's homeland, from where the movement toward the liberation of Germany, from the French yoke, originated. The holy flame was lit here.

We also experienced harder and harder times. Even today, we are living in dangerous times and, what's even more difficult, in dependency of others and divided from our brothers. We have no idea what ordeals will still confront us. Truly, we have to steel ourselves.

May the 150th anniversary of Kant's death remind us to keep some of the spirit that was part of our ancestors also alive in ourselves. Let us follow him and his infallible thoughts and the purity of his actions.

Note by the editor of *Hermann Apelt, Reden und Schriften* (Theodor Spitta):

> Apelt was a member of the Philosophical Society in Bremen and very familiar with the history of philosophy. He wrote this little jest to one of his friends:

Der Großpapa ist Philosoph gewesen.
Papa hat Philosophen übersetzt.
Der Enkel nun zu guterletzt
Begnügt sich, Philosophisches zu lesen.
Ob, was er liest, er auch versteht,
Das liegt auf einem andern Brett.

Grandpapa was a philosopher.
Papa translated philosophers.
The grandson finally
Tries to read philosophy.
Whether he, what he reads, also understands
That is another thing!

Well, he sure tried!

Zwei Königsschicksale[39]

Speech about Two Kings

At the Rotary Club

December 1959

I selected this speech because first it might have been one of my father's last speeches before his death in 1960 and second because it brings back two important events of world history: The invasion of Spain by the Moors in 711 and their expulsion by the Spaniards in 1492. My father was highly motivated to present this speech by his trip to Spain in 1958 where he was most impressed by the Alhambra. (See my father's letter to me from October 20, 1958 earlier in this book.)

While I was traveling in Spain last year, I felt both strange and important when our bus passed the battle field of *Xeres de la Fronteira*, where on July 26, 711, the fate of the West Gothic Empire was decided: King Rodrigo lost crown and land, and the rule of the Moors was founded for the next 800 years in Spain. A few days later, I stood at the Alhambra where the last king of the Moors, the unfortunate Boabdil, had to leave on January 2, 1492, in order to hand over the keys of his city Granada to the Castilian sovereigns Ferdinand and Isabella. That was the end of Moorish sovereignty in Spain.

At the beginning and the end of this Moorish rule, a devastating tragedy happened to the two kings, Rodrigo and Boabdil. Both men seemed to be affiliated with tragedies. There are the old sagas (not always the same as history) that tell us that Rodrigo had compromised the beautiful

39 Hermann Apelt, Reden und Schriften, page 401

Cava, daughter of the powerful Duke Julian. Therefore, the father wanted revenge and called for the Moors to kill Rodrigo.

Unheil kündeten die Winde und der Mond stand voll im Licht,
Als der König Don Rodrigo bei der schönen Cava schlief.
From the Spanish translated by Geibel

Disaster was told by the winds and the moon shone fully
When King Rodrigo slept with beautiful Cava.

The Moors came in droves and won the battle of *Xeres de la Fronteira*. Though Rodrigo was a courageous fighter and withstood the Moors with his West Goths for seven days, he was besieged. This is what the old saga tells us:

Als der Feind nun siegreich vordrang	When the enemy advanced victoriously
An dem achten Tag der Schlacht,	On the eighth day of the battle,
Wichen Don Rodrigos Haufen	Rodrigo's troops receded
Und die wildeFlucht begann.	And the wild flight began.
Da verläßt sein Zelt Rodrigo	There Rodrigo leaves his tent
Um zu fliehn aus seinem Land.	In order to flee from his land.
Einsam flieht der Unglücksel'ge,	Lonely flees the unfortunate one,
Niemand folgt ihm auf der Fahrt.	Nobody follows him on his path.
Müde schleppt sich fort sein Streitroß,	Tired crouches forward his battle horse,
Welches kaum noch schreiten kann;	That is hardly able to walk;
Sucht sich, ungestört vom Reiter,	Searches, not minding his rider,
Durch die Felder selbst den Pfad.	His path across the fields.
Denn bewußtlos durch Erschöpfung	For unconscious by exhaustion
Sitzt der König, wie erstarrt,	Sits the king, benumbed,
Todesmatt vor Durst und Hunger,	Dead-tired with hunger and thirst,
Daß es jedes Herz erbarmt.	That it pities everyone.
Ganz von hellem Blut beronnen	Completely covered with blood

Gleicht er einem roten Brand.	He looks like a scarlet flame.
Voll von Beulen ist sein Harnish,	Full of bumps is his armor,
Der mit Edelsteinen prangt.	That used to glow with precious stones.
Einer Säge gleicht sein Degen	Like a saw his sword looks
Von den Streichen, die er tat.	From the strokes he did with it.
Und sein Goldhelm hängt zerklüftet	And his gold helmet hangs destroyed
In die Stirn ihm tief hinab.	Over his forehead.

This might be the place in the old saga that Delacroix had in mind when he sketched the staggering picture of the fleeing king. This is the picture that our *Kunsthalle* purchased that we still own, and it connects us in an ideal way with the blood-covered field in Xeres, as well as connecting us in a material way with the wine from Xeres, the sherry.

The saga continues telling how Rodrigo watches his fleeing troops from a hill:

Und aus seinen Augen weinend	And crying bitter tears from his eyes
Ruft er jammernd dergestalt:	He calls thus:
"Gestern war ich Herr von Spanien,	"Yesterday I was ruler of Spain,
Heut von keiner einz'gen Stadt.	Today not of a single town.
Heute keins im ganzen Land.	Today none in all the land.
Gestern hatt' ich mir zu dienen,	Yesterday I had to serve me,
Kriegsgefolg und Dienerschaft,	Warriors and servants,
Heut' ist auch kein Mauerziegel,	Today not even one brick,
Den ich mein noch heißen darf.	That I may call my own.
Weh! Unselig war die Stunde	Wow! Cursed be the hour
Und unselig war der Tag,	And cursed be the day,
Da ich ward zur Welt geboren	When I was born into this world
Und ererbte Kron' und Land.	And inherited crown and land.
Denn verlieren sollt' ich alles	Because all of it I lost
Wiederum auf einen Schlag.	Everything in one blow.

Komm! O Tod! Was säumst Du länger,	Why do you tarry,
Aus des schnöden Körpers Haft	From the prison of the body
Meine Seele zu erlösen?	To rescue my soul?
Grüßen will ich Dich mit Dank."	I shall greet you gratefully."

The king flees into the remotest mountains, meets a shepherd, and asks him where he could find a village or a cottage to find some rest. The shepherd shakes his head, in this wilderness there is only one remote farm where an old hermit lives. People think highly of him.

Dessen freute sich der König.	Whereupon the King was glad.
Denn zu bleiben hofft er dort.	For he hoped to stay there.

He asks the shepherd for some food. The shepherd gives him dry meat and bread.

Schlecht gefiel das Brot dem König,	The bread did not please the king,
Schwarz bedünkt es ihm und grob,	It seemed black to him and coarse.
Da ergriff ihn tiefer Kummer,	There deep sorrow grabbed him,
Tränen brachen ihm hervor.	Bitter tears quelled from his eyes.
Denn er dachte vor'ger Zeiten,	Because he thought of past times,
Welches Mahl er da genoß.	What good meals he had enjoyed.

The King gives the shepherd two gold pieces—ring and necklace. Then he looks for the hermitage. The hermit steps out and asks, what made him come to this wilderness. The king answers while he is crying:

"Bin Rodrigo, der Unsel'ge,	"I'm Rodrigo, the unfortunate,
Der ich war ein König sonst,	Who used to be a king,
Und ich komme, meine Sünden	And I'm coming here
Abzubüßen hier am Ort."	To atone for my sins."

Then the hermit says:

"Richtig wählet ihr die Straße,	"You chose the right way,
Die zu eurem Heile frommt,	That will bring you salvation,
Wenn euch eure Missetaten	If God our Lord should
Gott der Herr vergeben soll"	forgive your trespasses."

The hermit prays for enlightening:

"Welche Buße für den König	"What atonement for the king
Sich gebühr' als Sündenlohn."	Should be adequate."

And God shows him a vision:

Das in eine Schlangengrube	That into a pit with a big snake
Ihn hinabzutun gebot.	He was supposed to go down to.
Denn allein durch solche Buße	For alone through such atonement
Werd' er seiner Sünden los.	He would be redeemed from his sins.

Rodrigo hears this gleefully and climbs into the pit without hesitation. After three days, the hermit comes by and asks the king how he fares in the company of the snake.

"Noch durch Gottes Schluß," versetzt er,	"Because of God's will," he answers,
"Hat die Schlange mich verschont.	"Had the snake not touched me.
Aber bitt' für mich, mein Bruder,	But pray for me, my brother,
Bitt' um einen sel'gen Tod."	Ask for a pleasant death."

The hermit consoles him. But when he comes by a second time, he hears a pitiful wailing coming from the king. When he asks what the matter, Rodrigo answers:

"Gott erbarmt sich meiner Not.	"God takes pity on me.
Denn es frißt die Schlange schon,	For the snake is already eating

Frißt von meinem sünd'gen Leibe,	Eats from my sinful body,
Ach, zum wohlverdienten Lohn,	Ah, for a well-deserved reward,
Weil allein aus seinem Lüster	Because from alone from all his appetite
Solch unsäglich Elend sproß."	Derives such horrible pain."

The hermit encourages him.

Bis sein letzter Hauch entfloh.	Until his last gasp came.
Also starb dort Don Rodrigo,	So died Don Rodrigo,
Stieg zum Himmel grad' empor.	And rose straight up to heaven.

So the legend ends, but history teaches differently. It denies the saga about the beautiful Cava. History rather derives the destruction of Rodrigo from the hatred of both sons of his predecessor Witiges. He had grabbed the throne pushing those two aside. In the battle at Xeres it was he who gave orders. Both side wings he had put under the command of the sons of Witiges (trusting them blindly). On the last day of the battle those two betrayed him and went over to the Arabs. Therefore the battle was lost for Rodrigo. The Arab commander Tarek killed the king. With the report of victory, Tarek sent the head of Rodrigo to the high commander Musa who sent it to the Caliph at Damaskus.

The Moors gained the entire Iberian Peninsula with this victory.

Nur Asturien blieb in Freiheit, weil so fest des Landes Art.
Only Asturia stayed free since it withstood the enemy.

So says the saga.

Also the Sierra Nevada in Spain could not hold up the conquering Moors and even France might have endured the same fate as Spain, had not in 732 Karl Martell put his troops between Poitier and Tours and sent the Moors back over the Pyreneans. This battle was followed by battles of *Karl dem Großen,* with the legendary Roland who died in the valley of Ronceval.

Soon the Spaniards tried to take back the land. In 1085 Toledo came back into Spanish hands and in 1094 El Cid marched into Valencia.

Like Roland, the hero of the French Roland song who later became the hero of the great Italian epics (*Pulci, Bojarder, Ariost),* El Cid became the center of a new Spanish romance series. We know these stories from Herder's translations.

In 1244, Seville was taken back after 500 years. In the end, only the fortress Granada remained in Moorish hands, but also occasionally as vassal and tributary under the Castilian crown.

As in the beginning of the Moorish sovereignty, there was Rodrigo, so stands at the end King Boabdil of Granada. But the roles have changed; then the Moors were the conquerors and now they are the conquered ones.

Boabdil (Abu Absdalla) was called by his subjects *El Zogoybi* (the Unhappy One). This is a label that fits both kings, him as well as Rodrigo. Both are connected to guilt. It was the historian Gines Perez de Hita who wrote about this Moorish king, though in spite of the historical title, *Geschichte der Bürgerkriege von Granada* (History of the Civil Wars of Granada), the book conveys the character of a knights' story. It is probably based on old sagas. According to Hita, Boabdil was a cruel tyrant who abused his wife, killed his children, and had the noble house of the Abencerages murdered.

One must always be aware of being in the shady border area between story and history, in the twilight of poetry and truth, and that the *when* and the *how* even the *whether* stay in most cases questionable. And this is also true about the revenge motive for murder of the *Abencerages*.

What you hear nowadays at the Alhambra is different from how Hita tells us. There we learn that the sultan heard rumors that his favorite wife was meeting at night with one of the Abencerages in the garden of the Generalife. He, the sultan, decided to hide at the time of the rendezvous. He listened, and his suspicions were confirmed. However, because of the dark night he could not recognize which of the five brothers was the culprit. In order to be sure to pick the right one, he invited all five of the Abencerages to a party at the Lions' Court and had all of them murdered. Red spots on the floor of the so-called Abencerage Room still prove the horrible act of revenge.

Washington Irving (my main source) thinks that Boabdil was accused wrongly. These misdeeds were actually committed by his father, Abu Hassan. And surely, he was right in assuming that this man, who had a record of having committed other such cruelties, was more apt to be accused than the unlucky Boabdil. A proof for this is the fate that befell Boabdil and his mother Ayxa la Horra. Maybe even it was not Abu Hassan, but his father, Ciriza.

Irving tells us that Abu Hassan, as an older man, married a beautiful Christian prisoner of noble descent. She adopted the Moorish name Zoreyde. They had two sons. She was ambitious and strove to secure the father's throne for them. For this purpose she worked on the suspicious nature of the king and started rumors that children of the king's other wives and mistresses were plotting attacks to kill him and to secure the throne for themselves. Some of them were murdered by the enraged father. Even Ayxa la Horra, the virtuous mother of Boabdil, who had captured his heart completely, became a suspect. He imprisoned her and the son in the tower of Comares and would have murdered Boabdil had not his mother helped him escape by letting him down from the tower at night with a rope made from her and her servants scarves, Boabdil was able to flee to Guadix.

Irving's conclusion is that this father is the more likely murderer of the Abencerages. Boabdil had demonstrated proof of his mild and friendly character during his brief, stormy, and unfortunate rule. He understood how to conquer the hearts of his subjects through benevolent and gracious manners.

In the year 1482, he was able to dethrone his father Abu Hassan, as this man had done to his father Ciriza. His sovereignty only lasted eleven years. He had to fight his uncle, the so-called Recke (hero), who tried to take the throne from him, unsuccessfully. Boabdil's relationship with Ferdinand von Aragonien hovered between friendship and hostility, between independence and dependency. Twice he suffered imprisonment but was released upon certain conditions. Twice he broke his promises. Ferdinand, a cold and devious calculating character (a contemporary of Machiavelli, equal to him in thought and action) pulled the net tight around him and had him give over the besieged Granada and the Alhambra to the Spanish authorities.

While surrendering he was said to ask that the gate through which he left the magic castle should be sealed up so no other could leave after him. Queen Isabella granted him this wish. *(This tower was later detonated by the French.)*

Boabdil had sent his wife and his mother ahead so they would not watch his humiliation. But while looking back once more to Granada he broke out in tears. It is said that his mother said to him, "You are doing well, crying like a woman over what you could not defend like a man."

Indeed, one cannot say that Boabdil lost his beautiful kingdom as a hero. The accusation of being a weakling had stuck to him, more rightfully than the attribute of being a callous murderer. When this story was told to Karl the Fifth, he responded: "If I had been he or he me, I would have preferred to make the Alhambra my grave rather than retreating to Andarax without a kingdom." Later Boabdil left Spain and moved to Africa and offered his services as a soldier to the King of Fez.

Ein jeder hat, er sei auch wer er mag,
Ein letztes Glück und einen letzten Tag.

Everyone has, might he be who he may,
A last chance of happiness and a last day.

And this verse also holds true for my father's life.

Afterword

It has been a pleasure to get to know my grandfather via these words written by my mother. I am very grateful that she has taken the time to translate many of his letters and speeches for the rest of the family.

The experience of editing the words of my mother and her translations brings me great satisfaction in my profession as a literary agent. My grandfather was an eloquent speaker who could find the right words to express his deepest feelings and make those around him enjoy the depth of his thoughts, whether about history, local Bremen politics, literature, philosophy, the arts, or other human beings including his colleagues, friends, and family. His clever poetry and riddles make me smile as I picture him interacting with my mother when she was a young girl.

On my mother's upcoming 90th birthday celebration on April 21, 2011, the family plans to gather in New York City to honor Mathilde Apelt Schmidt, the last of the children of Senator Hermann Apelt still with us on this earth. We will also acknowledge the publication of this book in English, with his stories and his contributions for all of the generations following his long and fulfilled life, as a reminder of the legacy our grandfather has left us.

New York City
November 2010
Doris Schmidt Michaels

Acknowledgments

I would never have written this book without my niece's discovery of the book *Hermann Apelt, Reden und Schriften.* Phyllis Kreider, daughter of my sister Cornelie Ernst, wrote me an e-mail in 2009 saying, "Tita, you *have* to read this book. It has all those speeches and writings of your father (her grandfather). You must have it. If not, I'lll send you mine. Let me know what you think of it."

Phyllis knows German and if *she* somehow received this German book, I should at least have it in the house. Sure enough, during spring cleaning, I dusted my bookshelves and there it was, on the uppermost shelf, sent to me by my mother in 1962, two years after the death of my father, and still unread by me. I read it, loved it, and decided to translate some of the speeches and writings and also add my own comments. When I shared this idea with my daughter, Doris Schmidt Michaels, a literary agent, she became excited about the idea and promised to help me edit the book along with her colleague, Delia Berrigan Fakis.

My father began his studies of law in Tübingen and continued these studies in Leipzig, and then practiced in Bremen.

Therefore, I researched all available sources, including the archives in the places he studied. Then I put my manuscript together and sent it to my daughter, who went over it not only professionally with her team, but also with all her heart. I thank her for this. I also want to thank my daughter, Barbara Schmidt Cruz, for her meticulous work on the final version of the manuscript. Leo Hermann Schmidt and Martin Walter Schmidt, my two sons, were behind me all the way. I could not have written this book without Leo Waldemar Schmidt, my husband of 58 years, who helped me with computer problems when they occurred and provided me with hot coffee and drinks while I was working. I am grateful to all of them.

I also thank my relatives in the United States and in Germany for showing me appreciation for writing this book and giving me valuable input. My niece, Hedwig Freytag, daughter of my late sister Julie Kulenkampff, went to the Rotary archive to retrieve valuable research material for me. I am grateful to all of them as well.

I decided to have the book self-published with iUniverse who had assisted me with my previous books: *My Life in Two Continents, 2006; The Lake Dwellers, 2007; Happiness, a Matter of the Mind, 2008;* and *The Old Castle in Austria, 2008.* My representative for this book is Joseph King at iUniverse.

Castro Valley, January 2011
Mathilde Apelt Schmidt

My Father

Hermann Apelt

Der Bremer Senat 1948.
Vordere Reihe von rechts: Hermann Apelt, Theodor Spitta,
Wilhelm Kaisen, Emil Theil und Adolf Ehlers

The Bremen Senate 1948
Front row from the right: Hermann Apelt, Theodora Spitta,
Wilhelm Kaisen, Emil Theil, and Adof Ehlers

Ernst Friedrich Apelt
mit Otto 1850

1850
My great grandfather, Ernst Friedrich Apelt, 1812-1859
My grandfather, Otto Apelt, 1845-1932

1886
My grandfather, Otto Apelt, 1845-1932
My grandmother, Cornelia Apelt, née Rassow, 1853-1882
My aunt Else Ernst, née Apelt, 1874-1946
My father, Hermann Apelt, 1876-1960
My aunt Mathilde Apelt, 1880-1961?

My father, Hermann Apelt still with hair.
Probably around 1894
He lost most of his hair after a fencing accident in 1896

1909
The year he married my mother on August 23

1911
with first child, Cornelie

1912

Reading the paper on our verandah

on Sunday morning

1916

At the front in France during World War I

1921
In our garden, the year of my birth

1921
In our garden with daughter Julie

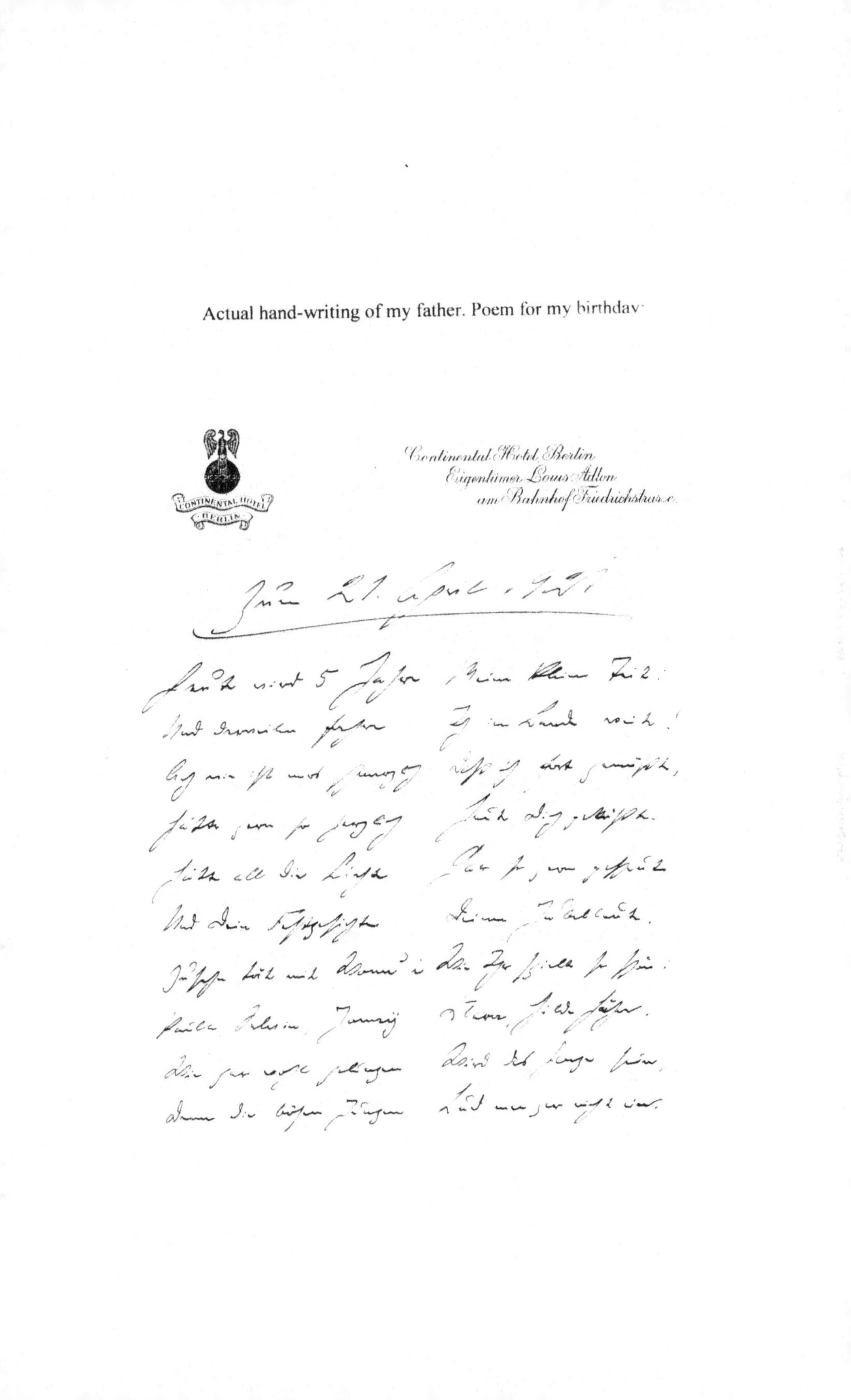

Actual hand-writing of my father. Poem for my birthday

Continental Hotel Berlin
Eigentümer Louis Adlon
am Bahnhof Friedrichstrasse.

CONTINENTAL HOTEL
BERLIN

Zum 21. April [illegible]

Heute wird 5 Jahr Mein kleiner Fritz:
[illegible]
[illegible]
[illegible]
[illegible]
[illegible]
[illegible]
[illegible]
[illegible]
[illegible]

Zum 21sten April, 1926.

[illegible]
[illegible]
[illegible]
[illegible]
[illegible]
[illegible]
[illegible]
[illegible]

[illegible]

1928

Father and I share reading a postcard

Silver Wedding Anniversary

August 23, 1934
Silver Wedding Anniversary
At the Burgstall, the Rassows' estate in the Alps

August 23, 1959

Left to right: Onkel Gustav Rassow, my mother, my father,

Tante Ilse Rassow, housekeeper

Dorothee, Julie, Mathilde

(Cornelie was already married to Walter Ernst)

Vacation, 1935

1937
On top of the Dolomites with his friend Ulrich

1937
Father with grandson Walt Ernst

1943

In our garden with my mother before the house was demolished (in 1945)

1949
At the Bremen Port showing a guest around

1950
Talking to a Dutch captain

1952
On vacation with my mother

1953
With grandchildren Phyllis and Madeline Ernst in Dayton, Ohio

1953

With sister Thilde at our home

shortly after moving into the rebuilt house

1957

In our garden with granddaughters Christine and Charlotte

Father shows the ports to his grandson Walt Ernst

1959

August 23, 1959

1959
Getting ready for the
Golden Wedding Anniversary
Herr Arendt will drive the Golden Couple

Golden Wedding Anniversary

Golden Wedding Anniversary in Scheeßel
(unfortunately there is no picture of their actual wedding in 1909)

1959, before or after the Big Day
Trip to the Bremen Port

Peace at last

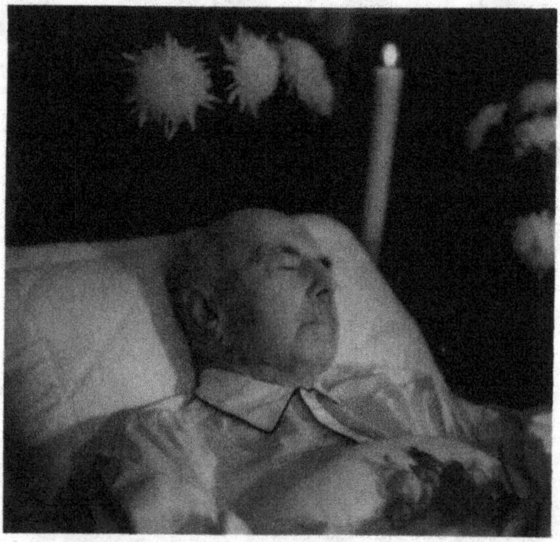

November 11, 1960
The day my father died.

November 15, 1960

Der mit Blumen und Kränzen geschmückte Katafalk im Rathaus

Staatsakt im Rathaus

Bremen nahm Abschied von Senator Dr. Hermann Apelt

Bremen took leave of Senator Dr. Hermann Apelt